Praise for *The Sacred Year*

Dorothy Day once said, "Don't call me a saint, I don't want to be dismissed that easily." In this book, Michael Yankoski refuses to limit faithful living to daredevil Christians, and he creates a commonwealth of sacred treasures for all to share. He reminds you that the Christian faith is more like a marathon than a sprint . . . and it's not just about what you do but who you are becoming.

— Shane Claiborne, Author, Activist, and Friend of Jesus

Michael Yankoski is such a good writer that it would be easy to hitch a ride through his Sacred Year without ever setting foot on the ground he covered. This book wants more of you than that. If you decide to accept its invitation, then you too will own up to what is ailing you, turning aside from the shallows of your life-as-usual in order to go deep. The spiritual practices in this book can help you do that, but they don't promise to keep you safe. Instead, they promise to open you to the Spirit who alone can make you whole.

— Barbara Brown Taylor, *New York Times* Best-selling Author of *Learning to Walk in the Dark*

Bright lights don't need spotlights. Michael's been a bright light for a long time and he's written another terrific book. He doesn't want the spotlight anymore; he just wants a deeper faith and a more meaningful life. *The Sacred Year* was like the sound of soft rain and the crackling of a fire to my tired soul. If you're like me, you'll put down this book, pick up your calendar, and make a couple changes. You'll want to cancel a few things and start a couple others; you'll want to be more intentional and engaged than you've been; and you'll want to live a more active love.

— Bob Goff, *New York Times* Best-selling Author of *Love Does*

Michael Yankoski uses crisp, engaging language as he addresses the "chaos of questions about whether spiritual practices are relevant" in today's fast-paced life. With engaging honesty and vivid narrative, he addresses the deep fissures that erode Christian public presence and testimony. You will not only love reading this book, you'll find it draws you deeper as you discover unforgettable patterns for your life in Christ.

— Luci Shaw, Author of *Adventure of Ascent* and Writer in Residence, Regent College

In our age in which churches and society are cursed with superficiality, it is a rare book that calls us to a deeper life. Michael Yankoski's *The Sacred Year* is one such book, artfully weaving the story of his own quest for a meaningful faith. This book is destined to become a spiritual classic, and it merits the sort of mindful attention that it calls us to nurture.

— C. Christopher Smith, Co-author of *SLOW CHURCH* and
    Senior Editor of *The Englewood Review of Books*

Occasionally a story of someone else's spiritual journey provides a map by which to navigate your own. *The Sacred Year* does that. Michael Yankoski's candid, open-hearted reflection on the practices that led him from exhaustion to plenitude and the encounters that inspired those practices is rich with memorable stories, wisdom from a wide communion of saints, and practical guidance. This book belongs on a shelf next to those of Wendell Berry, Richard Rohr, Kathleen Norris, Norvene Vest, and Ched Meyers, among other companions on the journey in our generation. From the discovery of silence to the rediscovery of breadmaking to the spaciousness of simple living to new ways to pray, we are invited in every chapter to deepen our conversations with self, others, and God, assured of surprise at every turn of the journey.

— Marilyn McEntyre, Fellow, Gaede Institute, Westmont College;
    Adjunct Professor of Medical Humanities, UC Berkeley;
    and Author of *Caring for Words in a Culture of Lies*

This book is a joy to the soul and a delight to the heart. Beyond that, and unless I am very, very mistaken, it is also destined to become a classic within the genre of contemporary spiritual and religious writing. I cannot praise it too highly nor recommend it too earnestly to anyone who yearns to feast on good words about holy living.

— Phyllis Tickle, Compiler of *The Divine Hours*

As part of the same community for a number of years, I had the privilege of observing some of these practices that Michael Yankoski describes in this captivating book. What I can say without equivocation is that this story rings true, not only of Michael's life, but of the ache and longing for a deeper life that reverberates within many of us. If you are looking to recover truth in your own life, then *The Sacred Year* is a very good place to begin this path of retrieval. And don't be surprised if you not only find truth but also something of the Way and the Life as you read.

— Tim Dickau, Author of *Plunging Into the Kingdom Way*

Michael Yankoski writes with passion and imagination. His memorable characters and vivid images celebrate practices that lead us deeply into the life of God. *The Sacred Year* has the power to transform and cultivate our desires so that we seek the God who is our life. May it be so.

— Jonathan R. Wilson, Pioneer McDonald Professor
of Theology, Carey Theological College

The Sacred Year offers a truthful deconstruction of the dysfunctional reality of rampant consumerism and the celebrity-making apparatus that has become American Christianity. Michael carves a way forward out of our existential crisis toward the story of spiritual depth. This vivid descriptive story of the necessary spiritual journey should be considered essential reading for all American Christians.

— Soong-Chan Rah, Milton B. Engebretson Professor of
Church Growth and Evangelism, North Park Theological
Seminary, and Author of *The Next Evangelicalism*

Michael communicates with humility without being self-deprecating, with candor without being narcissistic, and with story without being egocentric. *The Sacred Year* flows out of that style and is a compelling invitation to participate in spiritual practices. As a testimony to God's work in the world and a realistic assessment of our humanity, this book could well be described as good, true, and beautiful.

— Rod Wilson, PhD, President, Regent College

Michael Yankoski has written a wonderful, sensitive book about the way we awaken to life and learn to live with intentionality and purpose. His metaphors are rich. His life experiences real. His insights riveting. By teaching us to attend to everyday realities, Yankoski opens the windows of our senses to our own life with God. Ultimately, Yankoski invites us to embrace this life in order to enjoy the journey.

— Dr. Gayle D. Beebe, President, Westmont College

Michael Yankoski has given us a great gift. *The Sacred Year* is a book to savor, inviting us to consider how a return to the good rhythms of contemplation, gratitude, Sabbath-keeping, and even cave-dwelling can lead us out of the shallows of a distracted, "carnival Christian life" and into the deep and wondrous waters of mature faith. Read this book and follow Michael into the Deep!

— Leah Kostamo, Author of *Planted: A Story of Creation, Calling and Community*

The Sacred Year is the perfect book for anyone tired of the rat race, craving a life of greater depth and meaning. As a recovering workaholic, I find myself on almost every page of Michael's surprisingly personal and deeply moving story. Like a compelling novel, you'll find it hard to put this book down. But read it slowly, savoring each bite, and it will restore your soul.

> — Ken Shigematsu, Pastor of Tenth Church Vancouver and
> Best-selling Author of *God in My Everything*

I love how Michael Yankoski takes us on an honest exploration of the soul. He pauses long enough to see the colors and nuances of the beauty in and around us. The attention he pays to everything around him births a gift for us to learn from. I loved *The Sacred Year* as it gently describes the angst and wreck-full pace we blindly assume. Yet, Michael lets us walk with him as he embarks on a quiet revolution to still himself to hear the voice of God. Of course you should buy this book! It's a refreshing drink of water that comes from a deep well of contemplative activism.

> — Dave Gibbons, Author of *XEALOTS: Defying the Gravity of Normality*,
> Founder of *XEALOTS.ORG* and NEWSONG CHURCH

Yankoski's stories and insights are a necessity for those of us who've found ourselves run-dry, who recognize our spiritual anemia, and who are looking for instruction and a push toward a life of depth and flourishing. Most books promise life-change; *The Sacred Year* delivers it.

> — Ken Wytsma, Lead Pastor of Antioch in Bend, Oregon, and Author
> of *Pursuing Justice: The Call to Live and Die for Bigger Things*

Though forged in the crucible of personal crisis, Michael Yankoski has written a book full of joy, humor, personal vulnerability, and wide-eyed wonder. *The Sacred Year* brims with a childlike enthusiasm, and a new convert's sense of "Wow!" at the discovery of those ancient spiritual disciplines that are also known as the means of grace. The reader will laugh with him as Michael laughs at himself through his sometimes bumbling and painful recovery from the addiction to hurry. But make no mistake: this is a thoughtful and well-reasoned apologia and guide for those who would know the power and pleasure of learning to quietly go deep with God, one's self, and others.

> — Ben Patterson, Campus Pastor, Westmont College
> and Author of *God's Prayer Book*

THE SACRED YEAR

Mapping the Soulscape of Spiritual Practice—
How Contemplating Apples, Living in a Cave, and
Befriending a Dying Woman Revived My Life

MICHAEL YANKOSKI

W PUBLISHING GROUP

AN IMPRINT OF THOMAS NELSON

Published in Nashville, Tennessee, by W Publishing, an imprint of Thomas Nelson.

Published in association with literary agency of D.C. Jacobson & Associates, LLC, an Author Management Company, www.dcjacobson.com.

Thomas Nelson titles may be purchased in bulk for educational, business, fund-raising, or sales promotional use. For information, please e-mail SpecialMarkets@ThomasNelson.com.

Any Internet addresses, phone numbers, or company or product information printed in this book are offered as a resource and are not intended in any way to be or to imply an endorsement by Thomas Nelson, nor does Thomas Nelson vouch for the existence, content, or services of these sites, phone numbers, companies, or products beyond the life of this book.

Unless otherwise noted, Scripture quotations are taken from *Holy Bible*, New Living Translation (NLT). © 1996, 2004, 2007. Used by permission of Tyndale House Publishers, Inc., Wheaton, Illinois 60189. All rights reserved.

Scripture quotations marked ESV are taken from THE ENGLISH STANDARD VERSION. © 2001 by Crossway Bibles, a division of Good News Publishers.

Scripture quotations marked NIV are taken from the Holy Bible, New International Version®, NIV®. Copyright © 1973, 1978, 1984 by Biblica, Inc.TM Used by permission of Zondervan. All rights reserved worldwide. www.zondervan.com

Scripture quotations marked KJV are taken from the King James Version. Public domain.

Scripture quotations marked TJB are taken from THE JERUSALEM BIBLE. © 1966 by Darton, Longman & Todd Ltd. and Doubleday & Company, Inc. Used by permission.

"A Poet's Advice to Students" by e.e. cummings in *Journal of Humanistic Psychology*, Vol 12, Issue 2, p. 75. Copyright © 1972 by SAGE Publications. Reprinted by permission of SAGE Publications.

"VII" by Wendell Berry. Copyright © 1998 by Wendell Berry from *A Timbered Choir*. Reprinted by permission of Counterpoint.

"Lore" by RS Thomas. Copyright © 1993 by RS Thomas from *Collected Poems 1945-1990*. Reprinted by permission of Phoenix, an imprint of Orion Books Ltd., London.

"The Reconciliation of a Penitent," from *The Book of Alternative Services of the Anglican Church of Canada*. Copyright © 1985 The General Synod of the Anglican Church of Canada. Published by ABC Publishing (Anglican Book Centre). Used with permission.

"On Top" by Gary Snyder. Copyright © 2005 from *Axe Handles: Poems*. Reprinted by permission of Counterpoint.

Library of Congress Control Number: 2014942545

ISBN 978-0-8499-2202-2

Printed in the United States of America

14 15 16 17 18 RRD 6 5 4 3 2 1

To Danae:

For all the ways you help thaw me toward the Holy

And

To Regent College and Grandview Calvary Baptist Church:
For all the ways you embody the hope of the Kingdom of God

Earth's crammed with heaven
And every common bush afire with God;
But only he who sees, takes off his shoes.

—Elizabeth Barrett Browning[1]

Compared with what we ought to be,
we are only half awake.

—William James[2]

We only believe
As deep as we live

—Ralph Waldo Emerson[3]

The time is fast approaching when one will
either be a mystic or an unbeliever.

—Karl Rahner[4]

Listen to your life. See it for the fathomless mystery that it is. In the
boredom and pain of it no less than in the excitement and gladness:
touch, taste, smell your way to the holy and hidden heart of it because in
the last analysis all moments are key moments, and life itself is grace.

—Frederick Buechner[5]

Contents

Section III: Depth with Others

Introduction

Not long ago, an Australian acquaintance e-mailed and asked if we might meet for coffee. Though I didn't know him well—we'd shared a few classes together in seminary and I'd seen him in the audience of a local speaking event a few months earlier—I agreed. The next week, we met on a rainy Vancouver day at a trendy shop with tall, blue-ish windows that, along with the sound of the deluge hitting them outside, made me feel like I'd stepped into an enormous aquarium.

We shook out our umbrellas while we waited in line, bemoaning our decision to live in a part of the world categorized as a temperate rain forest. We grabbed our coffees and swam over to a dark wooden table right at the edge of the fishbowl. After all the usual niceties people employ to try and cover the obvious fact that they don't know one another very well, he leaned forward on the table and furrowed his brow.

"I've got to tell you, Mike," he said, dropping his voice a little. "I'm jealous of you."

I almost choked on my Americano and tried to cover with a laugh.

"I mean it," he said, straight-faced. "I want to be where you are. You're living the *life*! A published author, a public speaker, but more than all that, you're a force for good out in the world. I want to be where you are."

"Huh," I said, leaning back in my chair.

When I didn't speak, he filled the silence. "I was at that event you spoke at a couple of weeks ago, and the whole time I was listening to you, I kept thinking to myself, *I'm on the wrong side of the stage. I'm on the wrong side of the bloody stage. I should be up there, teaching, talking, compelling people to get off their couches and make the world a better place. Talking about how to change the world.*"

But I didn't say anything, and instead I marveled at the scene: two of us—an Australian and an American—sitting there in the fishbowl with the crowded Vancouver street bustling outside, the other blue-hued people swimming around inside, all of us trying to make sense of this thing called life, trying to figure out exactly why it is that we've woken up here on this pale blue dot.

He'd thrown me a curve, so I decided to respond in kind. "Have you ever had an existential crisis?" I asked.

It was his turn to sit back in silent surprise.

What I shared that day in the coffee shop was—in an abbreviated form—what *The Sacred Year* is all about. I confessed how exhausted and jaded I found myself after almost a decade as a "Christian speaker," as "a person out there having impact on the world." I started with the moment my existential crisis reached fever pitch, the moment when my life stretched out both before and behind me into infinite meaninglessness and a thousand unanswerable questions swallowed me whole, the moment when the carefully constructed facade I presented to the world came crashing down around me and I felt utterly exposed and very, very cold. I shared about the seed of clarity that moment embedded in me, how I slowly came to see that my life had become fragmented and shallow, with so much energy and focus going toward being up on stage *talking* about living a life of depth with God and the *idea* of genuine love for others that I had actually stopped pursuing the way of living necessary for sustaining genuine intimacy, authenticity, and depth. I shared how all of this inner turmoil launched me on a desperate journey away from the shallow, and facade-obsessed existence I had been living, and toward an existence in pursuit of deeper self-knowledge, intimacy with God, and a more manifest love for others. I told him how much I believed the infatuation with "changing the world"—however well intentioned—could actually be distracting us from the more important and critical work of the spiritual life, the *genuine* life with God that can't help but affect the world around it. And although I confessed openly that I didn't have all the answers, I admitted that I thought I *had* found something. Not just a thing, really, but a *way*—evident in the lives and traditions and stories of the past faithful—of intentionally structuring and ordering life around spiritual practices, practices that shape and form us into a particular kind of people. And, although I'd begun with a whole chaos of questions in mind about whether "spiritual practices" were relevant today—Who *cares* about what people of faith did fifteen hundred years ago? Do spiritual practices even *work?* What *purpose* might they serve given our frenetic and high-pressure lifestyles?—as I began to engage in these practices I discovered (to my astonished delight) that these "means of grace" were fundamentally changing the way I lived, moved, and had my being in the world.

It was slow change, to be sure, but definite—like living water reshaping stone.

In the pages that follow, you'll find the details of what I told that Australian acquaintance on that rainy fishbowl day—the full story of my Sacred Year. May you encounter deep nourishment, deep encouragement, and deep hope in what follows, through the ups and downs of one honest questioner's year of spiritual practice.

Michael Yankoski
Vancouver, British Columbia
January 2014

CHAPTER I

What Color Is Jaded?

Midway upon the journey of our life
I found myself in a dark wilderness

— DANTE, *INFERNO*[1]

O thou lord of life, send my roots rain.

— GERARD MANLEY HOPKINS[2]

There were only a few lonely travelers in the otherwise vacant boarding area as I arrived for yet another 5:00 a.m. departure. I was several years into the speaking tour for my first book, *Under the Overpass*, traveling from city to city, telling the story of my friend Sam's and my intentional journey as homeless men. The allure of travel and bright lights had long since worn off by this point, and more and more I was finding the unanchored life of an itinerate speaker increasingly corrosive.

One of my fellow travelers—a large man with a stained Harley-Davidson shirt and a beard like a muddy waterfall—had passed out across a row of chairs. He was snoring loudly, and every so often his steel-toed right boot twitched menacingly. A tattooed arm extended out toward his nearby suitcase, and as I sat down to await the start of the boarding process, a shiny silver bracelet flashed against the background of blue ink on his forearm. When I looked closer I saw it wasn't a bracelet at all, but a handcuff—he had handcuffed himself to his suitcase.

"Your attention please," a perfectly timed electronic voice blared over the boarding area speakers. "Please do not leave your luggage unattended. All unattended baggage will be confiscated and may be destroyed."

Ha! I smirked. *Nobody's* going to confiscate *his* stuff.

Over the next few minutes several more early morning zombies straggled in, all of them greedily nursing steaming cups of dark, gritty stimulant beneath shadowy eyes and hollow cheeks. These recent additions brought the total number in the boarding area to ten, including myself. A cold light inside a nearby vending machine began to strobe in an irregular, distracting way.

The speech I'd delivered the night before had gone well. The audience was kind, and only one person snored audibly. (It only took a second before his mortified wife elbowed him hard in the ribs.) When the time came there was an engaging Q&A session, with some of the audience members texting in questions while others just raised their hands politely or stood up and used the provided microphones at the back of the room. When it was all over, I stood in the foyer for more than an hour, shaking hands, answering still more questions, and signing the occasional dog-eared book.

This was my third speech in as many days, and tonight I would be in yet another city, in another room, standing before another audience without knowing anybody's name, trying yet again to weave words into a tale worth hearing, a tale—if I was really on top of my game—that might just produce zero snoring audience members and maybe, just maybe, might be worth their remembering the next day.

An airline employee arrived and began fumbling behind the desk with the computer, cursing every so often as he banged a fist on the malfunctioning printer.

Just then, something new strolled into the boarding area: a surprisingly bright-eyed, sandy-haired fellow with flawless clothes, straight teeth, and an impressive tan. He swaggered in, quickly surveyed the rest of us, and evidently unimpressed by what he saw, chose a vacant corner for himself. Once he'd lounged himself in a chair, his phone rang—a ringtone from that old hard-rock song about driving the highway of life.

"Hiya, babe," the man drawled into the phone, flashing a shiny grin that had probably worked miracles for him in the past. But soon his face darkened and his jaw muscles rippled under that tanned skin at whatever the woman on the other end was saying. "Now Nikki, hold on a minute," the man said firmly.

But Nikki didn't hold on. She just kept right on talking, and his face turned crimson.

"Good morning, ladies and gentlemen," the boarding agent announced. "We're now ready to begin our boarding process. Unlike you crazies, sane people sleep in Saturdays. That means we'll be boarding all groups at once. Please make sure your boarding passes are out and available as you approach the podium."

With his free hand, Mr. Harley-Davidson pulled out a bristle of keys and started working on his handcuff. We stood—most of us, that is— and made our way toward the podium, trying to remember where we'd stuffed our tickets to ride.

The guy with the tan stayed seated in the corner, the situation escalating.

"Now that's not fair!" he yelled. "We talked about this and you said—" But Nikki cut him off again.

"Good morning, Mr. Yankoski," the gate agent said once he'd scanned my boarding pass.

"You're in a better mood than I am," I mumbled.

"Enjoy your flight."

"You too," I said, and staggered down the jet bridge. As I neared the plane I could still hear the guy on the phone behind me, shouting.

I seem to have relatively good luck on airplanes. I've only had drinks spilled on me three times, lost my luggage twice, and been projectile-vomited on by a newborn once. And that's just the daytime flights. On my last red-eye I sat next to a broad-shouldered, flailing-snoring-farter who was remarkably capable at making sure that I didn't sleep for more than a few minutes at a time during the whole five-hour flight.

So it was par for the course when the Shouter threw his bag onto the seat directly across the aisle from me, ensuring that I'd have a front-row seat to the rest of his early morning tirade. I crammed in both of my earbuds and cranked up the volume to try and drown out the yelling.

3

I'd almost managed to fall asleep when the flight attendant knocked on my shoulder.

I looked up, blinking at her for a moment, surprised by how well she could harmonize with Bon Iver. Then the song ended and her lips kept moving.

I yanked out an earbud. "Huh?"

"Turn off your MP3 player please, sir," the flight attendant said again. Then she turned to the man across the aisle.

The Shouter hadn't abated. "That's absurd, Nikki! You always do this. This is just like last time. I can't even—" But Nikki cut him off.

Now it was the flight attendant's turn to get frustrated. "Sir! I'm not going to tell you again. The main cabin door is closed. We are ready to depart. *Turn off your phone!*"

"Nikki, I've got to go," the man yelled. "Yeah, uh-huh. Like I believe that."

"Sir!" the flight attendant shouted, stamping her foot.

The man held up a silencing finger at the flight attendant and bellowed into the phone.

"Well excuse me, Nikki, for ruining your miserable little life!" With that the man ended the call and hurled his phone at the floor of the plane, where it shattered into several pieces. He glared up at the flight attendant. "There. It's off now. Are you happy?"

She was more than a little surprised, as was I. So were the other nine zombies on the plane that morning, all leaning out into the aisle to see what was happening. Somebody needed to get this guy some Valium, and fast.

"Thank you, sir," the flight attendant said. After a sarcastic curtsy she walked away.

The man swore under his breath, clicked off his seat belt, and started picking up the shrapnel from his phone.

Once he was safely restrained in his seat, I ventured a question across the aisle. "Rough morning, huh?"

The man bared his Hollywood-straight teeth and glared out the window at the darkness. "You have no idea." He slipped the wedding band from his finger and began playing with it absentmindedly.

As we accelerated down the runway, I put my earbuds back in, reclined my seat a full half-inch, and tried to sleep. When we landed an hour or so later, the man across the aisle leaped up and stormed to the front of the plane before I'd even managed to click off my seatbelt. As the main cabin door opened, I heard him toss an awkward "sorry about that" to the flight attendant.

She responded with a halfhearted smile. "Don't worry about it, sir. I'm sure it happens all the time."

He stiffened at this, obviously contemplating a retort, but then thought better of it and vanished off the plane.

I didn't expect to think more about what I'd seen that morning. It was just another marital argument; another shouting, cussing couple; another man with a confident, polished exterior and a frazzled, fraying interior.

Then I arrived at the conference.

The Change Our World conference it was called—or something both audacious and cheesy as only a crowd of well-meaning Christians can be. Thousands of people had come from all over the country to attend and learn and discuss ways they might individually and collectively help shape our world for good. It was a well-attended, well-funded, and well-produced affair. Even the welcome folder I was handed at check-in felt posh, with lots of swag and full-color prints crammed inside.

My arrival time meant I had missed most of the first session, but I was able to slip into the auditorium just before the afternoon session started. Duplicate images of a flashy, bouncy timer counted backward on the two jumbo screens at the front of the room, with each tick-tock of the clock accompanied by an amplified drumbeat that made you feel like you were getting punched in the stomach in a dark alley. You could feel the energy in the room rising as the zero-minute approached, and when at last we reached liftoff, the theme song from *Rocky* began screaming over the expensive speakers.

The emcee bounded up on stage with a bright shirt and manicured fingernails, all visible and larger than life on the expensive jumbo screens. "Welcome, welcome, welcome, my blessed brothers and sisters, to the Change Our World conference!" he yelled into his microphone. A blinding shot of a chemically whitened smile burst on the screens, and the audience cheered. "I don't know about y'all, but I can feel it down deep in my bones—God is in the *house*." The audience cheered again, and I rolled my eyes.

The emcee raised his hand like a rock star and hushed the audience. "Now we have a real treat in store for y'all this afternoon. Our next guest here at Change Our World has been an internationally renowned Christian comedian for more than twenty years. He's been featured on every radio show you can think of and has even been a guest on the major network late-night talk shows. But despite all that, everybody knows he has a real heart for the Lord, and a heart to change the world too. Just like all of you. So, now join with me and let's give him a raise-the-roof, Change Our World welcome!"

The music and the cheering reached fever pitch as a surprisingly bright-eyed, sandy-haired fellow with flawless clothes, straight teeth, and an impressive tan swaggered out onto the stage.

I blinked several times, speechless. There he was—the Shouter from across the aisle—peacocking his way back and forth across the brightly lit stage, tan and radiant as ever.

The world gave a sort of sickening half-turn at that point. I couldn't help but cringe at the sight of him up there—for I saw myself in him as well—all swagger and smile, a spectacle strutting his song and dance for all to see, making others laugh with a memorized routine at a conference that pitched itself as helping "make the world a better place" while inside . . . well, who ever really knows what's going on down in our depths. Except that every so often we watch in horror as the turmoil within splashes over the sides of our carefully maintained facades and we chew out an innocent bystander, or sleep with a coworker, or wake up in a cold sweat after a nightmare in which *we* were the hamster running, running, running endlessly on the miniature Ferris wheel.

Before he'd even gotten into his routine, I stood up and bolted from the darkened auditorium, wondering if I was going to be sick. I ran toward the greenroom reserved for the conference's speakers and musicians, hoping to hide out there and collect myself until it was my turn to step on stage with my own song and dance. I practically crashed into three members of the headlining band as they stormed past me, pushing their way out of the greenroom with evident disgust. Inside the greenroom, the band's well-dressed manager was midstream in her harangue against two of the conference organizers.

"This is unthinkable," she seethed, her long silver earrings flickering like lightning with each syllable. "Completely unacceptable."

"Really, I am so very, very sorry," one of the conference organizers said. Her tone was genuinely apologetic, and she looked like she was about to burst into tears.

But the manager didn't hear a word. "Sometimes I wonder if you people even *read* the contract before you sign it. How can you mess up something as simple as this?"

The same organizer looked at me standing there in the doorway, a pleading expression on her face, and gently asked, "Would you mind excusing us for a little while, so the band can have their privacy until we get this sorted out?"

"I don't mind at all," I said. I scurried out of the room before the band manager could throw something at me. And I *didn't* mind. Whatever they were so furious about, I certainly didn't want to be there when the band returned.

The Shouter and the run-in with the high-maintenance band manager sparked an existential crisis on the plane flight home. Handcuffed to my suitcase, strapped into my seat at thirty thousand feet, I couldn't help but wonder if I was just another pawn in the brightly lit song-and-dance called "American Christianity," leading a life offstage that didn't actually warrant what I was saying on stage. Was my life deeply grounded in the living God and thus an indication of faith, hope, and love, or were the edges of my own life cracked and fraying?

When at last I arrived home from that trip, I decided to disappear for a week to a local Benedictine monastery. It was either that or check myself into the psychiatric ward of a local hospital for close observation.

It's hard to say what I was hoping for as I fled east from Vancouver toward the rolling, green farmland of the Fraser Valley. I'd never stayed at the monastery before, but several friends had highly recommended it to me, describing the quieter, more intentional life within the cloister's walls as a sort of healing balm on all their frenzy. After everything I'd been through in the past few days, I was looking for something—*anything*, really—by which to buoy and anchor myself amid the turbulence.

I parked my car outside the monastery and went through a sort of curved entryway. A young monk, dressed in a black habit and reminding me of someone I knew but couldn't place, welcomed me and offered to show me the way to my room.

As we walked the dark corridor, the silence of the place resonated all around us. We walked for quite a while, turning here and there down this hallway and that, passing the occasional black-robed monk who nodded and smiled at us but did not speak as we passed. There were no bright lights, no thudding speakers, no countdown timers, just the heartbeat of a life of work and prayer that was deeper, more substantial than words.

Suddenly I realized who the monk reminded me of. "Has anyone ever mentioned that you look like Luke Skywalker?"

The monk laughed and nodded. "It's the habit," he said, pulling on the coarse material he wore. "You know that George Lucas modeled the Jedi Knights after real monks, don't you?"

I thought for a moment, rearranging my mental chronology a little. "Of course he did," I said after a lengthy delay. "At least, I think I knew that."

"Here's your room," the monk said, stopping beside a door. "Dinner will be served in the main dining hall this evening at six o'clock, but be advised that it is a silent meal. Breakfast begins every morning at six thirty, and you're of course welcome to join us in the main chapel for any of our prayer services. But know that you are not obliged to do anything while you are here. Stay in your room the whole time, if you'd like, and rest. Or join in with the rhythms and life of this place. May I answer any questions?"

I shook my head, thankful to be welcomed as I came—unsure and overwhelmed, disoriented and confused. "No, I don't have any questions at all. I'm just thankful to be here."

"Well," Luke Skywalker responded, "we're glad that you're here with us too. We welcome you in the name of Christ."

Part of the package deal offered by the monastery to retreatants was the opportunity to meet daily with a spiritual director. Part Gandalf, part psychoanalyst, part drill sergeant, spiritual directors exist in a class of their own. Perhaps the most unique aspect is that the relationship is largely one-way, and thus free from the mutualities and shared niceties of almost every other category of human interaction.

After a luxurious eleven hours of sleep, I signed myself up to meet with a monk named Father Solomon the next afternoon. At exactly three o'clock I knocked on his office door, and a rotund man of a wrinkled and grandfatherly age pulled open the door with such force that the breeze blew the white hair off his shoulders. He adjusted his glasses, smiled broadly, and welcomed me into the small office, crowded from floor to ceiling with books: philosophy and theology, poetry and literature.

We each settled down into a comfortable blue chair, and Father Solomon asked how I was finding my first day of retreat.

I answered cordially enough, saying something about how much I was appreciating the change of setting and pace of life. Then I tried to return the formalities.

"So, Father Solomon," I said, searching for words, "how long have you been here at the monastery?"

Father Solomon didn't answer me at first, but instead measured me with a kind gaze from beneath a twin tangle of white eyebrows. "Chitchat will not be necessary, no matter how well intentioned. After all, we're not here to talk about me. You're under no obligation to pretend."

Though he wore a gentle smile as he spoke, I could tell he was watching me closely, gauging my every response.

"Oh, okay," I said, shifting in my seat. "But I'm just making conversation. That's what people do, right?"

"If this were a standard friendship, then yes. I suppose you'd need to conjure up some interest in my life," Father Solomon said with shining eyes. "But this is no standard friendship. Think of me as an impartial sounding board, one who cares deeply for and about you, but who has no vested interest whatsoever in the course your life takes. I don't need anything from you. I don't want anything from you. You're here for what—a week?" I nodded. "Then that means we have a total of five hours together. Consider these hours a gift. Just receive and be thankful."

"Okay," I said slowly, trying to find my footing on very unfamiliar but surprisingly supportive ground.

"Tell me about the storm that has brought you here."

"Is it that obvious it was a storm?" I asked, shocked to learn that I was being so unintentionally transparent.

"Well, not *obvious*, per se," Father Solomon said with a smile. "Sometimes I can just tell."

So I told him about the storm, about my dissatisfaction with the masquerade of faith I'd encountered not only at the Change Our World conference but also deep in myself, about the externalized "show" of religion I found myself caught up in that was largely devoid of any deep or abiding sense of truth or awe or wonder, of the religion that I'd once believed in but now found ironically and tragically devoid of the divine. I talked about the dislocation of being in a different city every night, of being told how great it was that I was "out making a difference in the world," and yet how strange and dishonest this felt given my own deep questions and inner turmoil. I even tried to put words to the gnawing hunger I sensed at the center of my life, the hunger that remained no matter how much I ate—a mirage that kept retreating into the distance.

At last I fell silent and waited for the sage to speak, but all I received at first was silence. Father Solomon pressed fingertip to fingertip in front of his face, occasionally stroking the coarse whiskers on his chin. When at last he spoke, it was with extraordinary grace and wisdom, though he aimed straight at the ache in the center of my life.

"The thrill of a carnival only lasts for so long, doesn't it?"

I frowned.

"A carnival is a wonderful place to go every now and then," he continued, "but a terrible place to live."

My mind spun for a few moments, trying to understand what he meant. At last my jaw dropped, and I saw in a single, crystallizing moment how perfectly the word *carnival* brought into focus the life I'd been living: the bright lights, the addictive cotton candy, the chipped-paint facades everyone was trying to maintain—a whole careening show haphazardly supported by a rusted-out interior that was threatening to crack.

Another image came at Father Solomon's words: a barren-leafed, withering tree. I could see the tree's roots in my mind, brittle and atrophied, no longer deep enough to support the life above ground. The meaning was clear: this was my life; and if I was to survive, what I needed was a kind of deeper sustenance, an abiding nourishment that would infuse my wearied, withered soul with new vitality, new life.

"Yes," I said at last. "Yes. That's it exactly."

Father Solomon thought silently for another few moments, chewing on his lower lip. "Might I offer you a suggestion?" he said at last.

"Of course."

And that's when my Sacred Year began.

What Father Solomon suggested that day was a season of life marked by intentionality, by dedication to what he called "spiritual practices." At first I had little idea what he meant. As a Protestant, all that really came to mind when I heard "spiritual practice" was quasi-erratic Bible reading and occasional, desperate prayers. I'd never really fasted before, had never spent more than five minutes in silence if I could help it. Beyond that, the realm of spiritual practice was a vast and uncharted wilderness.

I asked a lot of questions over my additional meetings with Father Solomon that week at the monastery. He patiently answered all of my questions and suggested several ways that I could learn more. Turns out there are more spiritual practices than I had ever imagined. Father Solomon and I discussed confession and pilgrimage and creativity, along with silence, simplicity, service, and even the intentional embrace of our own human finitude and mortality.

"Just about anything can become a spiritual practice," Father Solomon suggested on my last day at the monastery. "If you approach it in the right way—with intentionality, humility, receptivity, hope. And of course with an attentive eye on the lookout for the activity of the divine."

I was surprised by this claim, and Father Solomon chuckled at my raised eyebrows but then told me about another monk who lived a long time ago—named Brother Lawrence—who had extraordinary encounters with God while washing dishes in a monastery in France. And Saint Francis of Assisi, who believed that learning from the animals and birds was an avenue to God that most human beings couldn't even begin to fathom. And the modern writer Kathleen Norris, who reportedly found God permeating the everyday, quotidian aspects of her life, like cooking meals and hanging laundry.

Though I found all of this exciting and hopeful, a worry was growing inside of me during our conversations, a question that I knew touched on complicated theological ground and which I myself didn't have any clear thoughts on.

"But aren't spiritual practices kind of like trying to work our way to God?" I blurted out at last, struggling to find the right words. "You know, trying to make ourselves holy, or earning our own salvation, that sort of thing? Most days I have a hard enough time just keeping my head above water, and, to be honest, I don't have the strength to try and make God love me or even like me."

Father Solomon's face went grave, and he closed his eyes for several long moments. I wondered if I'd offended him somehow. When at last his response came, they were words of comfort, though the gravity of his tone shook the room like an earthquake, echoing in my soul like a song. "That's not the way this works, Michael," he said. "You needn't put that much faith in your own strength, for your strength is a mere atom beside an ocean of God's unending love. God is the Source. The Origin. The Ground of All Being. The One from whom and through whom and to whom are all things. You can't 'make God love you,' any more than you can *make* a star or a planet or even a human being. Any more than you can make yourself."

I didn't respond but sat there in the silence, listening.

Father Solomon spoke again, and the shaking of my foundations continued. "The God who called you into existence *ex nihilo*—out of nothing—is the same God who holds you in existence this moment and every moment. Were he to withdraw his hand, you would vanish without memory. All things would. No, you can't *make* God love you. You can't make God *like* you. But nor do you need to; he already does. Never forget that that is *why* he made you—because he *wants* you to exist. And not just exist. He wants you to *live life in all its fullness.*"

When Father Solomon at last opened his eyes they were moist with tears, tears that coursed down into the deep wrinkles of his face, irrigating deserts as they went. But somehow these tears weren't embarrassing; I didn't look away but instead took in the monk's weathered old face and hoped—just for a moment—that what he was saying might actually be true. And in that moment, a warmth wrapped itself around me like a Caribbean breeze, so quick and fleeting that I wondered if I'd imagined it, but so evident that it left me breathless.

Father Solomon was talking again. "Spiritual practices are a way of mapping your own personal soulscape. Helping you become more acquainted with who you are, who God is, and the people he's placed you into this life alongside of.

"It's rather like sailing," he said. I thrilled at the thought of this monk out there on the open ocean, white hair billowing in the wind, drops of sea spray clinging to his whiskers. A veritable Old Man and the Sea.

"When you're sailing, you learn to be constantly attentive to the wind—how it is blowing over your sails, what direction it is coming from, how fast it is moving, that sort of thing. Does that make sense?"

I nodded.

"This attentiveness to the wind becomes the main task—no, that's not the right word—the main *art* of sailing. We must both attend to the wind and then *respond* to whatever it is that the wind is doing. We trim our sails, adjust our course, sometimes we even exchange one sail for another—whatever it takes so as to be in the most receptive place given what the wind is doing. Our attentiveness to the wind *allows the wind to move us.*"

"And spiritual practices are like that?" I asked. "Like adjusting our sails and making sure we're in a receptive place given what God is doing?"

"Exactly." Father Solomon was smiling as he spoke. "And—if you'll indulge me for a moment—this metaphor becomes all the more fascinating given that in Jesus' time there was only a single word for 'breath,' 'wind,' and 'spirit.' 'The Spirit of God,' 'The Breath of God,' and 'The Wind of God' are all accurate translations of a common New Testament phrase, a phrase that basically means *GET READY: God is up to something!*"

I fell silent, wondering what shape the sail of my soul might be, where it might take me if I allowed my Maker to set the course. Then I remembered something Father Solomon had said during our first meeting. "Interesting that you knew a 'storm' had brought me here to the monastery."

"Very interesting indeed," Father Solomon said with a smile. "Now the question is: How will you respond to what the Wind is doing in your life?"

An idea took root as I departed the monastery and meandered my way back to the city. Though I was skeptical about how much of a difference these ancient spiritual practices could make in my life, I took great confidence in Father Solomon's belief that they could help me "adjust my sails" and be as receptive to the Breath/Wind/Spirit of God as possible. Maybe it was desperation, maybe it was faith (is there a difference?), but I decided to give it a year, decided to dedicate a set period of time to surrendering as deeply as I could to various spiritual practices and discover what might happen along the way.

I wanted to find out where the Wind might take me.

Maybe it wouldn't make any difference at all, and I'd find myself at the end of the year just as disillusioned and disoriented as I'd been when I first sought shelter at the monastery. But maybe—just maybe—the Wind would be strong enough to blow me beyond the carnival and toward a rooted, nourished, flourishing life.

"God help me," I whispered as I drove.

And for the first time in a long time this wasn't just rhetoric.

I actually meant it.

SECTION I

Depth with Self

CHAPTER 2

Single Tasking: The Practice of Attentiveness

*It ever was, and is, and shall be, ever living Fire, in
measures being kindled and in measures going out.*

—HERACLITUS[1]

Spirituality is seeded, germinates, sprouts and blossoms in the mundane.

—THOMAS MOORE[2]

I t is more than a little awkward when my wife, Danae, barges in on me,
sitting here at my desk, white-knuckling the sides of my chair, staring
at the apple.

"What are you doing?" she asks after a startled pause.

But I can't take my eyes off the apple. "Come back in an hour," I say.

"Really?" She sounds worried.

"I need to focus."

She hesitates but then retreats, gently closing the door behind her.
I hurry to lock the door, before returning at once to my seat before the
oracle.

This apple is beginning to speak, and I don't want to miss a single
word.

⁒

Interesting but relatively useless facts stick in my mind like darts in a dartboard. Like this one: Did you know that so long as it is stretched very, very thin (only a molecule or so thick), a single gallon of water could cover an area five square miles in size?

A friend recently fired that one at me. I winced as its tip hit home, realizing it at once for what it was: a mockery of my current state of being, a chafing metaphor for my life.

Bull's-eye.

"But if you could focus that same gallon," my friend continued, "pouring it into a straw about the size of a human hair, it would reach all the way down the center of the world, four thousand miles beneath the ground on which you stand."

Decreasing breadth increases depth. That's just the way things work in this three-dimensional world of ours.

As I begin my Sacred Year, it's painfully obvious which dimension I've been slogging along in. I feel stretched—just a few molecules thick. A few molecules *thin*, rather. Maybe *gaunt* is a better word. Or as Tolkien puts it: "like butter that has been scraped over too much bread."[3] Yes! That's it. Scraped gaunt, with lots and lots of dry and burned places throughout. I may be present and accounted for, but I'm certainly not very with-it. There isn't much of me in the "here" (wherever *that* is), and even less of me in the "now" (what time is it again?).

I'm trying to remember how I got this way. I don't recall always being this out of it. Nicholas Carr blames our use of electronic technology for scraping us gaunt. In his book *The Shallows: What the Internet Is Doing to Our Brains*, Carr points out that our habitual electronic multitasking between smartphones, websites, news feeds, and social media is dramatically rewiring the neurological pathways in our brains. According to Carr, all our browsing and liking and streaming and retweeting has conditioned the ability to focus right out of us. "In the choices we have made . . . ," writes Carr, "we have rejected the intellectual tradition of solitary, single-minded concentration. . . . We have cast our lot with the juggler."[4]

"Tell me," a wise friend once asked, "What is it you are doing with the singular gift of your life?"

Juggling? Is that what I'm doing with my singular gift?

It seems so, for I am a professional juggler—fit for a carnival. And this "skill" (if you can call it that) affects more than just my plugged-in, online habits, spilling out into the way I live the rest of my life. I multitask incessantly, launching more and more things into nail-biting, ulcer-inducing flight: objectives and goals, people and deadlines, phone calls and text messages and unanswered e-mails, fears and expectations, ego and masks. I spread myself impossibly thin beneath the imperative that *more* is better—bigger is better, faster is better, broader is better—with the end result that I stagger through life in a harried frenzy, jittery and nervous as any addict.

I see it in other people too: the conversations with coworkers or friends who aren't really listening, though perhaps they're trying to convince me they are, dolling out half-baked questions, half-baked because the little ovens inside their skulls are so crammed full that nothing is getting the heat it needs. Who do they think they're fooling, with eyes that don't see me, glancing down surprisingly often at the glowing screens or trolling the room for another momentary distraction?

Is a disorder still a disorder when it becomes commonplace? How many of us *don't* career our way through the world at seventy or seven hundred miles per hour, checking our watches every few seconds, wondering whether we'll make it or not, finish or not, arrive or not?

Diagnosed or not, we are an ADD culture, and I find myself agreeing with Carr that this isn't just a genetically inherited reality but a habitual, conditioned reality that we've *chosen* for ourselves. Day after day and decade after decade, we've taught ourselves how to give only a bit of our focus, a sliver of our fractured attention to everything we do. We rarely focus on something, rarely delve deeply into anything, all so we can scrape ourselves just a few molecules thinner over an ever-broadening area, so that we can fling yet another thing up into the air to join the juggled horde.

I'm starting to wonder if pushing along the breadth axis, if sacrificing depth in every area of my life, will be sustainable in the long run, or, frankly, if it is even worth it. Spread out as I am over the five square miles of my life, it is becoming obvious that I just don't have the mental or spiritual or emotional energy to care very much about very much. Days and people and things all blur into the obsolete and indifferent past, just as today will, and as tomorrow will, too, unless something changes.

The urgency of all this snapped into focus for me on that fateful plane flight home from the Change Our World conference, after the Shouter and the band manager set me to wondering if I was in fact living in what Thoreau calls "quiet desperation."[5] Perhaps it was the depth of the desperation that frightened me so much, for I found myself almost hoping that the plane wouldn't make it to its destination, found myself almost hoping the whole juggled charade that I had been masquerading as my life would at last come to an end.

"So that's what I'm doing with the singular gift of my life?" I ask myself. "Juggling so much that I'm relieved at the thought of it all coming crashing down?"

And yet I've encountered a radically different way of living in Father Solomon. During those hours of spiritual direction while I was on retreat at the monastery, he kept using words that seemed foreign and strange, but intriguing and inviting too: *Notice. Attend. Observe. Contemplate.*

How can I attend, or observe, or contemplate when I've got so many things up in the air that I have only half a second to notice each one before I must let it go or allow the next thing to crash?

John Muir is someone who knew how to notice things, who knew what he was doing with the singular gift of *his* life. One mid-December day in 1874, Muir was huddled in a friend's rustic cabin in the Sierra Nevada Mountains, just east of Sacramento. He had been stuck there for a while, forced inside by a torrential rain. When at last the rains subsided, a sun brilliant as good news lit up the land. And a wind blew up with such raw power that it snapped and leveled hundred-year-old trees around the cabin at the rate of one every two or three minutes. Energized by the sun and stirred by the wind, Muir leapt up, found his jacket and tie, and flew his coop, insisting that outside "the danger to life and limb is hardly greater than one would experience crouching deprecatingly beneath a roof."[6] Leaning into gusts as strong as a hurricane, Muir explored the wild, living country for hours, glorying in the sound of the singing trees, the radiant sunlight, the sheer exhilaration of winter's quickening freshness.

Then—on a whim, perhaps—he climbed up the highest tree on the highest peak in the area and clung there like a flag, holding on and holding out for dear life. His description of this afternoon is extraordinary, borderline mystical:

> I was therefore safe, and free to take the wind into my pulses and enjoy the excited forest from my superb outlook. The view from here must be extremely beautiful in any weather. Now my eye roved over the piny hills and dales as over fields of waving grain, and felt the light running in ripples and broad swelling undulations across the valleys from ridge to ridge, as the shining foliage was stirred by corresponding waves of air. . . .
>
> The sounds of the storm corresponded gloriously with this wild exuberance of light and motion. The profound bass of the naked branches and boles booming like waterfalls; the quick, tense vibrations of the pine-needles, now rising to a shrill, whistling hiss, now falling to a silky murmur; the rustling of laurel groves in the dells, and the keen metallic click of leaf on leaf—all this was heard in easy analysis when the attention was calmly bent. . . .
>
> I kept my lofty perch for hours, frequently closing my eyes to enjoy the music by itself, or to feast quietly on the delicious fragrance that was streaming past.[7]

I love the sensuous nature of Muir's experience: we see, we hear, we smell, we touch, we taste the wild and stormy world through his ecstatic and deep attentiveness to the surrounding details.

Like I said: Muir was someone who *notices*.

To notice something is to sense it. Have you ever noticed that your senses are organized in a hierarchy of increasing intimacy? If your eyesight is good, you could probably make out a single apple on a tree from a few hundred paces away. But you must be within about fifty feet to hear it thump onto the dry ground. And even then, you must stoop from only a few feet away and pick it up if you want to feel its sun-warmed skin. Its sweet fragrance materializes at a few inches. But to taste it? To taste it you must drop all your defenses and allow the distance between you to diminish to intimacy.

Given this sensual hierarchy, why is it, do you think, that the psalmist upended the "obvious" order of things and began instead with intimacy before bothering to get around to objective visual observation: "*taste* and see that the LORD is good"?[8] Could it be that intimacy is a prerequisite to seeing something fully? That only once we've "taken the Wind into our pulses," as Muir put it, dropped our defenses far enough so that the thing can become *part of us*, that it is possible to say that we truly "know" something?

Did Muir break off a few pine needles, I wonder, as he scaled his windy perch, crushing them between his teeth, and letting their spice and musky pungency quicken his pulse so he could finally *see* "the light running in ripples and broad swelling undulations across the valleys from ridge to ridge"?

We have only five senses, you know. Five tiny windows through which the world around us can come crashing into the rustic cabins of our minds.

And sadly, one of the unintended side effects of my juggling, of being spread only a few molecules thin, is that my "windows" have all had blinds pulled down over them, leaving me numb and indifferent. The more I juggle, the more the world becomes bland and bleak and barren.

When was the last time I actually threw open the shutters and *tasted* a meal or *listened* to the music in the trees? I was a boy the last time I climbed a tree, and, come to think of it, I can't remember the last time I actually remember *seeing* one. They disappear, don't they?—blurring as they do while we speed past or fly over. Juggling.

In February of last year, city maintenance workers replaced a section of cracked sidewalk close to my home. After pouring the new cement, they roped the section off, placing SIDEWALK CLOSED signs at either end to keep absentminded walkers from inadvertently mucking up their work. At least two creatures disregarded their signs entirely. The first was a lone dog, or a solitary coyote perhaps, that left a trail of clover-shaped prints a quarter-inch deep along the entire length of new sidewalk. These tiny catchments now rake and grab the world, grabbing ahold of it like Velcro as it courses along above them, hoarding leaves and bits of dirt inside themselves, the colorful beads of a broken necklace, a few drops of rain.

The second creature was one of us. Hasty letters were scrawled along one of the edges of the new concrete, freezing a moment in time: "DJ – 2/20/12. 2:15." I picture DJ as a lonely insomniac, out for a rainy stroll two and a quarter hours after midnight, who, upon seeing the SIDE-WALK CLOSED signs, stops and stoops. "Oh well, why not?" she says as she scrawls in the cement. "I might as well leave my mark on this fleeting world of ours."

Eons ago a volcano erupted near what is now called Laetoli, Tanzania. Great clouds of volcanic ash spewed out of the mountain, blanketing the surrounding area with several inches of fine, powdery ash that swirled like dry snow in the wind. Not long after the ash settled it began to rain, and as the rain mixed with the volcanic ash a sort of natural concrete formed. Before the concrete had set, five creatures disregarded the SIDEWALK CLOSED signs and left their mark on this fleeting world of ours, evidence of their existence that is still there today. A few moments frozen in time. The first creature was a bird, walking in a haphazard and roundabout way like any pigeon does; the second something like a rabbit, leaping skittishly here and there, nose twitching in fear, whiskers tinged with ash.

And then along came three hominids, strolling in a family of sorts: a male, a female, and a child, their bare feet leaving a trail of footprints some ninety feet long.

One of these walkers—as the concrete evidence reveals—paused for a moment midway along this ninety-foot stretch of wet sidewalk. Writing about the ancient footprints, Mary Leakey—the paleoanthropologist whose team discovered the Laetoli footprints—notes that the creature "stops, pauses, turns to the left to glance at some possible threat or irregularity, and then continues to the north. This motion, so intensely human, transcends time."[9]

It transcends time, this turning aside to look. It transcends time and also brings to mind another barefoot refugee named Moses, fleeing a volcano he himself had created with the best of intentions, who paused one day midfrenzy and turned left "to glance at some possible threat or irregularity."

What Moses saw—glory of glories—was a burning bush.

Would the bush have burned, I wonder, if Moses hadn't noticed it—if he'd just sped past with his face aglow from an electronic screen, mumbling half-baked questions? Juggling?

Someone once suggested that perhaps the best translation of *Selah!*—the Hebrew word we find sprinkled like seasoning throughout the Psalms—is *"Shut up! And pay attention!"*

I like that.

I need to stop—to be jolted out of my comatose coasting. I need to be surprised and awed and enlivened by things rather than just letting the world blur past me in my drive-by, fly-by, race-by life.

I need to hear the *Shut up!* too, need to quiet the incessant monologue of judgment and comparison and ridicule and mockery and fear that roils inside me, long enough to notice something, to encounter something other, something outside of myself.

Selah! is an invitation to be like Muir, to throw open the blinds and let the world come streaming in like the sun. It's an invitation to fly my coop and step outside this dingy little cabin, to be sensuous and ecstatic, to romp around the world and climb up the highest tree on the highest hill in the neighborhood and cling there for a while, billowing in the Wind like a flag, holding on and holding out for dear life. It's an invitation to *attend*, to *observe*, to *contemplate*, to *notice*, to *pay attention!*

But wait—that last phrase is not the right way to talk about this.

The first four seem true, but the last feels too mechanistic, too economic: "*Pay* attention," this phrase boasts, and, in a sort of exchange, you'll "receive" something in return. "*Be* attentive" gets more at the heart of *Selah!*, for attentiveness is not something you can buy at any price but rather something you must become. Attentive is a way of being in the world, an inherent availability and receptivity, a connection, like the tension that keeps bridges standing, uniting different bodies across the void with a thin filament of intention.

Selah! the psalmist cries again and again. *Notice! Look, see, listen, hear, touch, feel, smell, taste!* Be intentionally attentive to the world around you, attentive as a partner in a dance. Close. Warm. Intimate. Embracing for a while and letting the sparks fly.

Speaking of sparks, thinkers as different as the Greek philosopher Heraclitus and the Jewish mystic Baal Shem Tov believed there was something like a "divine spark" tucked away inside each and every individual thing—a pearl of great price waiting to be found. While incredibly exciting at first, this can get overwhelming pretty quickly. After all, there are just so many *things* out there. Maybe that's why we've done our tragic best to cram and confine God into a few specific holy places, into churches and synagogues and mosques, because the thought that the Almighty One might be out there somewhere, *anywhere*, is—well—just a bit too much for us to handle. After all, there are (give or take a few billion) something like one hundred billion stars in our galaxy alone, and about that many molecules of water in the tiniest of snowflakes. (Remind me, if you would, how many snowflakes there are in a blizzard?) And that same number—one hundred billion (give or take a few, remember)—is about how many of us *Homo sapiens* have lived on this planet, which also happens to be around the total number of hazelnuts harvested in Oregon in the last decade, or the number of grains of sand that would fit into my car if I packed really, really carefully, and—oh yeah—about the number of neurons crammed inside each of the stretched-thin, half-baked ovens we all carry around inside our skulls.

Give or take a few billion, of course.

The great challenge of numbers this huge is that while we humans are somewhat adept at getting them into our heads, we are dismally incapable of getting them into our hearts. Exponents are always an abstraction, rocketing us instantly from the real into the ethereal: a child can do the math and add a hundred billion together with another hundred billion to get two hundred billion; you can hold down the zero key long enough to get a googol (a *googol*, by the way, is actually a number: 10^{100}, or a 1 followed by 100 zeroes) just as well as I can. But as Stalin allegedly noted with ominous calculation, "The death of one person is a tragedy. The death of a million a statistic."[10]

Our hearts, it seems, can be scraped only so gaunt before they crack into an acre of arid indifference. We are woefully incapable of caring well about very much, and it doesn't matter where the commas go: if we have to use even one it's probably a good indication that we're juggling a few too many, that somewhere in the forest we've misplaced the tree we might climb up, that we've forfeited the one tiny snowflake for the blinding blizzard.

A friend of mine, a musician, told me of a particularly sharp lesson he'd received from the master under whom he was studying. "You have far too many records," the master insisted. "Get rid of them. Go from a hundred albums to maybe four or five, delve deeply into them, and then—then!—*perhaps*—you will truly learn to love the music they contain. Perhaps *then* you may come to truly know them."

A hundred billion stars? A hundred billion people? A hundred billion neurons and molecules and hazelnuts?

Has anyone seen the singular gift of my snowflake amid the hordes? I remember seeing it there on the shelf, next to the other records, but I seem to have misplaced it now, somehow.

Is *Selah!* the reason Moses saw the burning bush at all? Did his turning left that day somehow fan the divine spark ablaze? Let the glow out? Was his *attentiveness*, his *observation*, his *contemplation*, his *noticing*, the thing that set the whole thing off?

Is *Selah!* what Jesus meant when he cried, "Whoever has ears, let them hear"?[11] Perhaps *Selah!* is the answer to our endemic ADD, the cure to my own frenetically juggled, fractured life. What if it is a first step toward health after the cracking of my scraped-gaunt-like-butter-over-too-much-bread life, a way of focusing my meager gallon as best I can, a way to notice a few particulars instead of trying to juggle blizzards?

A chance to *Selah!* comes not long after I return from the monastery. Peter, a friend and retired schoolteacher, owns a hazelnut farm not too far away. Every year he allows a few of us to glean from his orchard once his commercial harvesting is finished. The commercial process requires a great vacuum that inhales everything in its path: fallen hazelnuts, sticks and leaves, bird feathers. It swallows the hazelnuts into its holding tanks and then spits out the less savory parts in its wake. The machine is incredibly efficient, vacuuming up thousands of pounds of hazelnuts in just a few hours. But despite its efficiency, nature's profligacy prevails, and last year, by scrounging around on our hands and knees, we were able to squirrel up hundreds of pounds of hazelnuts in a single afternoon.

As we are en route to Peter's farm, a friend reminds us that the fourteenth-century English mystic Julian of Norwich—whom Thomas Merton has called "the greatest of all the English mystics"[12]—had a thing for hazelnuts. She reads a section from Julian's *Revelations of Divine Love*:

> At the same time [God] showed me something small, about the size of a hazelnut, that seemed to lie in the palm of my hand as round as a tiny ball. I tried to understand the sight of it, wondering what it could possibly mean. The answer came: "This is all that is made." I felt it was so small that it could easily fade to nothing; but again I was told, "This lasts and it will go on lasting forever because God loves it. And so it is with every being that God loves."
>
> I saw these three properties about this tiny object. First, God had made it; second, God loves it; and third, that God keeps it.[13]

As we are getting ready to depart Peter's orchard with our hordes, I stoop down and pluck up a single, average hazelnut. It is small and unimportant, and very lovely besides: a pleasant oak hue with dime-width mahogany ridges encircling its circumference. There is a little mud obscuring its shine. I wipe it clean with my thumb, and when I press it to my nose I smell the gift of good land. I hold the hazelnut up to the sunlight, wondering if I might catch a glimpse of the spark within. The autumn sunlight breaks through a cloud and ricochets off the hazelnut— a blinding flash that burns the moment in my mind.

Instead of dropping this hazelnut back to the ground or chucking it into the bags with all the rest, I hide it safely in my pocket.

Selah!-ing a hazelnut is as good a place to start as any, I figure. Anything much smaller than that would get lost in the lint. Maybe it will still be there, decades from now, a quiet memento of the first moment I noticed I was noticing something—a souvenir of my first *Selah!*

I resolve to palm the hazelnut whenever I find I've worked myself up into a frenzy, whenever I feel myself slipping into a multitasked, ADD, juggled frame of mind. With it in sight, I'll echo Julian: "This lasts and it will go on lasting forever because God loves it. And so it is with every being that God loves."

One afternoon, after the hazelnut has been riding around in my pocket long enough to become a burnished brown, a blizzard blindsides me. While I'm shouting at someone on the phone, texting to delay my next call, writing a half-baked response to an urgent e-mail, wolfing down a tasteless meal, I find myself wondering: *How much coffee have I injected so far today? Can I have another fix?* I know I'm addicted, but you don't understand—everything is getting lost in the chaos. I'm falling behind, getting snowed under, losing my grip.

Nearing panic I rub a sweaty palm along my thigh and—*gasp!*—feel the hazelnut in my pocket.

"*Selah!*" I shout, and I suddenly notice the apple on my desk.

An hour seems about right.

Divided evenly between my five senses, the Oracle of the apple will have twelve minutes to break through each of my shuttered windows. Maybe then I'll fly my coop, romp around in the hills, climb a tree, and let the Wind come coursing into my pulses.

I am not disappointed.

Within the first thirty seconds I realize I've never actually *seen* an apple. Not really, anyway. How many sides does an apple have? I know, I know. An apple is round, right? It doesn't *have* sides. But are you sure? Viewed from the top, this particular apple *does* have sides. Five in fact, and five corresponding little knuckles on which it stands. *Knuckles* is an accurate word, especially given the wrinkles that stretch between each of them, just as the thin skin creases lengthwise between my knuckles when I ball my fist. The whole skin is freckled with texturey (wait—I'm getting ahead of myself) mustard-hued flecks. When I try to count them I get to 467 and then can't recall whether or not I've already covered this terrain before.

And the color! Don't *ever* let anyone tell you an apple is red. To generalize is to miss the thing entirely, to lose the spark in the blizzard, to lose the hazelnut in the harvest.

The inside of this apple's belly button is as yellow as a Number 2 pencil, and is shaped like the underside of the sea star, which I now see was there all along, hiding between the knuckles in the apple's southern hemisphere. And the skin isn't a single color at all, but rather a full gradient: fresh blood, last night's merlot, hummingbird throat, sunflower crimson. Anything but plain old *red*. As I'm spinning the apple in my hand a solar flare erupts on the surface, borrowed from a NASA photo, a "coronal ejection" rising up from the darkened surface of the sun, a ghostly sheet of pale yellow hanging there against the fiery backdrop.

There are thirteen soft spots on this apple—evidence of a relatively hard life. I'm not sure how one would measure this, but it takes about as much of a concentrated squeeze to bruise the apple as it would take to break an egg. I feel the cell walls crush beneath my fingers as I squeeze. The mustard-colored flecks on the apple's skin have a texture, but I must admit I don't discover this with my fingertips; they aren't sensitive enough. Instead I use my tongue tip, which has many more touch receptors. Using my tongue like a magnifying glass, I feel the tiny raised islands of texture—a one-in-a-million, a one-in-a-hundred-billion story etched here in braille on this particular apple's papyrus.

We smell because fields of tiny neurons in the olfactory regions of our noses wave in the air like a forest in a storm. Men typically have a much less sensitive sense of smell than women, but by all accounts the human ability to smell pales in comparison to most members of the animal kingdom. Nevertheless, I inhale the apple, and to my surprise encounter far more than I expect. The grapefruit my apple neighbored in my kitchen fruit bowl has rubbed off; I can smell its spicy tang even now. And—though I can't figure out how—this apple has also somehow picked up faint hints of vanilla along the way. When I bite into it, I find that the apple's inside smells vastly different from its outside. Who would have known? If the apple's fragrance were a song, the skin would be treble—the high, lighter notes—while the interior is obviously the midlevel and bass—the deeper, throatier tones. The eighteenth-century German poet Friedrich Schiller kept a jar of rotten apples in his desk. Apparently the sharp and prickly scent of their decay helped him focus his mind and increase his creativity. Perhaps I'll start my own jar of apples and keep watch while they rot.

Apples don't say much, of course, but they do sound. *Crunch* is a stale way of putting it. This apple's flesh is so fresh it tears like a sheet of paper when I tug at it. While I'm chewing, it dawns on me that I'm hearing it not the way I hear most sounds—through vibrating air—but instead the sound is traveling through my teeth and along my jawbones until at last it reverberates in my skull—a much louder and direct route to my eardrums. And shifting the bite from left to right has as much effect as turning the balance dial on a stereo. By the time I've spun the dial back and forth a few times, the tear of flesh is now applesauce and sounds softer: melting slush being scraped from a car window.

And taste . . . Well, intimacy delights most behind closed doors—an intimate dance between the beholder and the beholden. But I will let you in on a little secret: the seeds of an apple taste remarkably like a common ingredient used in sweet breads, cookies, and other delicacies. I'll leave it to you to *Selah!* and discover how the spark therein tastes.

The point is this, it seems: the more you look, the more you will see; the more you listen, the more you will hear. "Further up and further in!"[14] is how C. S. Lewis puts it in his *Chronicles of Narnia*. There is always more to know, always more to *Selah!*

But the way to find it is not to spread yourself just a few molecules thin, to lose yourself in the blizzard. The way down into the depths of attentiveness is to stop juggling a thousand and one things and focus instead on the singular.

The precise.

The particular.

The One.

Given all our cultural, egotistical, and neurological momentum toward juggling, learning to *Selah!* individual, particular things, to embrace them like a partner in a dance, to construct bridges of intentionality and plunge a straw four thousand miles down into the heart of things, is rather hard work. It takes time, and coordination, and—well—practice.

And this practice *has* spilled over into other areas of my life. After carrying around the hazelnut in my pocket for a while, and being attentive to about a dozen apples, I'm finding that I'm a much better conversation partner. Especially when I've turned off my cell phone. And I don't just mean "silent" mode either, but actually *off*. My wife and I now make a habit of doing this whenever we're out with friends or enjoying time together. I've begun chewing each bite of food at least fifteen times, making sure I roll the balance dial back and forth at least three or four times per bite. It sounds easy until you actually try it. I'm slowly learning not to juggle incessantly but to instead marshal my mind, shepherd my thoughts. The practice of *Selah!* is spilling into other areas as well: the afternoon stroll in the snowy woods, the book I'm reading, the friend I'm talking to. I do my best to no longer dish out half-baked questions.

Kids, I discovered recently, can be wonderful tutors in *Selah!*, in this practice of single tasking. My niece, Tirzah, is almost two years old, and is as much a tangle of joy and curiosity and passion and emotion as her head is a tangle of red curls. She can't quite pronounce both syllables of my name yet, and instead contents herself by calling "Mile, Mile, MILE!" whenever she wants to get my attention.

I was multitasking her recently, forgetting the hazelnut in my pocket and juggling an e-mail, a phone call, and a promise to babysit.

When Tirzah realized that I wasn't actually talking to her, she toddled a bit closer to me, stretched out both hands, and started shouting, "Mile! Mile! Mile!" as loud as she could. I turned away at first, but my cold shoulder only managed to increase her volume. She ventured a little closer, shouting again, and then a little closer still, hands outstretched expectantly.

"I'm sorry," I told the person I'd just called. "Might I call you back later?"

As I turned toward her, my first emotion was exasperation, singed at the edges with anger. "What is it, Tirzah?" I asked, trying hard to control my tone.

"Dance," was her one-word response.

Turns out I've eaten hundreds of apples and slept through countless blizzards. Nearing thirty, I've rushed my way through almost eleven thousand days, and at least as many conversations. How many of them have I been truly attentive to? How many have I truly known?

"Mile! Mile! Mile!" cry the divine sparks all around us, inviting us to diminish the distance into intimacy.

Though the blizzard threatens, the hazelnut in my pocket grows warm, the pearl of great price waiting to be unearthed, waiting to be fanned into flame.

So I slip off my shoes, turn toward the left, and offer an outstretched hand.

Let the Dance begin.

Selah!

CHAPTER 3

Life and Death:
The Practice of Daily Examen

Let me know you, O you who know me; then
shall I know even as I am known.

　—SAINT AUGUSTINE[1]

Our wisdom, in so far as it ought to be deemed true and solid wisdom,
consists almost entirely of two parts: the knowledge of God and of ourselves.

　—JOHN CALVIN[2]

True humility is found in knowing yourself and God.

　—CATHERINE OF SIENA (PARAPHRASE)[3]

To be nobody-but-yourself—in a world which is doing its best,
night and day, to make you like everybody else—means to
fight the hardest battle which any human being can fight; and
never stop fighting.

　—E. E. CUMMINGS[4]

A reclusive man dwells on the perimeter of a Pacific Northwest island's secluded bay. He just might be of Elvish lineage, directly descended from Tolkien's Middle Earth. I say this because of the exquisite artistry by which he handcrafts wooden boats. The man has spent more than a year crafting a single vessel, working by sunlight, moonlight, and candlelight in his woodshop. The completed works of art glow from within with warmth and care and love. To witness one of these vessels is to find yourself filled with awe and longing, for they rest on the surface of the sea like a soft kiss or a leaf, proving that beauty and utility need not be either exclusive nor shoddily mashed-up as is so often the case in our mass-produced world.

I am floating now on one of these leaflike creations, a quick and agile "jolly boat," appropriately christened *Kingfisher*—though the elemental realm of this beauty is water, not air. It is early morning and cold. Sparklingly clear. The sun has just shown its face over a nearby peak, catching the *Kingfisher* in a fiery glow.

A group of us are pulling silently on our oars, with a man named Loren as our captain. Loren is a friend and professor and Renaissance man, as well as a poet, farmer, theologian, philosopher, chef, and seaman. With his plaid wool shirt, French beret, and grizzled beard, Loren looks almost mythical as he stands in the bow of the boat—the perfect captain for the *Kingfisher*. Looking over the bow, he shades his eyes from the glare of the morning sun, studying the vertical horizon between rocky cliff and sea toward which we are rowing.

"There it is," he says aloud. Loren sits down again, gripping his oar and falling in with the rest of us as we glide across the sea.

"There *what* is?" I ask.

"The current," Loren says between strokes.

"You can *see* the current?" I ask, astonished. What can I say: I grew up in Colorado. "A current that is beneath the ocean?" I pause my own rowing to owl my head around, trying hard to see what Loren sees.

Characteristically laconic, Loren nods. And keeps on rowing.

Unable to make any sense at all of the water off our bow, I turn back around just in time to catch Loren's half grin, as though he is simultaneously bemused that I know so little about the sea and yet pleased nonetheless that I am willing to inquire.

"How do you know it's there?" I ask.

"The surface of the sea is like a text." Loren explains as he rows. "It is possible to read it, to interpret it, to discover meaning in it."

Though I consider myself a lover of both the words and the sea, I've never before acknowledged the kind of resemblance Loren is describing. But Loren has sown a metaphor in my mind, and it has taken hold.

"Of course!" I say with a smile. "We talk about reading a person's body language, or even their facial expressions, and finding meaning there as well. Why not read the surface of the deep?"

"That's the idea," Loren says, still rowing. "And we talk about reading between the lines as well, unearthing meaning that is buried; meaning that, while present, is difficult to detect, more implicit than explicit."

I stop rowing completely and stand up, trying to get a better view of the water off the bow. "All I can make out is the cliff and sea. There is no meaning for me there."

Loren continues rowing, but speaks from his decades of experience. "Do you see the smaller riffles nearest to the cliff, the three-foot-wide mirror-calm gap, and then the continuation of the similar smaller riffles immediately beyond it, stretching out towards the channel?"

Loren's language is precise, instantly bringing to clarity what I'm seeing, making perceptible what was otherwise invisible. There it is: the mirror-calm roadway stretching along the contour of the cliff, continuing on as far as the island allows vision. "Oh," I say, hearing the astonishment in my own voice. "Yes, I see it now."

"That smooth roadway is the current," Loren explains. "It moves along the island in a southerly direction when the tide is ebbing out to sea, and in a northerly direction when it is flowing, flooding back into the sound."

And we are getting close to this smooth roadway. Two more full strokes and we are nearly there, less than a boat length from it.

I sit back down.

"Toss your oars!" Loren commands.

Our response is immediate, the entire crew lifting their oars up out of the water, lifting so they are all standing vertically in the boat. The cool drops of seawater spark like gems in the sun as they slide down the oars and over our hands, baptizing us with liquid fire.

The *Kingfisher*'s momentum carries us toward the mirror road. With a gentle adjustment on the tiller, Loren directs our little leaf through the smaller riffles and into the heart of the current. The effect is instantaneous—the *Kingfisher* shoots forward, gaining a knot or two in speed from the silent, mighty power moving beneath the surface, this power that is in fact a dance of sun and moon and earth and sea, and older and longer and deeper than any of us.

"Astonishing," I say, closing my eyes, feeling the movement carrying us.

We are at rest now, borne along by an ancient power working constantly and tirelessly in the depths.

⁓

Just north of Seattle, my wife, Danae, and I are on a Saturday afternoon hike through lush temperate rainforest with friends, Jennie and Andrew. Jennie and Andrew have both worked in the medical profession for decades, Andrew at the helm of a hospital and Jennie as a doctor advocating for healthcare rights on behalf of at-risk migrant workers. It is a glorious day, the sunlight filtering down through the trees and the damp, *living* smell of the forest rising fragrant all around us. The conversation is good as well, meandering like the pathway upon which we walk, ranging over topics both personal and universal. Nearing the pinnacle toward which we are walking, Jennie asks me a question that will set me thinking for months.

"Michael," she begins, "where are you most yourself?"

In many ways it's a straightforward question. It makes sense given some of the content of our earlier conversation, given my acknowledgment of the occupational and existential questions that roil within me: *How do I get ahead? Where do I belong? What am I doing with my life?* But I'm not exactly sure what she's getting at, and so I ask back, "What do you mean?"

"Well," Jennie says, "during our whole conversation I've had the distinct feeling that you don't actually know who you are."

I slow down in order to hear well what Jennie is saying—for she's spot on, in fact.

"Go on," I say.

"You are working four different jobs," she continues. "You travel and speak all over the country. You're on the boards of different organizations, et cetera, et cetera, et cetera. The way you carry yourself, you look like you're someone who is always going somewhere. From the outside, you seem like you know exactly what you're doing, like you have it all together. I would never have guessed that you are wrestling with all the existential angst you've mentioned during our hike."

"Really?" I ask. This is surprising to me—the first hint of the substantial gap between how I perceive myself and how I am perceived by others. "All that existential angst is what drives me to do more—it's the great engine of my activity in fact, the great fire fueling my activity." I look at Danae and smile as I say this, for she knows this up close and personal.

"That makes complete sense," Andrew says. "There are basically two poles to existential anxiety. Some people are incapacitated by it; others are driven into ever-increasing action."

It's more than a little vulnerable to have the inner workings of my being out on the table for discussion, but in the context of friends, I resist the urge to backpedal.

"The problem with doing more and more," I say, "is that it makes answering your question—where am I most myself?—almost impossible. The question of being—'who am I?' or 'where am I most myself?'—gets buried under the urgency of doing—'what must I accomplish today?'"

"Of course you're not alone in this, Michael," Jennie adds after a moment of silence. "Our whole culture is oriented around external productivity. We value internal depth—knowledge of the true self—so very little."

"I find it so much easier to just work, you know?" I say. "To throw myself into doing and making, than it is to plumb the depths of my inner self and ask the questions of being."

"That's true," Andrew says, thoughtfully. "But for what it's worth, I'd counsel you to work hard at getting to know your true self. Go deep. Find out who you truly are. Who you've been created to be. Otherwise you'll wake up one day at my age—utterly exhausted and perhaps having accomplished a great deal—though you may still not have the faintest idea of who you actually are."

I like to think of words as little pieces of mental Velcro we all go around sticking to the world. "Clock," I might say, and if we were together you might look at your wristwatch or perhaps your phone. "Table" or "chair" or even "sky" are similarly well-stuck pieces of mental Velcro, with obvious and evident objects to which we'd all agree they refer. But of course there are some things in our world—love or death or beauty, to name a few—that are notoriously resistant to our attempts to cleanly grasp them with our little pieces of Velcro—the sheer magnitude of their reality evades and transcends the stick-to-itiveness of our feeble Velcro patches. While our words might adhere for a while, after time the stickiness wears off and the words fall to the ground like a dry leaf in autumn, bereft of potency and vitality, merely a "dead, or petrified metaphor" as C. S. Lewis's friend and Oxford professor Owen Barfield once described them.[5] Thus each successive generation must call in their poets and mystics, the sticky-makers among us, and task them with trying to make the Velcro stick again.

"True self" and "false self"—terms I discovered in Richard Rohr's book *Immortal Diamond*[6]—are the stickiest pieces of Velcro I've yet come across to describe a very disorienting reality: while sometimes it seems I'm living out of who I truly am, there are other times in which it is all too evident that I'm living out of a lie. Of course Richard Rohr is not the first person to suggest this. The Russian novelist Alexandr Solzhenitsyn believed this fundamental division exists inside all of us, noting that "the line dividing good and evil cuts through the heart of every human being."[7] And centuries before him, Saint Augustine, in his fiercely perceptive autobiography *The Confessions*, spoke of the felt difference between his "disintegrated" and "integrated" selves.[8] Each generation of writers, it seems, seeks to acknowledge this fundamental division between different sources, different motivations for how we live and move and have our being in the world.

The reality all these pieces of Velcro are trying to stick to is this: inside each of us there seems to be an essential kernel, a "diamond,"[9] as Rohr calls it, of individual being, granted to us by the Creator God (or rather, created *as* each of us by God), that is waiting to come into mature existence in all its uniqueness and beauty and individuality. And yet in opposition to this incomplete true self there is a whole army of false selves as well, each one a masquerade that is a kind of antiself or quasi self. Inherently opposed to the well-being of the true self, these false selves manifest as elaborate constructions, masks, selves that while certainly "real" are not in fact who we *actually* are, not who we've been created to be. If the true self is the gift of the Creator God, anchored therefore in the "Ground of All Being," then the false self is like an ethereal chameleon, changing as circumstances demand.

Jennie's question to me on that Saturday hike—"where are you most yourself?"—exposed the deep rift at the core of my being, bringing to articulacy the subconscious question that had been gnawing at me for a long time: *Who am I, really?* I know a great deal about who people expect me to be—about the external pressures and expectations from culture and family and friends. I know a great deal about the internal expectations I put upon myself—productivity and creativity and success. But who is my true self? Who have I been created by God to be? What is the nature of my essence actually like?

This lack of depth-knowledge of the true self is as ironic as it is tragic. Think about it: If asked I could tell you what the weather is like in Dubai, Sydney, Los Angeles, and New York, all in less than twenty seconds. Pressing a little deeper, I could also provide not only the current conditions but also the average wind speed, annual precipitation, and typical hours of sunlight for each metropolis.

Want to know about sixteenth-century mysticism in France?

Catherine of Siena's birthplace and date?

No problem.

Two new Wikipedia windows and I'll have a rough sketch for you in less than thirty seconds.

But if you inquired into the "ecosystem of my soul," as one friend describes it, into the average climate of hope I experience therein, or the source and texture of the despair that may have been darkening my internal world during the past week; or about the elemental makeup of this internal "ecology"—fruits of the Spirit, let's say: love, joy, peace, patience, kindness, goodness, faithfulness, gentleness, and self control,[10] as opposed to the seven deadly sins: lust, gluttony, greed, sloth, wrath, envy, pride—I'd be hard pressed to respond with more than a blank stare.

Truth be told I don't really *know* what's happening down in the deep places of my self. Who knows what currents are moving there, way below the surface?

Wikipedia aside, who would have ever predicted that we might misplace our very selves?

Shortly after that hike with Jennie and Andrew, I'm back at the monastery, in the dining hall, or refectory, as it's called. The vaulted hall is utterly silent except for the quiet sound of thirty or so soup spoons dipping and lifting and then scraping a simple but delicious black bean soup. The silence has palpable weight to it, and fragility too—as though it were an enormous pane of glass that we have all lifted together and are now holding above our heads. There is a strange community that emerges from the strenuousness of this communal silence. Although none of us are interacting in the usual manner during the meal—with chitchat and comments about the weather—we are in fact working together, collaborating, and participating, each of us upholding our respective corner of the silence.

I can't help but wonder what might happen if I dropped my fork or—God forbid—sneezed. The thought almost makes me burst out laughing, but I force the laugh into a smile and maintain my portion of the silence.

When we have all finished eating, our used plates and cutlery are cleared by the two monks to whom the responsibility has fallen this week. Once the plates are cleared, someone strikes a bell that—in contrast to the heavy silence of the meal—seems loud and deep as a gunshot as it ricochets around the refectory. The ringing of the bell is warm and bright and—like the silence before it—seems to have a physical quality to it. A pounding on the door of my mind, demanding my attention.

I'm so bell-shocked by the ringing that I don't realize that everyone else in the room has risen from the tables, pushed in their chairs, and begun quietly reflecting on the meal. Brother Nicholas, the young monk who is seated next to me, taps me on the shoulder and motions for me to stand. I push out my chair with a loud screech and stand up awkwardly, miming the monks and looking down at the empty table before me, wondering what I'm supposed to be doing.

"What is the bell for?" I ask Brother Nicholas a few minutes later when we've all departed the refectory for the adjacent corridor.

"The bell," Brother Nicholas explains, "is an invitation to reflection. 'Stop! Notice!' it says. 'Now you are *here!* Here you are *now!* Mark this moment. What have you just done? Why did you do it? How did the doing of it affect you? Did it bring you toward life or toward death?' In this way it's both an invitation and a warning: don't let what is now passed slip by unexamined."

"After every meal?" I ask. "Seems like a lot of work to end every meal."

"In a way," Brother Nicholas says. "I suppose we believe that living well requires a great deal of intentionality in general. We seek to reflect not only upon our meals together but upon everything we do. After working in the garden, scrubbing a toilet, making a meal—we take a few minutes to look back upon the thing and take note of how it affected us. It's like we're holding up a magnifying glass, trying to see as clearly as possible how God was at work in us during that activity. We are searching for the ripples of the divine that radiate throughout the ordinary."

Sounds like *Selah!*

Imagine that! Igniting one's attention to time's passage; holding up the magnifying glass of intentionality to consider what has just slid by, noting how the moments affected us and what they may have revealed to us about the immortal diamond we are within, doing our best to make sure we don't lose those moments in the ever-flowing stream of unending hours.

Imagine that: doing something—even something ordinary and

mundane as eating a meal (or living a life)—and then afterward, actually *knowing* that you've done it. Savoring it. Rolling it around in your consciousness like a morsel of fresh-baked bread in the mouth, contemplating, tasting, appreciating, examining it.

This is what the Daily Examen is: a magnifying glass for exploring the ecosystem of the soul, a bell ringing out clarion and strong amid all the fog of unknowing, a mirror-smooth roadway atop our internal oceans that—if carefully followed—just might lead us past the limits of our current knowledge into the wisdom of the true self.

But I don't see this at first.

It seems rigid and formulaic at first, off-puttingly so, in fact.

Saint Ignatius of Loyola—the founder of the Jesuits and creator of the Daily Examen—was a military man, and a militaristic regimentation can be perceived at every turn in the Examen's structure. But as I slowly practice the Daily Examen more and more regularly, I begin to see the enormous help the structure provides. It's like a ladder: Rigid, yes. Strong and dependable too. And that's the point. You can't climb very high on Jell-O.

The Daily Examen has five basic steps, and I've found envisioning these steps as "movements" in a musical piece makes them seem less regimented. You begin with gratitude, then move into a petition to God for clarity, crescendo with a minute-by-minute, hour-by-hour review of the day's events, descend into confession for the wrongs committed, and wrap things up with express hope of living well in the time that is to come.

I begin practicing the Daily Examen at the conclusion of my days, taking fifteen minutes to step through these five movements.

My practice is laughably thin at the start.

"What happened today?" I smirk as I enter the third movement of my second Daily Examen, the "review of the day."

"Not much," comes my snide retort. "I ate breakfast, and then went to work, ate lunch, did some more work, and then—what did I have for dinner? Oh who knows. And after that? Forget it! I'm too tired to even remember, and I have a great deal to do tomorrow. That about sums it up. Time for bed."

It goes on like that for a while.

Do you remember the movie *The Karate Kid*? I feel like Daniel—the young karate student—being asked to "wax on, wax off" the long line of cars belonging to the karate master, Mr. Miyagi. "What's the point of this?" I keep asking myself as I sit down at the end of another long day and begin going through the motions of the Daily Examen yet again. There don't appear to be any results, and I am starting to get discouraged. "Am I really getting to know my true self through this?" I ask.

The next day a project I've been working on for nearly five years collapses with a single e-mail: Definite no-go. Pack it up. Head on home. Story's over. Hundreds upon hundreds of hours of work, shattered into obsolescence.

Just like that.

And as I read and reread the e-mail I am visibly shaking, the outward manifestation of an inner crumbling.

In *The Karate Kid* we find out later just how integral the seemingly nonsensical motions prescribed by Mr. Miyagi actually are in forming Daniel's muscle memory. The endless hours of "waxing on" and "waxing off" are shown for what they are: conditioned responses aimed at deflecting the opponent's attacks. They've become natural—second nature, in fact.

When I come to the Examen on the night of that project's collapse, a quick and superficial gloss over the day's events isn't even remotely possible. It's time to go deep, straight to the epicenter where the throb and an ache are continuing to churn, the point from which all the fear and insecurity and pain are radiating out like dark lightning.

During the first two steps of the Examen's rhythm—gratitude and petition—it becomes clear that the former weeks of work have conditioned me well, setting me up and familiarizing me with the contours of the practice for just a moment such as this, when I really need to not be checking off a list but instead entering deeply and naturally into the flow of the Examen itself.

Tonight the expression of gratitude for the gifts I have received in my life—family and friends and health and life and a home and food—is especially poignant. And the petition for God's assistance is not merely a mental exercise but the entire posture of my raw self, the self in desperate need of knowing who it truly is, who it has been created to be apart from external falsities and expectations. The first two movements feel fluid, familiar, foundational, allowing me to enter the heart of the Examen—the Review of the Day—with confidence and expectancy—a patient submitting before the examination of an expert doctor.

And that is where a whole array of realizations snap sharply into focus, where the ringing of the bell becomes close and incessant, rousing me from the continuity of my days to a place of unique clarity.

For I can suddenly see how bound and wound up my identity had become in the hoped-for success of the project that had just gone up in smoke. I see suddenly that for years I'd been living in a hypothetical world of the someday-success of the project, this imaginary world holding an array of would-be scenarios and conversations, from imagined red-carpet photographs to live TV interviews. Through the magnifying glass of the Daily Examen I suddenly realize I'd crafted a whole imaginary world in which I had wealth and influence and power, all of which I promised myself—of course—that I'd use for good. What I failed to see until that Examen, however, is that in the repetitive imaginings of this world of success, my sense of identity and well-being had become completely bound up in it.

"You'll be okay then," my imagined self said. "Once all of these things happen you'll be important, loved, established. *Then* you will be who you are."

In the Examen all of that is revealed for what it was: a falsehood and lie upon which I had been building my trust and my hope for security, my longing for importance and influence in the world. It had cracked like chaff and blown away in the Wind—all at a single e-mail—threatening to unhinge my sense of well-being and identity as it shattered.

There is a special piece of Velcro for a created object to which we ascribe such unequivocal power, to which we look for our salvation, peace, happiness, and prosperity: idol.

What snaps into focus for me in that evening's Examen is what a great and grievous idol I have allowed the project to become, and how sneakily this idol has been feeding a false self's sense of self-worth, way down deep in the core of who I am.

As I grow in the practice of it, the Daily Examen becomes a great bell resounding through my days and weeks and months, inviting me to stop for a moment and observe—like the monks in the monastery, like the captain of the *Kingfisher*—the currents moving way down in the depths of my life. It becomes an invitation to look and observe and notice how I am affected by the events of my days, to see how I have been moved and how I am moving in response. And all in the hope that perhaps—after a lifetime of practice, after innumerable cycles of "wax on, wax off"—I might have become so familiar with the shape and texture and essence of my true self that the unearthing of the immortal diamond will at last be nearing completion.

Then I shall have been made who I am, having at last become—fully and completely—my true self, and letting *it*—not the shape-shifting chameleons of my false selves—live and move and have its being in the world.

CHAPTER 4

Daily Bread: The Practice of Sustenance

*Blessed art Thou, O Lord our God, who bringest
forth bread out of the ground.*

—JEWISH PRAYER[1]

*For people who really love it, food is a lens
through which to view the world.*

—RUTH REICHL[2]

*Food is the daily sacrament of unnecessary goodness,
ordained for a continual remembrance that the world
will always be more delicious than it is useful.*

—ROBERT FARRAR CAPON[3]

Planting seeds inevitably changes my feelings about rain.

—LUCI SHAW[4]

*Gardens work powerful enchantment as they take us body and
soul out of the busyness of life and into a place set apart.*

—THOMAS MOORE[5]

Cultivate (v): to prepare and work in order to raise crops; to grow or tend; to produce by culture; to form or develop by education or training; to train; to refine; to promote the growth or development of (an art, science, etc.); to nurture, foster; to devote oneself to.[6]

My love affair with bread began in a back alley of Paris at around 6:30 a.m. on a Thursday.

I was eighteen years old and had been invited—thanks to a friend's airline-pilot father—to tag along on their family's weeklong vacation in Paris. They'd rented a flat equidistant between the *Basilique du Sacre-Coeur* and the *Louvre* and, for the mere cost of my food, I'd been offered a week to wander through a two-thousand-year-old city in the heart of Europe.

We were a rather introverted group, not to mention fiercely independent besides. And the Paris flat—although exquisite in many ways—was surprisingly smaller than it had appeared on the website. By the end of the week I was craving some solo time, yearning to get out and explore the ancient city on my own.

So on that Thursday morning, I stepped out the front doors of the apartment complex at around 5:30, just as the eastern skyline was hueing toward dawn. I turned left, then right, then right again down the vacant but somewhat familiar streets until—on a whim—I decided to duck down an unknown alley, turning left and then right and right again, and then left a time or two just for good measure until I was completely and entirely lost.

I didn't mind at all.

After all, how often does one have the chance to get lost in a foreign city's predawn glory?

Watching the city come alive was like being present for the birth of a child or the marriage of a friend—anticipated, of course, and yet breath-haltingly beautiful nonetheless. One moment the only sound I knew was my own meandering footsteps down a cobbled street, and then the next—so loud that I jumped with surprise and felt my heart pounding within me—the trees overhead erupted with the cacophony of birdsong, each invisible beak heralding the coming day with abandon.

I was *Selah!*-ing the city as I sauntered along: cool air, dusty scent, rough texture of stone, sound of groggy French. I gazed up past the darkened buildings into the brazen, blazing sky, awing at the neon-hued mares' tails and mackerel scales of the high clouds.

As I continued my wandering it gradually dawned on me that I was moving deeper into the unknown depths of the city.

"Hei," a sharp voice suddenly called out from close behind me, startling me out of my reverie.

I spun around, noticing in an instant that while I'd been gawking at the sky I had strayed into a less-than-savory district. Razor wire stretched across doorways, and there was graffiti on almost every window.

Three men in dark hooded sweatshirts were walking rapidly toward me, hands crammed down in hidden pockets.

"*Ne bouge pas!*" one of the men shouted again in a threatening tone.

"*Je ne parle pas Français,*" I shouted back. "I don't speak French" was one of the few broken phrases (along with "I need a toilet" and "I'm hungry") that I'd been able to pick up during my week in Paris.

"*Ne bouge pas!*" came the shout again, even more intimidating than before.

I quickened my pace, rounding one corner and then another, then ducking down an alley that—*gasp!*—ended in a high brick wall.

The hooded figures were gaining on me now, shouting and heckling, filling me with adrenaline.

As I ran I caught sight of my only hope: the warm, yellow light shining from an open back door halfway down the dead-end alley. The shopkeeper—a baker dusted from head to toe with white flour—was out in the alley, pulling deeply on his morning cigarette.

"Hey!" I shouted, waving at him. "Hey! Help!" I sprinted toward the baker.

"*Voulez-vous de pains?*" the baker asked, inhaling deeply on his cigarette.

The three men chasing me rounded the alley at that exact moment, and I saw the baker's eyes double in size. He tossed his cigarette away and began hurriedly beckoning me into the bakery.

An empty wine bottle shattered on the wall next to me just as I ducked into the store at a full sprint.

The baker slammed the door behind me, threw the dead bolt, and yanked the shades down over a wire-mesh window.

We stood there a moment looking at one another, wincing as another bottle shattered against the door.

"*Merci*," I said.

"*Voulez-vous de pains?*" the baker asked again with a smile.

"*Je ne parle pas français!*" I said, shaking my head wildly.

"You want breads?" the baker asked through a thick accent. "Right place," he said, motioning to the space around us. It was old and warmly lit and smelled of yeast and honey and milk. Despite the pounding of my heart, I realized how hungry I was.

Before I could answer, the baker grabbed me with a floury hand and pulled me deeper into the bakery, past racks of croissants and industrial ovens stacked full of slowly rising baguettes.

When at last we reached an enormous stainless steel table, the baker shoved a large mixing bowl toward me.

"Taste," he said thickly. He dipped a pinky finger into a bowl of light-brownish bubbling glop and shoved the whole mess of it into his mouth. He smacked his tongue loudly on the roof of his mouth several times, rolling the stuff from side to side with evident pleasure.

"Good, no?" the baker said.

Unsure of what exactly it was that I was sampling, I took a smaller amount on my own pinky and was startled by the strange combination of sour candy and pancake batter.

"What is it?" I asked, smacking my own tongue on the roof of my mouth.

"The seed," the baker answered with evident pride.

"The what?" I asked, laughing. Something was obviously getting lost in translation.

"The seed," the baker said shortly, and I stopped laughing. "Look."

He led me around to another side of the bakery where hundreds of sourdough baguettes were cooling on racks.

"The seed," the baker repeated again, smacking his tongue. "We bury the seed into the *pâte*. It grows into these delicious breads."

"Ahhh," I said, realizing what I'd sampled: sourdough starter. "Good indeed." For emphasis I smacked my tongue again and nodded.

"Here," the baker said smiling. He grabbed a still-warm baguette from a cooling rack and handed it to me.

"Oh." I patted my pockets in what I hoped was a universal sign of pennilessness. "No money."

"No, no," the baker said, pushing the loaf into my hand. "A gift, a *gift!* For your trouble," he explained, motioning toward the back door. "Delight it, *delight it!*"

The baker led me the rest of the way through his shop, through the cafe at the front, and to the glass door that opened out onto a familiar street. After looking both ways to be sure the hoods weren't waiting for me at the front, the baker pulled open the door.

Once outside I turned to thank the baker, but he didn't even let me speak.

"A gift!" he said with a smile. "Delight it, *delight it,*" he called out after me.

I turned toward the sunny street and, pressing the still-warm loaf up against my nose, inhaled deeply.

"Delight it indeed," I said with a smile.

The memory of what it felt like to take refuge in a bakery and then be sent away with a fresh loaf in hand is what first got me interested in baking. But it was only a passing interest, an occasional act. But once that memory had been sufficiently leavened by Father Solomon's invitation into this Sacred Year, I started baking a weekly loaf of bread. The more I *Selah!* this ordinary and everyday goodness, the more convinced I am that homemade bread is one of the most direct gateways to upper-case-J

Joy. Why else would the Scriptures name simple, ubiquitous food—bread and wine, not to mention milk and honey before that—as *the* foremost indications of divine love and provision? Call me a simpleton or even a fool, but with a steaming piece of fresh bread straight out of the oven, all gooey and dripping with golden honey butter, and accompanied by a small glass of wine, I shall call myself blessed far beyond my deserts.

Baking your own bread is a deeply attentive act, worthy of contemplatives everywhere. Each loaf becomes a hard-won pearl of great price unearthed by intention and care. Each time I press a freshly homebaked loaf up against my nose and inhale, I'm reminded of the first time I took an hour to eat an apple. No matter what's going on in my life, making bread brings me to a place where I just can't shake the sense that God really *is* good and that one day . . . all just might be well after all.

But beyond being contemplative, baking my own bread is in fact an act of defiant real-world rebellion. It is the antithesis of the fast-cheap-nourishless food pandemic we're facing in our world today. Baking my own bread is slow and costly, and incredibly nourishing as well. Just this morning I spent fifteen minutes grinding flour, mixing the dry ingredients together, stirring it into the yeast and warm water. Then I left the dough to rise in a warm place for about six hours while I went about the day's other work. When I hit my next writer's block I'll go downstairs, turn on the oven to 450 degrees, and hide the bread within for forty minutes.

All told, two homemade loaves of sourdough will require approximately thirty minutes of my day. In the calculus of modern economics I've paid dearly for these two loaves, more than doubling the cost of store-bought bread in labor costs alone, not to mention the required ingredients.

I could double the cost again if I sat in front of the oven window and watched the bread rise, though of course this is optional.

In terms of nourishment: assuming you do not legitimately suffer from the strangely fashionable "gluten sensitivity" of our day, homemade whole wheat bread provides an extraordinary complement of protein, carbohydrates, vitamins, and minerals—far more than the store-bought "enriched white flour" bread ever could. Popeye should have had a loaf of whole wheat bread alongside his spinach.

That reminds me.

I use whole wheat whenever I can for the same reason I reject racism and believe in the incarnate God: any notion of "purity" or "holiness" that excludes people, degrades community, or diminishes life originates not in the heart of God, but in the pit of hell. Some may think the connection between white flour and—say—Nazism a bit extreme, but I think it bakes. After all, "pure" is the adjective that was used not only to market "pure white flour" in its early days, but also as the basis for Hitler's vision of the "pure Arian race." Not to mention the motivating force behind segregated toilets, white-only restaurants, and two-tier movie theaters in the United States.

Nope. I'll have none of that, thank you.

Such notions of purity are altogether useless. All they've done is mask evil and promote death. Give me whole grain bread and whole grain communities. They're richer, heartier, more nourishing all around.

But I digress. Back to bread.

It took humankind untold years to discover how to make the stuff— how to mix the right amount of flour with the right amount of yeast and the right amount of water—and only a few decades of "specialization" for the average North American to lose these eons of history, culture, myth, and magic entirely. I mean no disrespect if you're a machine operator in an industrial bakery. But I know the secret you keep under the levers you pull and the buttons you push, and I have set myself to bring the glorious goodness of bread baking back into my own home. Why shouldn't my kitchen hold the same aura, goodness, wonder, and fragrance of that Parisian bakery?

It's actually quite easy. Here's the basic no-knead recipe I've been making weekly during the Sacred Year, adapted from the brilliant book *Healthy Bread in Five Minutes a Day*.[7]

Ingredients

4 cups whole wheat flour (fresh ground is best, but if you or a
neighbor don't have a grain mill, preground will do)
4 cups unbleached all-purpose flour
1/4 cup vital wheat gluten
1 tablespoon salt
2 tablespoons active dry yeast
3–4 cups of lukewarm (around 100° F) water

Method

1. Stir the 2 tablespoons of dry yeast into 3 cups of lukewarm
   water, setting this aside for approximately 5–10 minutes in a
   warm place until the yeast begins to bubble.
2. Mix the dry ingredients together in a large mixing bowl, separate
   from the water.
3. Combine wet and dry ingredients, stirring them together. Add
   only enough additional water (approximately 1/2 to 1 cup) so that
   the dough becomes sticky, but not runny. Think Play-Doh-ish
   consistency, not cake batter.
4. Cover with a damp towel and set aside. Let rise 2–4 hours. (If
   the bread will be sitting out longer than 6 hours before you bake
   it, put the dough into a container in the refrigerator.)
5. DO NOT KNEAD.
6. A half hour or so before you want to bake the loaf, turn on your
   oven so it preheats to 450°.
7. When the oven is hot, cut the dough in half with a sharp knife,
   and shape each half of the dough into a loaf.*
8. Place loaves onto a greased cookie sheet with 2–4 inches of space
   between them and bake for 20 minutes at 450°, and then for
   another 20 minutes at 400°.**

*For extra artistry and flair, consider "scoring" (slicing with a sharp
knife or razor blade) the top of the loaf with quarter-inch-deep cuts in
the shape of a square or an "X" or three parallel slits. The bread will rise
into these cuts as it bakes, imprinting a delightful design on the crust.

** For a firmer crust, put another cookie sheet on the bottom rack in the oven, and pour in a cup of hot water just before you put the bread dough into the oven. This water will evaporate as the bread bakes, raising the humidity in the oven and providing a firmer crust.

I have no doubt that after a week or two of baking your own bread you'll agree with me that breadcraft is—in the highest sense—contemplation of the divine mysteries hidden like yeast right in the exquisite mundanities of life. You may even stumble upon a truth that is evident in so many things in our world, if we have the eyes to see and the ears to hear.[8] "Further up and further in," as C. S. Lewis puts it in *The Chronicles of Narnia*. Isn't it true that each veranda of attentive joy opens out onto still greater vistas? That the more we discover, the more we realize there is to see?

Bread is just the first step on a lifelong journey. Why not pastries? Or homemade pizza dough? Or sourdough English muffins?

Go on! Delight it!

Mahatma Gandhi once cautioned that "To forget how to dig the earth and to tend the soil is to forget ourselves."[9] Not wanting to forget myself, I've recently begun interrogating dirt, and few things have proven to be more surprising or pleasurable. You'll think me mad for saying it, but dirt is utterly *fascinating*, and not least because I soon came to see that we humans (and every other living thing besides) are animate pillars of the stuff. Think about it; there is something breathtakingly beautiful—if we but have the eyes to see it—in the everyday metamorphosis: dirt becomes plant, plant becomes food, food becomes human, human thanks God for the food, lifting up the bread and the cup in a ritual of thanks. Then the whole cycle repeats itself, and every garden plot, no matter how small, becomes a miniature Mount of Transfiguration.

Thus I do solemnly declare: if God is active anywhere, it's in the dirt.

Think about it: this stuff has the ability to alchemize dry, dead seeds into abundant, flourishing life. The amount of life and energy roiling in the seemingly static soil is beyond comprehension. Turns out that there is much more alive *underground* than there is above it. An eccentric soil scientist named Hans Jenny once contrived a way to sum up all of the invertebrate and microbial biomass found in the soil. The total weight of all the itty-bitty things living underground in the average acre of farm-land weighed more than ten draft horses.[10] In a single acre of a particular Danish forest there are something like *one and a half million* worms. The total weight of the worms alone: more than four thousand pounds.[11]

Tread lightly, ye minor human form. There's much beneath thee, upholding thee, supporting thee that thou dost not see.

And that's just the beginning.

Most of our weapons against infectious disease come from dirt. Before humans had systematized a defense against tuberculosis, John Wesley recommended that sufferers of the disease dig a small hole in the fresh earth and—get this—kneel down on their hands and knees and breathe into and out of the hole daily. Some who followed Wesley's recommenda-tion actually survived the disease and returned to relative health.

The reason?

Secretions from a common soil microbe—*Streptomyces griseus*—destroy the TB microorganism. In fact, *Streptomyces griseus* is the tiny critter from which the first industrial cures for tuberculosis were later mass produced. Those who followed Wesley's ground-breathing advice apparently inhaled in enough *Streptomyces griseus* to combat the rot in their lungs.[12]

Kissing the ground gave them new life.

It used to be that a good farmer could tell quite a lot about a soil by putting a bit of it in his mouth and mulling it around for a while. Its pH was immediately evident, with acidic soil spiking the tongue like citrus while alkaline soil feeling like a mouthful of chalk dust. Neutral soils simply tasted like—well—*dirt*.

I almost chip a tooth chewing on a clump of my garden plot's dirt. Fortunately I've had the foresight to dig down beneath the layer of manure, but the smell of it all is fragrant enough in the spring sunlight to trick my mind into tasting something that everyone knows should never, *ever*, be put into the mouth.

I gag and spit out the dirt, suppressing the urge to vomit, but just barely.

"What's the matter with you?" an elderly voice says with evident concern. It is Sweet Maria, the eighty-year-old Italian woman whose house is next to my community garden plot.

I hadn't known she was watching me as I shoved the handful of dirt into my mouth. Now she is standing next to me, shoulders rocked backward in an expression of total disgust.

"Hi, Sweet Maria!" I call, simultaneously wiping my mouth, trying to get the dirt off my lips and out of my teeth.

Don't let Sweet Maria's name or her age fool you: she's fiercer than a bulldog. Sweet Maria defends the community garden like a loving mother defends an only child.

One day Sweet Maria was hanging laundry onto her clothesline when a punk teenager walked by the community garden and mindlessly chucked an empty pop can into her six-inch-high tomato plot. The number, variety, and rapidity of the expletives that came coursing out of Sweet Maria literally stopped the teen in his tracks. Her tirade concluded with an absolute command: "Get back here and pick that up!"

And do you know what?

The kid did as he was told.

Watching his every move, Sweet Maria gave a quick snap of her wrists and cleared the wrinkles out of another T-shirt, hanging it out to dry.

That was months ago, the day after I'd given an entire afternoon to spreading a truckload of cow manure (the driver called it the "*true* black gold") across my garden, the steaming mass of it fragrant and sticky as I worked it back into the ground. All spring I have been patiently waiting and watching as the catalyst works, contemplating this astonishing metamorphosis, hovering over the surface of the dirt as the tiny lettuce seeds given to me by Antonio—Maria's second cousin—have become more fully themselves. First they were wee hints of life, looking more like a few splinters of dead wood than anything carrying the promise of life.

Then they put out their tiny seed leaves and slowly grew into enormous, purple-flecked heads of lettuce. So, too, with the hyperbola-shaped granules of beet seeds and the ocher BBs of arugula, the half-carat spinach diamonds, and the steel-colored pepper flakes of kale.

I have heaped high before me now a salad of exquisite consequence: grown not five blocks from where I'm sitting, in that unused urban lot turned garden, the fruit of intentionality and care and love tossed in a tangy homemade balsamic vinegar dressing. I spear through layers of green goodness and, cramming the cornucopia into my mouth, sit back in the sunshine and lift up my heart to God above with a hymn of praise that sounds strangely like chewing. Is this what Saint Paul meant by "groanings too deep for words"?[13] I certainly *feel* like the Spirit is interceding on my behalf.

As any gardener or farmer will tell you, coaxing life in all of its vibrancy and nutrition up and out of the soil is nothing short of cultivating a miracle. And—don't ever let anyone tell you otherwise—miracles are always fraught with difficulty. Gardening is no exception. Even once you've buried the dead seeds and borne witness to their miniature resurrections, there are all sorts of varmints you must defend your vulnerable produce from: aphids, slugs, raccoons, and rats, to name just a few. Urban gardening ratchets this need for constant defense up another few notches, for in the city you have all the normal challenges of gardening with the added vulnerability that in the city fellow humans become pest-like, intent on carrying off your hard labor for their own satisfaction.

Ryan—a friend of ours and urban gardener extraordinaire—was devastated one morning upon finding that more than a hundred pounds of carrots had disappeared from his plot the night before.

"I hope they're allergic to beta carotene," Ryan said wryly.

After surveying the brutality of our "dog-eat-dog" world, author and prophet Wendell Berry honed the decision we all face to a razor poignancy: "we are divided between exploitation and nurture." Berry continues:

The standard of the exploiter is efficiency; the standard of the nurturer is care. The exploiter's goal is money, profit; the nurturer's goal is health—his land's health, his own, his family's, his community's, his country's. . . . The exploiter thinks in terms of numbers, quantities, "hard facts"; the nurturer in terms of character, condition, quality, kind.[14]

Though any number of examples would suffice, Los Angeles strikes me as a city particularly characterized by exploitation: it's the heart of the entertainment and fashion industries that are notorious for using and abusing people. About 70 percent of US pornography is produced in the Los Angeles area.[15] The Port of Los Angeles is one of the primary portals for trafficked people into the United States,[16] as well as the thousand of kilos of cocaine that pass through every year.[17] And then there's the fact that Los Angeles is one of the most violent cities in America, particularly in terms of gang violence.[18]

Berry's diagnosis seems applicable to Los Angeles: efficiency, money, profit, numbers, quantities, and cold hard facts.

But then there's Ron Finley, probably the best-known gardener in Southern California. While eating my home-grown salad I watch a TED Talk Ron gave recently, and I have goose bumps throughout.[19] To hear Ron speak about the task of transforming his South Central LA community—one of the most dangerous neighborhoods in the whole urban morass of LA—is to catch a glimpse of resurrection.

His method: guerilla vegetable gardens.

"I use dirt as my canvas," Ron says. "I have witnessed my garden become a tool for the education and transformation of my neighborhood."

I'm not suggesting that we all move back to subsistence farming. But if community gardens can lead to a decline in violence in South Central LA, there is enormous weight to Ron's bold declaration that "Gardening is one of the most therapeutic, and defiant things you can do. Especially in the inner city." Exhausted by the exploitation he has himself experienced and has witnessed all around him in South Central LA, Ron is giving himself entirely to the difficult task of nurturing. And in doing so his life stands as a poignant standard against which we might all evaluate our own lives: Are we exploiters or nurturers?

What is my trajectory? I wonder. *Am I moving more toward exploitation of people, places, and the dirt? Or toward the nurturing of it?*

This is what Wendell Berry is getting at by ending his poem "Manifesto: The Mad Farmer Liberation Front" with the imperative "Practice resurrection."[20] When I first read this I smiled in a condescending sort of way, secure in my exploitative framework with the belief that this was merely a hopeful scribble from an endearing—if misguided—old man. Charming, yes, but foolishly impractical and therefore easily disregarded.

But through visionaries like Ron Finley and with dirt under my own fingernails, I have come to see Berry's imperative for what it actually is: an invitation to cultivate the common, everyday occurrence of the miraculous. To *Selah!* the tiny, "insignificant" granules of hope called *seeds* that anyone can put into the ground and thereby practice resurrection. In its highest and most austere moments the simple act of growing some of your own food just might be a way of not being conformed any longer to the pattern of this world but instead being transformed by the renewal of our minds.[21]

Inspired by Ron Finley, and under the cover of darkness late one night, I become a guerilla myself and trespass into a nearby abandoned lot to sow kale by moonlight. Three hundred seeds cost me all of $2.99—a penny each. Not steep at all considering the miracle of life I'll get to witness over the coming weeks. I broadcast the seeds widely, extravagantly. Some undoubtedly fall on stony ground, while others will be devoured by hungry birds. Some will be choked to death by the weeds that inevitably call the lot their home as well.

But some—thanks be to God—some will take root and grow to produce a harvest of their own. What might the return be? Thirty? Sixty? Maybe even one hundred times what I've sown?[22]

The rewards of nurture far exceed those of exploitation, if only we'd see and hear and wake up to the dance.

But this work of nurturing, of digging the earth and tending the soil, of practicing resurrection, isn't "good" enough for many people.

A friend of mine, an accomplished financier and real-estate developer, was once chided by a family member for his love of cultivating his garden.

"Let someone else do that," he was told. "Your time is far too valuable to be mucking about in the dirt."

This is an age-old sentiment, and all the more lamentable for its antiquity. The evidence of its longstanding existence is evident in everything from industrial agriculture to the history of the English language. Despite the fact that the word *Adam* means "red clay," despite the fact that we grow our food in it and live on the basis of its health, despite the fact that we will one day be buried in it, to many "civilized" people, dirt is "dirty," and by association, so are those who work with it. Take the word *villain* for example. *Villain* and *villa* and *village* are all related words, originating from the Latin word for *farm—villaticum.* And the farm, of course, is the polar opposite of the city—*civitas*—where everyone is "civilized" and where "civility" is paramount.

Thus do the civilized critics and financiers and industrialists alike point out that we should relegate the menial task of the cultivation of our food or the baking of our bread to the migrant workers or the minorities or the machines so that the rest "can get on toward more important tasks," like amassing wealth or weapons or even "changing our world."

But I'm no longer convinced by this logic, seductive and "liberated" as it seems. Cultivating a garden, baking bread, feasting with friends— these are all extraordinary acts of enormous particularity, of stewardship, of attentiveness, of care. And if the resurrection is anything at all, it is an act of great particularity, stewardship, attentiveness, and care, and I'm rather inclined to herald and participate in it in any way I can.

Mother Teresa meant something similar—I think—with her bold declaration that "we can do no great things, but only small things with great love."[23] Is the burial of a single beet seed, or the watering of a squash plant, or the weeding of a wheat patch, too small an act to be done with great love? Call me crazy, but I'm thoroughly convinced that the mounding of a potato plant in the hope of feasting on and sharing the future unearthed spuds is a distinct—albeit small—way of anticipating and practicing the resurrection.

Of course I could buy my bread and vegetables and let someone else do the hard and tiresome work on my behalf.

But why on earth would I want to pay someone else to do for me that which is deeply pleasurable?

Should I hire someone to enjoy my dinner for me as well?

The sun has just vanished beneath the Ugandan horizon as leaders of the community called Otongo begin gathering under the great Bell Tree, a one-hundred-year-old behemoth that yawns ten stories up into the vibrant sky. A rusted-out car wheel hangs precariously from one of the largest of the Bell Tree's branches, strung up by a shockingly thin chain. The heat of the day still radiates up from the dirt, making my dusty feet sweat, but delightfully cool ribbons of wind are wending their way across the land from the nearby lakes, bringing refreshment with them like a sigh. The full and fragrant smell of wood smoke is ubiquitous in the land, arising from the hundreds of cooking fires that spread out toward every horizon. For hours now people have been bending over their fires, taking turns preparing the evening meal as other, tired bodies come in from the fields and slump down onto rough-hewn stools.

Danae and I have been in Otongo for three weeks now, living out of our backpacks and tent. The community that has welcomed us here has brought a new depth to the word *hospitality*, opening their lives and meager resources to foreigners from far away.

With an unspoken signal someone picks up a piece of rebar and begins hammering on the rusted-out wheel. The "bell" for which the Bell Tree is known rings out clear and resonant across the darkened land. Many people have already gathered beneath the Bell Tree, and even more begin arriving at the sound of the bell. A fire is lit, bathing the tree's belly and all the faces seated there in a radiant glow, releasing its fragrant incense.

Victoria—the widow who let us pitch our tent on her property—is smiling widely, her teeth flashing like ivory in the warm firelight. "The land was very good to us this year," she says with a laugh. "But it is not always this way." Her face drops. "Sometimes the rains do not come when they should and the ground is stone. Those are hungry times. We eat grass like the cattle." Her mouth tightens as she speaks—this is no hypothetical statement.

"But when the rain is good, the ground lives." Victoria places another piece of steaming cassava into my rough-hewn bowl, on top of the mingled *sim-sim* and *skuma-wiki*. "And when the ground lives, we feast and delight it."

The memory of that evening meal under the Bell Tree in Otongo comes rushing back to me unexpectedly as I am en route to my community garden. It is a Wednesday, and Wednesdays are garden pot lucks. Bright and clear and gloriously warm, the pavement still radiates the heat of the summer day as Danae and I walk down the hill toward the garden. I'm bringing a loaf of bread, and Danae has made a salad dressing we'll pour over greens cut straight from the garden.

When we arrive five or six others have gathered there as well under the watchful governance of Sweet Maria—and a vibrant spread has emerged atop an old door that has become a table. There is an exquisite cheese, brown rice with steamed vegetables, and gooey chocolate chip cookies. Someone has even brought a bottle of wine, a basic but adequate Merlot.

Danae and I sit down on overturned buckets around the doorway-tabletop and are handed glasses of the shining wine.

"To the King and the Kingdom," a friend says, raising her glass.

"To the King and the Kingdom," we all say in unison.

I pull out the fresh baked loaf of brown bread, and with care, cut still-steaming pieces for all. Someone else has brought honey from last year's harvest.

"Delight it!" I say. "Delight it indeed."

CHAPTER 5

Freedom in Downward Mobility: The Practice of Simplicity

If only simplicity were not the most difficult of all things.

—CARL JUNG[1]

What is prosperity anyway? Is it money in the bank, or is it a fulfilling life?

—WILLIAM BRYANT LOGAN[2]

A man can do worse than be poor. He can miss altogether the sight of the greatness of small things.

—ROBERT FARRAR CAPON[3]

What to do? Stay green
Never mind the machine,
Whose fuel is human souls.
Live Large, man, and dream small.

—R. S. THOMAS[4]

I loathe pruning.

I loathe it precisely to the extent that I crave possibility. I'm someone who stands beside a tomato plant and dreams of all the fruit that *could be* born out of this stalk here and that one there.

Why cut them off? Who knows what might come into existence someday?

Unfortunately there is a fundamental problem with this approach.

"You kids," Sweet Maria scoffs at me one afternoon as I stand admiring my tomato plant. She disappears into her house, returning a moment later with a pair of scissors. "You'll never get any fruit that way. You have to prune if you want fruit to grow."

"Oh, Sweet Maria," I say in a disregarding tone. "That's just one of those old wives' tales, like planting seeds on the full moon. There isn't any truth in it."

"No truth," Maria scowls and swears at my stupidity. "Try it and see. See if it's an old wives' tale."

So I do try it, although more out of a desire to prove Sweet Maria wrong than to see if she might be right.

Having planted identical tomato varieties in identical soil, and being meticulous about watering the plants the same amount, I allow only one difference between them: one plant I prune and the other I do not. Then I watch and wait to see not only which plant will produce more fruit, but also which plant's fruit actually *tastes* better.

Need I tell you the obvious? Sweet Maria is right after all.

Without question the tomato plant I prune produce more abundant, sizeable, and tasty tomatoes. The plant fulfills its purpose more fully as I focus and narrow the plant's energy by pruning off distractions.

The plant I let grow wild, however, is a sorry disappointment. It generates lots and lots of tantalizing flowers, but a surprisingly small number of these flowers actually matures into edible tomatoes. And the tomatoes that do actually come seem somehow stunted—they never actually grow and mature into the size of the tomatoes coming from the pruned plant. What's more, many of the tomatoes on the unpruned plant become diseased and rotted right on the vine, almost as though the tomato plant just doesn't have any extra energy to defend itself from disease. When I finally cut one of the unpruned tomatoes off toward the end of summer, hoping for a delectable feast, its flesh is starved for moisture and more or less absent of flavor, tasting mildly like wet sawdust.

Sweet Maria is watching from her nearby back porch, laughing and rolling her eyes at me.

"You were right, Sweet Maria," I admit, holding up two vastly different-sized tomatoes for her to see.

"Say that again?" Sweet Maria says, feigning and cupping a hand at her ear.

"You were right," I say a little louder.

"And that would make you . . . ?" Sweet Maria asks.

"And that would make me wiser for knowing you, Sweet Maria," I respond with a smile and an exaggerated bow.

It seems this general truth—that fruitfulness depends upon pruning, that bounty derives from limits—applies to more than just tomatoes.

Last week I planted a few fruit trees in our backyard. Three kinds of apples, a cherry tree, and my personal favorite, a deep purple plum. The "Fruit Tree Pruning Manual" given to me by the garden center was explicit: if I hope for the trees to become established, healthy, and enduringly productive, I must be merciless in pruning them back during the winter months.

It's almost like there's a fundamental law built into the nature of the universe: *limitations and boundaries enable fruitfulness.*

Strange how adamant our culture is about disregarding the necessity of limitations and boundaries in all forms. Limits rub us the wrong way, and so we cry, "Foul!"

"That impinges on my freedom!" Or "Our forefathers died so we wouldn't have to have limitations!" (Okay, maybe *you* don't insist that this is why our forefathers died, but I have had someone say this to my face after a talk I once gave!)

I'm an American, a child of the Enlightenment. The idea of not being able to do something I want to do is an affront to my sense of autonomy and my understanding of "freedom" as well.

But I can't help but wonder if perhaps I've misunderstood what *freedom* actually means.

Is it *really* the ability to throw off limits, to do without boundaries, to do whatever I want, whenever I want?

I'm back at the monastery, asking Father Solomon about it.

"That's not at all what freedom means," Father Solomon says with a frown. "That might be what many—or even most—people today *think* freedom means, but it is really a gross perversion of the original concept."

"How so?" I ask, getting ready for an argument. Threaten someone's notion of freedom and you can guarantee *some* sort of push back.

"Do you know how ranchers used to kill wolves?" Father Solomon asks.

I'm thrown off by this sudden change of direction. "I—I have no idea," I stammer. "But how did we get from the definition of freedom to wolves?"

Father Solomon doesn't answer my question outright but keeps going with the wolves. "A hundred years or so ago, when a rancher wanted to kill some wolves, this is what he'd do. At the end of winter, just before spring melt-off when the wolves were ravenous with hunger, he'd take a piece of meat—say the leg of a deer or an elk or something large like this—and bury several razor blades into it, with the edges facing out. Then he'd take the leg out and chain it to a tree. The wolves, utterly famished, would smell the meat from miles away and descend upon it. The meat would have frozen solid by then, but the wolves wouldn't care. They'd begin licking the meat to melt it, slicing their own tongues on the embedded razor blades, growing all the more ravenous at the taste and smell of fresh blood and yet all the weaker as they bled to death in their famished frenzy."

Father Solomon pauses a moment, letting the gruesome scene settle into my mind.

"With a little luck a rancher could wipe out a whole pack of wolves in this way," Father Solomon says.

I swallow hard, still wondering what on earth this has to do with freedom. "I still don't see. How did we get from the definition of freedom to a dead pack of wolves?"

"Picture an alcoholic," Father Solomon explains another way. "Would you say an alcoholic person is *free* so long as no one prevents him from—say—walking into a bar and drinking himself under a table?"

"I don't know," I say, trying hard to think. "That's complicated. Obviously it isn't *good* for the alcoholic to drink himself under the table. But if nobody stops him from doing what he wants to do, then yes, I would say that he is free—in the sense that he is able to do what he wants."

"What you're missing is the crucial connection between what is 'good' and what *freedom* actually means," Father Solomon says, passion in his voice. "Freedom isn't about being able to do whatever you want to do whenever you want to do it. Freedom is about being able to *choose* and then *act* toward *what is good*. It is about the opportunity to grow toward one's *telos*—the Greek word which means "purpose" or "maturity" or "goal"—for which you've been created. Freedom means both a lack of *external* coercion that prevents you from moving toward your *telos*, but also a lack of *internal* coercion that prevents you from moving toward your *telos* as well. Does this make sense?"

"I think so," I answer, trying to take it all in. "But the idea of internal coercion is strange. Are you saying I can be enslaved by something that I actually *want*?"

"Of course," Father Solomon says. "Haven't you experienced that before: wanting something you know to be destructive? The language sometimes used to speak about this is 'disordered affections.' Affections—an attraction or an affinity for something—are a fact of life. But there are *ordered* affections and *disordered* affections. Ordered affections lead us toward life and light and love, toward our *telos*, toward God. Disordered affections lead us toward evil, toward death and darkness, away from everything that we have been created for."

My mind is spinning now, trying to see in the new light Father Solomon is shining on things. "So just because somebody 'chooses' something does not mean they are truly free—in the sense of *choosing his or her own good*—in that choice. Just because nobody stops the drunk from entering the bar doesn't make him free, doesn't mean he is living toward his good, toward his *telos*?"

"Precisely," Father Solomon says. "For in following his disordered affection, the alcoholic is actually acting out of his enslavement to alcohol. He is bound by his addiction, chained and oriented toward what is degrading to his well-being, what is contrary to his *telos*. He cannot at all be called *free*. He is like the wolf: drawn by hunger, yes, willingly licking the razor blades, yes, but ultimately securing his own death in the process. Rightly conceived, freedom leads unto life, not unto death."

I am silent, mulling this over, as alcoholics and bleeding wolves swirl together in my mind. "This is rearranging everything," I say at last.

"As it should," Father Solomon agrees, nodding. "The tragic irony today is that we've been pushed toward a new kind of slavery by the *rhetoric* of freedom, liberty, and self-determination. Instead we now find ourselves mired in the intensely arrogant belief that the pinnacle of freedom is a society of individuals running around pursuing whatever they *feel* like, without any thought whatsoever about what we've been created for."

The freedom conversation with Father Solomon sets my head spinning for weeks to come, especially the need to be free not only from *external* coercion but also from *internal* coercion. This is further emphasized when I encounter Thomas Merton's book *New Seeds of Contemplation*:

> It should be accepted as a most elementary human and moral truth that no man can live a fully sane and decent life unless he is able to say "no" on occasion to his natural bodily appetites. No man who simply eats and drinks whenever he feels like eating and drinking, who smokes whenever he feels the urge to light a cigarette, who gratifies his curiosity and sensuality whenever they are stimulated, can consider himself a free person. He has renounced his spiritual freedom and become the servant of bodily impulse. Therefore his mind and his will are not fully his own. They are under the power of his appetites.[5]

As I begin sitting with this question of internal coercion in my Daily Examen, a whole tirade of things become visible.

Like this one: my razor-like addiction to wealth.

Of course money is necessary for life, for buying food and paying bills, but the more I look within myself the more I see that I don't just want money sufficient to cover my needs. Oh no. The "disordered" part of my bond with wealth is that I relate to it from a standpoint of scarcity—I feel there will never be enough. And in this warped perspective there is only one logical response: I want more of it.

One particularly stressful afternoon after yet another larger-than-expected bill arrives in the mail, Danae and I get into a heated conversation about our finances.

"Why are you so stressed out about this bill?" Danae asks. "We knew it was coming, and we have more than enough to cover it."

"That's not the point!" I snap. "It's more than I thought it was going to be and thus at the end of the day we have less than I'd planned we would."

"But we have enough," Danae says adamantly. "More than enough."

"No, we *don't* have enough," I insist. "Not as much as I'd like, anyway."

"What do you mean by 'enough' then? We have money left over after paying our bills last month, and—all things considered—we probably will this month too. Isn't that what 'enough' means?"

"No," I snap. This conversation is needling on a nerve deep within me, and I don't like it at all. "*Enough* has always meant and will always mean a bit more than we have right now."

"Sarcasm isn't going to be helpful here," she says, not budging an inch. "Are you hungry right now?"

"No, but I—"

"Are you without clothing or shelter, exposed to the elements?"

"No, of course not, but that's not the point."

"What do you think Jesus meant by teaching his disciples to pray 'Give us this day our *daily* bread'?"[6]

"I don't *know* what Jesus meant," I say, stamping my foot. "Whatever he meant, I will feel better when we have a bit more in the bank, a bit more margin."

"Oh come *on!*" It's Danae's turn to get frustrated now. "*A bit more margin* is just a cover for a never-ending pursuit of *just a little more*. I want a little margin as well, and we have that. We have more than enough. If you don't actively start cultivating a sense of what *enough* really means, you're going to spend the rest of your life enslaved to the idea of *more*, forever pursuing *just a bit more*, without ever learning to experience the possibility of joy that comes from all the enough-ness around you."

Danae's words hit me like a slap in the face, and suddenly I am confronted with a vision of myself at the end of my life, grey and wrinkled, an old wolf still licking that frozen razor blade, still frantically hounding after *just a little more*, unaware that lights are getting dim and the curtain is starting to drop.

"Oh no!" I say, feeling my eyes grow wide as I look past Danae. "You're *right!*"

Suddenly I see how coercive the idea of *more* has become in my life. I drive myself toward it ruthlessly, utterly bound to the idea that bigger will be better, that larger will be stronger, that *just a little bit more* will be safer, sturdier, more stable. It's always future tense, never present, always just around the corner of the next accomplishment, the next milestone. I've been blinded and have blinded myself to the abundance around me by constantly searching for the evasive and fleeting and retreating *more*.

It is said that Qin Shi Huang—China's first emperor, living some 2,230 years ago—once told his adviser that he "longed to swallow the world."[7]

I can relate.

Haven't you felt that way at one point or another? To see, be, do *all?* See everywhere, experience everything, love everyone?

Left wild, human appetite is boundless, our capacity for rapaciousness without limits. Thus we are the dominant species on this third little rock from the sun, and we're doing our best to mainstream what was once unfathomable: circling the globe in twenty-four hours, feasting on food picked yesterday two continents away, leveling entire mountains for the ore and coal buried inside. The whole world has become raw material for the furnace of our insatiable desire, and we are driven like slaves toward an indefinite and evanescent *more*. And we call it *growth*, and it is *the* single indicator of economic health today.

Though I'm well acquainted with this insatiable desire for more, I can't help but wonder if our individual and collective appetite is actually oriented toward the purposes for which we and everything else have been created. Are we truly *free* in our desire to acquire?

Might it be that our insatiability is actually an addiction?

A disordered affection on a globalized scale?

Could it be that we human pack—seven billion strong and growing every second—are all unknowingly mutilating ourselves on the razor blades buried in the meat?

After all, unchecked growth in a living organism isn't called *health* at all.

Cancer.

That's what we call it.

And left untreated, it is lethal.

I thought for a while that this growth-obsessed cancer of ours is a kind of hypermaterialism.

And if asked, I would have said that by *materialism* I meant that we extract too much *meaning* from our stuff.

A recent trip to the dump shook this use of *materialism* right out of my vocabulary.

Of course there's a lot of junk at the dump. Stuff that nobody wants anymore, that can't be recycled, that can't be fixed. Every culture from every age has produced waste of some sort. And mining ancient trash heaps reveals enormous amounts of "material culture" for historians and archaeologists to categorize and classify: bits of broken pots, clay writing tablets with hastily scratched notes in them, scraps of clothing.

But future archeologists will have to scratch their heads and ponder carefully why it is that our culture tosses out such perfectly good stuff: hardly worn shoes and sweaters that aren't at all moth-eaten or stained, printers that just need a new toner cartridge, furniture that would fetch a quick fifty dollars at a trendy thrift store.

Given how ready we are to throw things out, how choked and brimming our culture's landfills are with perfectly usable goods, it seems the only conclusion to draw is not that we care *too* much about material things but rather that we don't care *enough* about them. We're constantly tossing things out, disregarding them, having our gaze and attention hijacked by "the next big thing," the *new release*, or the updated version of the recently obseletized gadget. Until—that is—"the next big thing" gets transmogrified by the passage of time, and then we toss that once-new and briefly beloved thing into the bin.

We aren't addicted to *things* anymore.

Now we're addicted to the *experience of obtaining something new.*

How would it make you feel to learn that this addiction is not at all natural or coincidental? That this state of perpetually needing to obtain something new is a calculated and cultivated reality in the hearts and minds of us consuming hordes? Does it strike you as repulsive that "planned obsolescence" is a technical term in design circles, and that a major automobile manufacture's R&D department spoke of the "organized creation of dissatisfaction"?[8]

Behold, fellow citizen of the consumer culture! I have news you must hasten to hear: we are not at all "free," bound by some $11 trillion[9] of consumer debt, addicted as we are to the latest and greatest, prone as we are to "shop till you drop," hungry as we are for "just a little bit more."

The coercion is all around us, poisoning the air of our culture under the rhetoric of "freedom." And the addiction burns within us as well, internally coercing us without end. Thus we spin through the five-step process of discovering, desiring, acquiring, depleting, and disposing an unending avalanche of stuff.

We are *conditioned* to never be content, to always be hungry, to lick and lick again the razor that is not only our death but the death of this world as well.

Father Solomon knows exactly what I am talking about when I ask him what it might look like to practice a different way of being in the world. And he—doctor of the soul that he is—speaks to me three words to ponder and embody:

"Purge. Reclaim. Delight."

Then he sends me on my way after the shortest meeting we've ever had.

"PURGE."

Henry David Thoreau once questioned the standard definition of *rich* by asserting that "I make myself rich by making my wants few."[10]

His was a simple game of logic: if being rich is having more than one wants, then there are two obvious ways of becoming rich: possess more or prune our wants.

Rabbi Abraham Joshua Heschel would seem to agree, though his advice is less about being rich and more about living peaceably in our world: "In regard to external gifts, to outward possessions, there is only one proper attitude—to have them and to be able to do without them."[11]

Both writers are saying something about our wants. And as we all know, our wants are different from our needs. We can do without our wants but we need our needs. Even Thoreau had what he needed at Walden Pond: food, water, clothing, shelter.

It seems to me that purging requires a clearer understanding of what the difference between a want and a need actually is. And this is less straightforward than you might think. While the UN Millennium Development Goals define the basic number of food calories *needed* to sustain life, a recent BBC special feature referred to super yachts (privately owned luxury yachts greater than seventy-five feet long) as a "necessity" of the super-rich.[12]

God help me if I ever call a super yacht a "need."

But is this just a question of perspective?

Do I *need* a place to live? The apostle Paul seems to have forgotten shelter on his list of necessary items: "We brought nothing into the world, and we cannot take anything out of the world. But if we have food and clothing, with these we will be content."[13]

Or was Saint Paul just alluding to the Jesus who had "no place to lay his head,"[14] to the Lord who instructed his followers to not worry about things like what they would eat or what they would drink or what they would wear?[15]

If Jesus and Paul both seemed unconcerned with shelter, do "house and home" live in the category of "need" or "want"?

Let me get back to you on that one—I don't yet have a suitable answer.

Arriving at a clearer distinction between a need and a want is precisely where Father Solomon's admonition to "purge" led me. For scraping out the excess is a way not only of "reducing wants" but also of learning "to have things and be able to do without them."

I start in my closet, pulling out one thing and then another.

"Are you sure?" Danae asks as I pull out another shirt.

"Yup," I say. "I haven't worn that in more than a year."

Danae picks it up and looks at it. "You're right. You haven't."

"What about this?" I ask, pulling out a suit I got when I was eighteen.

"I've never even *seen* that suit before," Danae says with a laugh. "Where have you been hiding it?"

I add it to the pile.

"And these?" I hold up a nice pair of shoes that also haven't been worn in more than a year.

"Gone," says Danae.

All told I clean out ten shirts, two pairs of jeans, that nice pair of shoes, my pristine suit, and a whole pile of T-shirts, that I will never wear.

In the process of purging my closet, though, Father Solomon's admonition to "purge" starts acting like a lens, dramatically affecting how I see not only the stuff in my closet and drawers but other places as well. While I used to consider the accumulation of items in my life an indication of my gradually increasing wealth, they now remind me of the hair and soap scum that accumulates in my bathtub drain until I find myself standing in two inches of tepid water. Or maybe a better image is the ominous plaque that collects in the arteries of our hearts until we are left gripping our left arms, sinking down to the floor in a panic.

Maybe this is a little dramatic, but you get the point: piles of superfluous stuff aren't healthy or attractive.

Thinking about it in this way makes downsizing not only easy but also enjoyable. Just like pulling out that big wad of hair and soap scum that has kept the whole shower from running smoothly.

I head to the garage next.

Snow skis. Old rock-climbing gear. A helmet I haven't worn in half a decade. All of it thrown into a box for the thrift store.

"Don't worry," I say when Danae opens the garage door warily. "We don't need any of this stuff."

"I know," Danae agrees, adding her own boxes to the ever-growing pile. "I decided to purge some of my own stuff as well."

We heap it all into our car and drive it down to the local thrift store and have to make four trips to unload all the miscellaneous stuff that results from Father Solomon's single word, "Purge."

And do you know what?

I feel free.

Four loads lighter at least. Is it any wonder? I've not been dispossessed of things that have any great significance or value to me, but I've gained instead a noticeable amount of mental landscape, clutter-free space-time. I will never have to move or organize or worry about those things— shirts, skis, rock-climbing gear—again.

Perhaps this is what freedom actually means: not the ability to crush oneself down with unending piles of useless clutter, but instead the lightness that comes from decluttering physical, mental, and emotional space-time of the causes and effects of the insatiable appetite for more.

Beyond working *backward* in the garage and basement and closet through past purchases, Father Solomon's admonition to "purge" begins shining *forward* into the future as well.

"Why do I want this thing?" I find myself asking before a new purchase. "Is it because it will truly add something important and valuable to my life, because it will help me on my way toward my *telos*, or is it because my mental or emotional 'arm' is being twisted, either by an ingenious marketing machine, or by my own disordered affections?"

"How will this thing affect my time?"

"How much of the singular gift of my life will this thing require?"

"Will it actually add value to my life for more than a few days?"

Despite the cliché that "we don't own our things, our things own us," few of us are clear-sighted enough to realize that everything we buy or acquire is going to require something of us. It's not just that we use our stuff but our stuff uses us as well. Everything we bring into our sphere of responsibility—whether a car or a shirt or a piece of electronic equipment or a home—requires something of us: our time, our attention, our care.

The invitation to purge has meant that I stop daydreaming so much about what something is going to *add* to my life when I buy it. Instead I've started trying to picture myself taking care of that thing, trying to visualize what it is going to *require of me if I acquire it*. These questions seem to help:

Is this thing actually something I want to give my time and care and attention to?

How will giving my time and care and attention to this particular thing affect the rest of my life?

What am I saying no to by saying yes to this particular thing?

By asking these questions Danae and I decide *not* to buy a second car with all of the requisite responsibilities and expenses that come with such a purchase: insuring it, maintaining it, Saturday-morning car washings. Because we live in a town that has dependable public transit and is relatively bikeable, we decide to purge our life of a future vehicle by instead making use of these simpler options.

But don't misunderstand me.

The point of purging is not about drawing lines in the sand: "Own fewer than seven shirts." "Only eat vegetarian." "Don't own a second car," and so forth. To do so is to continue to be enslaved by the desire to "keep up with the Joneses," just along a different trajectory.

What I've come to see Father Solomon was guiding me toward is a habit of mind and heart that is clear-sighted and honest—*free* might be the best word, in fact—in the way I think about and relate to the material objects that inhabit my life. It isn't about abstract rules: whether or how much to own, but rather about being free, uncluttered, oriented, alive.

Tell me, Mr. Thoreau: You made yourself rich by making your wants few. But I suspect you became more human, too, didn't you? Purging yourself of the nonnecessities of life?

"RECLAIM."

I once had the chance to meet a young boy named Geoffrey in Zambia. Geoffrey lived about an hour's car ride from Zambia's capital city of Lusaka, in a rural farming village. Geoffrey was an astonishingly creative boy who—at the age of twelve—found a way to rig up a homemade solar-power stereo system for his family to be able to listen to the local news and World Cup soccer games. Soon Geoffrey's home became a central hub in his village, with as many as thirty or forty people gathering around in the warm evenings, hoping to hear the news or listen as the game unfolded.

What made Geoffrey's ingenuity all the more astonishing was the fact that everything he used to rig up his family's stereo was garbage. Literally. Too impoverished to buy the parts new, Geoffrey had found all the various pieces while rummaging through the local trash heap. Having soldered a few wires to a broken piece of solar panel, he'd then hooked up a half-missing speaker to the casing-less innards of a government-issue radio. After a little more tinkering and persistence, Geoffrey had a working radio. With a little creativity and a few pieces of garbage, Geoffrey had figured out how to make something of great significance, something that brought his family and village together around shared interests.

Father Solomon's second word—*reclaim*—brings Geoffrey to mind. Here is a boy who had taken garbage and *reclaimed* it into something that not only provided hours of information and delight but also brought his entire community together.

I'm now on a bus, traveling from Vancouver to Seattle in order to catch a flight out for a speaking engagement. On my lap is a large pile of miscellaneous clothing items I've brought along with me on this trip. My purpose: to reclaim them by stitching and patching the holes and loose bits in each article of clothing.

Several people have done double-takes as they boarded or disembarked at various stops along the route, and I can't blame them. I can't help but be a very strange sight. Nobody else is darning their socks or patching the holes in their jeans or accidentally jabbing themselves with a needle whenever the bus rams through a pothole.

Nobody except this clown in seat 12B.

"Excuse me," a female voice says. It's the grandmotherly woman with plastic-jewel-rimmed glasses from across the aisle and one seat forward. She's looking at me with a bemused frown. "I've got to ask you something. Why are you doing that?"

"Doing what?" I ask, wryly implying that this is the most natural thing in the world.

"Mending your clothes," she says. "I'd expect someone my age to do that. But not someone your age. Why patch your clothes when you can just go and buy new ones? Or can't you afford to do that?"

Her tone is not aimed at insult, but rather inquiry. I'm happy for the dialogue, as I try to work out myself why I'm doing what I'm doing.

"I can afford new clothes," I reply. "But it seems a little silly, doesn't it, to throw out a perfectly good pair of wool socks just because there's a quarter-sized hole in one of the heels?" I hold up the sock I'm darning and poke my thumb through the hole. "Even from an economic perspective it makes sense. Let's say it takes me ten minutes to fix this hole, and it would have cost ten dollars to replace this pair of wool socks. That means that by darning them I'm saving ten dollars in ten minutes, which is sixty dollars per hour. That's a pretty good rate."

"A good rate," she agrees.

"But it's more than that," I continue thinking out loud. "We humans throw away such an astonishing amount of stuff every year, especially in the developed world. Resources are scarce, clean air and water and land are precious, and perhaps one of the ways of protecting what remains includes doing small things like this."

"Perhaps there is hope for your generation after all," the woman says with a smile.

⁓

After several months of mending and patching rather than tossing and replacing my own possessions, an obvious extension of "reclaim" springs into my mind: the practice of trying to reclaim not only my own things but also those that have been discarded by others.

So I start Dumpster diving.

You wouldn't believe all the great stuff you can find in a Dumpster, but I'll restrain myself to mentioning just one category of things: construction materials.

Close to where I live, eight or ten new houses are in the process of being built. As any builder knows, all construction projects result in a substantial amount of leftover material. Some of this is donated to places like Habitat for Humanity's ReStore outlets, where partially used construction material can be bought at a steep discount. But most construction sites—around here, at least—simply rent a "haul-away" Dumpster and toss every leftover thing in. Excess lumber, countless ends and pieces, tiles, half-used bottles of wood-glue, and much more all get thrown into the Dumpster on the grounds that they aren't "worth the cost" required to keep and reuse them. They are simply a "sunk cost" of the construction process, and aren't worth the time and expense it would take to make these items available to others.

Two things come immediately to mind regarding the mind-set that causes most leftover building material to end up in the landfill. Number one: as the old saying goes, "one person's trash is another's treasure." And number two: we need to explore what *worth* actually means.

From a purely economic perspective, you're right: it isn't "worth" paying someone twenty dollars to salvage ten dollars' "worth" of lumber. But what if the "worth" of something is derived less from the arbitrary price set by the market and much more from the meaning and satisfaction one derives from caring about that item?

Here's what I mean: In my office I have a beautiful black-and-white photograph of myself, my father, and my grandfather—all three generations of Michael George Yankoski. This photograph would have no cash value whatsoever on the market. And yet it is exceedingly meaningful to me, especially given the fact that my grandfather is no longer alive, and because the photo was taken on my wedding day almost a decade ago.

Zero dollars of worth on the market, substantial meaning to me.

That's what reclamation is all about: *Selah!*-ing something and so granting great meaning to what would otherwise have little worth.

With a little bit of spit-and-polish and care, a substantial number of items from the Dumpster have become mainstays in our home: our dining room table, our living room coffee table, my office desk, Danae's office desk, the headboard of our bed, the supports for our bed, the storage shelves in our kitchen and laundry room. All of them from reclaimed wood.

A little bit of time, a little bit of care, a little bit of creativity, and the alchemizing power of reclamation becomes evident: that which was worthless suddenly has meaning.

Write me off as an idealist, but I'm beginning to see what Father Solomon meant. Darning socks and Dumpster diving for building materials just might be among the freest things I've ever done.

"DELIGHT."

Several years ago I was homeless.[16]

By choice, yes. Not that "choice" makes the concrete any softer.

My friend Sam and I chose to live on the city streets of several major US cities, including Denver, Washington, DC, Portland, San Francisco, Phoenix, and San Diego. We spent a great deal of our time trying to meet our basic daily needs: food to eat, a dry place to sleep, someplace private to use the bathroom. There were several multiday stretches where we didn't eat anything at all, once because we got lost and couldn't find the church that was serving a free meal, another because busking didn't go very well, another because the place where we'd waited in line for food for four hours ran out just as it was our turn to receive our meals.

There's nothing admirable or praiseworthy about not being able to eat when you're hungry.

And yet I began to notice something surprising during the months that Sam and I were on the streets.

Food tastes better and is more satisfying when we're hungry. Some of the best meals I have ever eaten were when I was homeless and hungry, whereas some of the least delightful ones were when I wasn't actually hungry and had only a few minutes to wolf something down.

It makes sense, though, doesn't it?

Water is more refreshing when we are thirsty, just as the chance to sit in front of the crackling of a wood fire is more warming on a cold winter's day, or a dip in a cool river more delicious in the high heat of summer.

Could it be that delight is in some way connected to the size of the gap between the want and its satisfaction?

Why do I spend so much time, then, pulling out my credit card several times a day to ensure that I'm never hungry, never thirsty, never hot, never cold?

Could it be that temporarily embracing—even *extending*—situations of felt need, of unmet desire, might in some way *enhance* our delight?

Fasting seems a good way to test this theory, to embrace Father Solomon's third recommendation, "delight."

Just one day per week, skipping breakfast and lunch, and thus going about twenty-four hours between dinner one night and dinner the next night.

As I write these words I've been fasting weekly for almost a full ten months, and the effect is regularly profound: the dinners I eat at the conclusion of my fast are by far the best and most memorable dinners I enjoy during the week. I tend to fast on Mondays, at the start of the week, and Monday night dinners aren't anything like the more elaborate meals Danae and I make when friends come over on the weekends.

Nevertheless, the simple fare of Monday evenings is elevated because of how hungry I am after not eating breakfast or lunch. Fasting *increases* the delight of food. Voluntary abstention from eating enlarges satisfaction; it heightens and deepens and expands the joy we experience when we finally sit down to a meal.

Doris Janzen Longacre insists that this is the case in her profoundly practical book *Living More with Less.* Intentional simplicity is not about draconian austerity or harsh restrictions. Rather, Janzen Longacre writes, "This book is about living joyfully, richly, and creatively."[17]

It sounds counterintuitive, but this is precisely why the priest and author Robert Farrar Capon warns that "too much of a good thing is as bad as too little."[18] And why twentieth-century author G. K. Chesterton boldly declares that "We should thank God for beer and Burgundy by not drinking too much of them."[19] I take all three of these sage writers to mean that there is a space somewhere in between "too much" and "not enough" that is rich and satisfying and joyful and creative.

And, having fasted regularly for several months, a new idea begins to take shape, that of eating on two dollars per day during the season of Lent as a way of cultivating an extended time of unfulfilled desire. Let me say that the regular diet of plain oatmeal in the mornings along with bland rice and beans and one-fourth an avocado for both lunch and dinner not only makes me lose a good amount of weight, but also makes my mouth water like it never has before at even the *thought* of chocolate or ice cream or deep-dish pizza. Even everyday fare brings on intense longing amid this Lenten fast: bread and butter, eggs over easy with buttered toast, quesadilla with sour cream and salsa. Even such "simple fare" suddenly seem enormously extravagant, simply by intentionally restricting my diet for forty days.

We are invited to a potluck on Easter afternoon, the very day my two dollars per day fast is ending. I've been to lots of potlucks and am normally not overly impressed.

This one is different.

I almost weep with joy when I enter their home and see the twenty-foot-long table loaded with a vast assortment of homemade dishes.

When it is time to eat I load the plate up with the extraordinary fare and prepare to feast.

"How's the food tasting, Michael?" a friend named Thomas asks me. Thomas knows what my Lenten fast entailed, and he is genuinely curious.

"Categorically delightful!" I say through a large piece of cheesy bread with garlicky bruschetta. "Delightful indeed!"

Here is a poetic equation, a mathematical riddle with the power to derail even the strongest acquirers among us: if you want to increase your harvest, you must learn how to mercilessly prune. If you hunger for a deep and abiding sense of "enough," do everything in your power to work against the malicious belief that "more" will get you there. Start cultivating instead the ability to see and acknowledge the abundance that is all around you, even if to do so—as Henry David Thoreau suggests—you must "decrease your wants." And if you are at all interested in becoming less consumeristic, become *more* materialistic.

Prune. Purge. Reclaim. Delight.

This is—or so I've come to believe—the fourfold straight-and-narrow path to freedom through downward mobility.

CHAPTER 6

Let There *BE!*: The Practice of Creativity

The person who aims after art in his work aims
after truth . . . no more and no less.

—FLANNERY O'CONNOR[1]

What is good is difficult, and what is difficult is rare.

—ROBERT FARRAR CAPON[2]

A pebble cast into a pond causes ripples that spread in all directions.
And each one of our thoughts, words and deeds is like that.

—DOROTHY DAY[3]

Writing is easy: all you do is sit staring at a blank sheet of
paper until the drops of blood form on your forehead.

—GENE FOWLER[4]

Hurry ruins saints as well as artists.

—THOMAS MERTON[5]

Theologians debate what it is about human beings that warrants the high and lofty term *imago dei*, "image of God." Some have pointed to the memory and understanding and will as possibly corresponding to the Father, Son, and Holy Spirit, while others were more convinced that the whole person—body, mind, and emotion—might mirror the Creator more closely than a merely cerebral model. Other specialists point out that the triune God is fundamentally relational, and thus it is humanity as a whole—not just individuals—who image the infinite God.

Though I'm only a closet theologian, I'm willing to bet the *imago dei* is at least somewhat related to our ability to create.

Have you ever stopped for a moment to think how incredible it is that we can bestow the gift of *being*, that we can call into existence things that once *weren't*? Of course the raw material is already there for us (only God creates *ex nihilo*, "out of nothing"), but whether it's a bridge, a building, a bowl, or a baby, the power to create is incredibly godlike. In a divinely imaged triad we unite our will, our imagination, and our body, and—echoing the Creator God—cry *Let There Be!* and—WHAMO!—what was once not now . . . *is.*

If only it were that easy.

As everyone who has ever tried to make anything knows full well, creativity is extremely hard. Bestowing the gift of being on even a very small scale is exceedingly difficult.

Take pottery for example. And I don't mean machine-made IKEA pottery, boxed up like a blizzard by the hundreds of millions and overnighted around the world, but hand-thrown pottery made by a real person, one pot and bowl and plate at a time, each piece individual and unique.

How hard can it be? I think smugly as I sign up for my first pottery class at a local community center. *It's basically just grown-up Play-Doh.* And besides, even before my little niece Tirzah could string a sentence together she was making all sorts of Play-Doh creations: bears, birds, snakes.

The class I sign up for focuses on "wheel-throwing," which—as I discover during my first class session—is a wonderfully apt phrase. All I do is throw clay—all over the room, in fact. And all over myself and everyone else unfortunate enough to be in the line of fire.

"Sorry about that," I mumble, trying desperately to gain control of the slippery chaos that's oozing between my fingers. A classmate wipes a gooey grey glop from her forehead.

"That's a bit too fast, Michael," Asia—the instructor—says from where she's hovering over my shoulder. Asia is an elegant and graceful woman in her midfifties with a pile of wild and wiry grey hair that she keeps at bay with the horn-rimmed glasses she is always losing on the top of her head. Laugh lines wreath her kind eyes, and she is constantly on the move about the studio, her forest-colored hemp clothing flowing behind her like a comet's tail.

"No kidding," I say beneath my breath.

This pottery class has been a rude awakening for me, a crash course in what every real artist already knows: no matter the medium, it's a devil of a task getting the raw material to behave like you want it to. Of course it doesn't help that my mind is all flashback to the day I learned to drive my parents' stick shift. There I was, pimple-faced and white-knuckled, awkwardly juggling accelerator, clutch, and brake in a start-and-screech tirade that was drawing wide-mouthed stares from other drivers.

Wide-mouthed stares seem to follow me like a shadow.

Back in the studio I goose the accelerator pedal on my pottery wheel, and another spray of clay takes flight.

"I'm so sorry," I mumble, not having the guts to look at the damage I've done.

Asia comets away from me, and without looking I can tell she's shaking her head.

After another disastrous half hour I flee the pottery studio under pretense of a bathroom break and hide out in the last stall until class is all but over.

When I return to the scene of my crimes I'm shocked by how much it looks like a toddler stumbled upon a can of paint and a lidless blender. Clay has literally splattered the ceiling. While some of the other students are sliding professional-quality vases and teapots onto the drying shelves, I start searching for a mop.

But then Asia gets our attention from the front of the room. "Next class," she says, "we'll be having a competition."

My heart sinks. The only thing more humiliating than being *implicitly* the worst is having the fact broadcast.

"What's the challenge?" I venture.

"Volume," Asia says with a broad smile.

I stare blankly at her, wondering at the meaning of this strange new pottery term, as impenetrable and mysterious as the rest: wedge, slip, glaze, score, cone.

"You'll start class with a fresh bag of clay," Asia explains. "And the winner will be the person with the least amount of clay remaining at the end."

My heart lifts a little. Since half my clay usually ends up on the wall or ceiling, I might actually have a chance at this.

"But here's the catch," Asia says with a wise grin. "You can't keep a single one of the pieces you make."

"What?" the other students gasp. For them, keeping their beautiful pieces was part of the deal, and disappointment is evident. Personally, I don't mind—I haven't made anything worth keeping anyway.

A middle-aged student raises his hand. "What's the point of spending an hour coaxing form from chaos if we can't keep it?"

"Trust me," Asia says.

"But what if I really like the piece?" The man keeps pushing.

Asia feigns exasperation. "Then you'll know that you've made it once and therefore that you can make something similar again."

I retreat back to my wheel, pushing the squeaky-wheeled mop bucket.

"Besides," Asia continues. "You all are too attached to the pieces you're making." I look down at the wobbly, off-centered bowl resting like dropped Jell-O on my wheel. *Attached* isn't exactly the word I'd use.

Asia continues from the front of the room. "As is true in all creativity, an essential part of mastering wheel throwing is indifference, objectivity, nonattachment."

Surprised to find that Asia's pottery class has Philosophy 101 thrown in for free, I halt my mopping.

Asia pauses for dramatic effect before continuing. "You must cultivate a perspective on your work that will allow you to evaluate and learn from the pieces you're making. This requires nonattachment. Only from that perspective will you be able to learn what worked as well as what didn't, and then move on to the next piece, incorporating and adapting and growing as you advance your skill."

"You mean we shouldn't care about our work?" a woman asks.

"Oh no," Asia says, shaking her head. "You should care a great deal. All artists care about their work, or else they wouldn't go to the bother of making it. But you mustn't allow your care to become attachment. There is a world of difference between the two. If care becomes attachment I can guarantee you that your skill will stagnate, that you'll be unable to learn or grow or progress."

We all nod, trying to make sense of this strange tension between caring deeply and yet being unattached.

"There's only one way to cultivate this unattached care," Asia continues. "And that's practice without concern for the results. Next class you'll throw as many pots as you're able to. At the end you will smash them *all* back into your bag of wet clay."

Her concluding tone is exultant. She looks around the room with eager expectation, hoping we've all caught the vision.

"I think I understand," the pushy man says slowly. "It's the old adage, I guess: practice makes perfect."

"No!" Asia cries, gaping in horror at the man.

We all blink in surprise at Asia's outburst. You'd have thought he'd suggested taking a bat to Michelangelo's *David*.

She takes a moment to compose herself before explaining. "That's exactly what I mean by attachment," she says. "If you're trying to make your pieces 'perfect' you're much too attached to them already. The weight of the 'perfect' in your psyche creates so much pressure that it can literally squash the creativity right out of you." She smacks her hand together like she's smashing a mosquito. "You need to let each individual piece of clay become what it is, let it be its own unique piece, its own thing. Forget the abstract idea of the 'perfect bowl.' It doesn't exist. Focus instead on the first two words of that axiom. Then you'll actually be onto something." Asia ends with a serene smile.

"The first two words?" I ask.

"Practice *makes*," another student chimes in. "Is that what you mean?"

"Exactly!" Asia cries, exultant. "That's *exactly* what I'm saying. *Practice makes!* And that's what next class is all about. That's how you'll improve as potters. Not by slaving away under the expectations of 'the perfect,' not by attachment to each and every piece. The only way forward is this: make it, evaluate it, learn from it, throw it away, start again."

"I'll be happy if I can make anything at all," I say under my breath.

I start mopping.

But do you know what? Asia is right. Though I write it off as nonsense at first, Asia's paradox of *care but not attachment* and the revised axiom *practice makes* turn out to make all the difference in the world. Two class sessions after the "competition" (no, I don't win the bar of dark chocolate Asia offers as the prize, though I do come in second place with only two pounds of clay remaining . . . I suspect the winner was kicking clay beneath the wheel) I have a delightfully productive hour and a half in the studio. When I come in that day things *just work*: the clay is malleable and responsive even as my hands are strangely attentive and able to understand what the clay is saying to me—what it can handle and what it can't, what it needs and what it doesn't. That might sound a bit crazy or anthropocentric, but there's no other way to describe what starts happening at the wheel. Throwing feels more like a dance than a war, more like a partnership than coercion. Not only does most of my clay stay within an acceptable radius of my wheel, but I actually end the class with two handsome bowls and a splendid pitcher.

"Those are very good," Asia shares with me as I get ready to smash the day's work back into my bag of clay. "Why don't you keep them?"

I blink in surprise. "Really?"

"If you want to, go ahead," she says, smiling. "You've gotten the hang of nonattachment, I think." She looks up at the ceiling where my clay from three weeks ago has dried.

I look back down at the pitcher and bowls, trying to decide what to do with them.

But Asia distracts me with a cautionary tone. "You must remember one thing, though."

I look back at her.

"As your ability grows, you must maintain a beginner's attitude."

"Huh?" I ask, surprised. "I was sort of hoping to move past the beginner stage as soon as possible."

"Oh, in terms of skill, you have," Asia says, picking up the pitcher and examining it. "And you will continue to improve. But as you advance you must try hard to not lose a beginner's attitude, by which I mean a beginner's joy, a beginner's humility, and a beginner's hope. This is the difference between merely making stuff, and being an *artisan*."

"What do you mean?" I ask, intrigued by this Pottery Philosophy 201.

Asia explains. "Every day in the studio is a new day. The clay is always unique, as is every piece. I've been creating with this medium for two decades, and I never know what is going to happen when I sit down at the wheel. Sometimes I think I'm going to make a bowl and I end up making a mug; sometimes I plan a plate and find a vase emerging in my hands. Joy, humility, hope."

"'The attitude of a beginner,'" I repeat, nodding. "I'll keep that in mind."

Asia smiles and walks away, her clothes and hair billowing behind her.

Either wisdom is found in many places, or Asia was quoting Flannery O'Connor:

> One thing that is always with the writer—no matter how long he has written or how good he is—is the continuing process of learning how to write. As soon as the writer "learns to write," as soon as he knows what he is going to find, and discovers a way to say what he knew all along, or worse still, a way to say nothing, he is finished.[6]

But why is this?

Remember the first time you picked up a violin, or sat down at the piano, or tried to move your feet in rhythm with the music? Or the first time you swung a bat, shot a free throw, cracked open a cookbook, kneaded dough, learned to sauté?

Do you remember how those early days felt? How strange and exciting it was when you started? How wonderful and mysterious and seemingly impossible?

There's something beautiful and clarifying and terrifying all at once in being at the beginning, in not really knowing what you're doing or if you're going to succeed at all or if the whole thing is going to hit the wall (or the ceiling) in utter failure. To be a beginner is to be full of hope-filled humility, to be overflowing with eager expectation that is simultaneously held in check by the obvious gap between your aspirations and current abilities. To be a beginner is to be pregnant with dreams but nascent with skill, and then to set about the work of cultivating the life of both.

It is precisely here—in this hope-filled humility—that nonattachment, indifference, and relative objectivity can exist. The stance Asia tried to help us all achieve. The beginner is by nature fluid and open, hungry for learning and skill, straining toward what is ahead, what is to come, what might one day be.

The nineteenth-century composer Johannes Brahms claimed that the mark of an artist is how much they throw away,[7] just as modern-day author Anne Lamott alludes to the *awful* first drafts every writer must create at the beginning. "All good writers write them," explains Lamott. "This is how they end up with good second drafts and terrific third drafts."[8]

To fail to be a beginner is, as O'Connor pointed out, "to be finished." But to embrace the attitude of a beginner is to be at the beginning, with the whole day, the whole project, the whole career ahead of you.

Not—mind you—that that makes sitting down every day in front of a blank page any easier.

If you haven't heard it from any other writers, let me fill you in on a little-known secret: the blank page is more terrifying than a firing squad, more intimidating than walking into a courtroom as the defendant. At least in a courtroom you can look the judge and jury in the eye, engage in dialogue, make your defense.

If only we writers were so lucky.

But—sadly—I don't have it so easy. The words I'm creating today will soar out into the world and be subject to scrutiny and cross-examination by an invisible judge and jury in the shadowy, distant form of reviewers, critics, and readers like yourself who will decide whether I am guilty or innocent, whether this project has merit or not, whether it should be relegated to the landfill or the thrift stores or even (maybe?) lauded and recommended to others.

Just thinking about this is enough to make any writer quake. If I dwell on this too long I start to sweat, feeling like a tiny microbe at the edge of a microscope's slide, just waiting for all the water to evaporate and my life to come to a sizzling end.

I need to get off this quick, or I'll soon punch Ctrl-Alt + Delete and scrap the whole thing.

But the attitude of a beginner is full of hope too. The hope of creating something true and good and beautiful, the hope of affecting others deeply with what one has long labored over, the hope that what one has set free in the world will bring life and joy. Flannery O'Connor describes the writer's hope best: "My task which I am trying to achieve is, by the power of the written word, to make you hear, to make you feel—it is, before all, to make you see. That—and no more, and it is everything. If I succeed, you shall find there, according to your deserts, encouragement, consolation, fear, charm, all you demand—and, perhaps, also that glimpse of truth for which you have forgotten to ask."[9]

So there it is: the extraordinary challenge of creating: imagination, hope-filled humility, practice. That's what Asia and O'Connor meant by the "attitude of the beginner." It's a disposition toward the work of creativity that is permeated with joy, buoyed by hope, anchored in humility. Meld this beginner's attitude with the wisdom and experience of hard-won skill, and you find yourself a master. This is as true for the potter, the poet, and the musician as it is for the person pursuing spiritual practice.

Whether or not I'll ever achieve the "writer's task" O'Connor described is yet to be determined. I've made two bowls and a pitcher, but who knows what will happen next week when I sit down at the wheel again.

But I mustn't concern myself with the perfect ideal.

Practice makes.

So I keep on making.

Stephen Nachmanovitch points out in his book *Free Play* that "the word *create* comes from 'to make grow,' as in the act of cultivating plants."[10] I like the implications of this, especially considering that God is *the Creator.* Can you picture a gardener God, in the greenhouse of the universe, cultivating everything that is, growing you, pruning me, fertilizing her, shaping him? It fills me with hope to think that God wants the world to grow and to flourish, to be fruitful and thrive. It's a stark contrast to the angry god so many of us find lurking about in our subconscious. Of course diseased branches must be cut off. But the good gardener does so in hope of health, not out of hate.

Might God be leaning over everything that is, with gaze hopeful and fixed, working all the while in our world like a careful, attentive gardener? Willing you and I and all the rest to grow and flourish?

Given the simultaneous months I spent tending my garden plot and throwing clay under Asia's supervision, I was delighted that Nachmanovitch pointed this out. It's astonishing how similar gardening and creativity is: the tilling of the soil, the planting of the seeds, the watering of the plants as they grow, the pulling of weeds and the difficulty of pruning, the hoped-for harvest. The same could be said for pottery: wedging the clay, coning up, pressing down, pulling, pulling, pulling, scraping, refining, drying, firing, glazing, firing. One "*fashions*" a text, as the Pulitzer prize–winning author Annie Dillard points out, just like one fashions a bowl or a garden or even a life.[11]

But beyond work and skill there is something more in this, something intrinsic to all creativity and all artistry: the sense that one is midwife to a mystery, steward of an extraordinary goodness, a captivating gift.

True, the gardener and the potter and the author is essential in the process, but—at least from the human perspective—none of these roles is ultimately the cause of that which one has been charged with guarding and caring for and directing. As a writer I sometimes feel like I am discovering the words more than I am creating them. As though they are in me, and my role is not to give them life but rather just to do what I can to help them out into the world, to not get in their way.

This notion of midwifing a mystery is one of the most astonishing things I learned from engaging the practice of creativity, stumbling upon it as unexpectedly as a miner upon a radiant vein of gold running straight through a slab of impenetrable stone.

Surprisingly, this is also true of spiritual practice. I'm as much of a newbie at fasting as I am at playing the piano, as wobbly on pilgrimage as I am on the pottery wheel, and the beginner's attitude is as necessary here as in the kitchen, the pottery studio, the writer's shack.

Father Solomon helped me see this when I was last at the monastery.

I was sitting in his office, having a chat about how things were coming along with my Sacred Year.

"How have you found the various spiritual practices are affecting you?" Father Solomon asks me. He eyes me keenly under one of his bushy grey eyebrows for a moment, but then turns away. There is a book titled *Renaissance Art* open on his desk and he starts flipping through it absentmindedly as I try to put into words the last several months.

"It's going well, I think," I say. I mention a few of the practices I've been engaging in, and he nods his head and—despite my worry that he's not paying attention to me—asks several probing questions once I've finished speaking.

"Tell me more about the pottery course you enrolled in," he enquires.

"It was awful!" I say loudly. Father Solomon looks up from the *Renaissance Art* book in surprise.

"At first," I continue. "But then I started to get the hang of it, and the clay became easier to work with as I slowly learned to coax the clay into doing what I wanted. It's like it became more malleable in my hands."

"Ahh," Father Solomon says, closing his eyes. "You can see now—can't you—why the prophet Jeremiah likened God to a potter? Why Saint Paul called us jars of clay?"

I nod and smile at the rich imagery, remembering Asia's words. *The clay is always unique. So is every piece.*

Father Solomon reaches the section on Michelangelo.

"Do you know how Michelangelo created the ceiling of the Sistine Chapel?" Father Solomon asks.

"It's fresco, isn't it?" I answer.

Father Solomon nods. "Do you know how fresco works?"

I shake my head, unsure of what Father Solomon is getting at.

"Fresco is basically painting with concrete," the monk explains. "It's a kind of plaster, really, which, once it hardens, is extremely durable. But what the artist gains in durability, they lose in malleability. It is painstaking work, with a fresh application of plaster necessary every couple of hours, for each and every section of the entire image. The artist first applies the plaster to the wall or ceiling, and then diligently applies carefully concocted pigments, achieving an overall composition of extraordinary nuance and clarity."

As he says this Father Solomon stops on a page in the *Renaissance Art* book showing a close-up of Michelangelo's *The Creation of Adam*, from the ceiling of the Sistine Chapel. It is a famous image, of course, but I can't recall ever seeing it in this much detail. God is there in heaven, of course, and Adam is on earth. But I'm seeing something now that I've never noticed before: the way God's whole being is reaching out, yearning toward the world, toward Adam, the gardener God caring with everything that he is about us. God's right arm is outstretched, finger extended toward us, intent, pointed, specific.

And there is Adam, looking haphazardly toward God, lounging back, indifferent, jaded, nonchalant.

"For years Michelangelo labored," Father Solomon continues. "Painstakingly applying the plaster, creating his tones and shades, applying them before the plaster dried. At one point he had to rip a whole section down and start over—the plaster was molding. But slowly

Michelangelo's creative energy was rewarded, and the masterpiece grew. Detail was added to detail, form to form, as one of humanity's greatest artists worked steadily toward the goal of the work he'd imagined."

Father Solomon lets his words hang in the air for a few poignant seconds before he turns to look at me. "How long does it take to fresco a soul, do you think?"

"Sorry?" I ask. I'm stretching to understand, but can't quite follow the logic. "Isn't God the artist here?"

Father Solomon nods. "Yes, of course," he says. "God is *the* artist, *the* Creator. But," and he looks off into the distance as he speaks, surveying all his long life and learning, "the older I become, the more convinced I am that we participate with God in the creative process of the soul. God is the capital-A Artist, if you like, and we are the lower-case artists, but nevertheless the relationship between God and human beings is much more dance than methodology, more delightful partnership than rote coercion."

"What do you mean?" I ask.

"I mean," Father Solomon muses, "what if what Saint Paul means in saying 'work out your salvation with fear and trembling,'[12] is that we are to partner with God in the artistic process of forming the human soul?"

Things snap into focus for me: the hope and humility of being a beginner, the persistent feeling that I am stewarding a mystery, that I am charged in my life with being a midwife to something that I do not own and can lay no claim to, and yet have substantial responsibility for. The deep joy of the hard work of it all.

Father Solomon smiles at the look on my face. We are quiet a long while, both of us looking at Michelangelo's infinite yet infinitesimal gap between the yearning God and the indifferent Adam.

"It will be glorious, won't it?" Father Solomon asks. "When at last the gap ceases to be?"

CHAPTER 7

Endless Finite Days: The Practice of Embracing Mortality

Death is the muse of philosophy.

—SCHOPENHAUER[1]

We know joy precisely to the extent that we know sorrow.

—WENDELL BERRY[2]

A man who keeps death before his eyes will at all times overcome his cowardice.

—A DESERT ELDER[3]

It is only in the face of death that man's self is born.

—SAINT AUGUSTINE[4]

All told, I've had two close encounters with death, one from a certain distance, the other up close and personal.

I am walking hand in hand with Danae along an idyllic, peach-colored beach on the east coast of Ecuador. We've been in the country for three weeks now, high up in the Andes Mountains working on a research project, and are thankful for this brief respite by the sea. The sun is slipping itself down toward pied and shimmering waters, and the delicious smell of fried plantains wafting toward us from a beachside vendor sets our mouths watering. It is a lazy end to the day, warm and humid. A pleasant breeze blows in off the sea carrying the sea's spray with it. I lick my lips and taste salt.

Suddenly a woman's scream pierces the warm air. Electricity on the spine. Rush of chills. Pounding heart.

We quickly scan the beach, searching for the source of the screams, and then see her there, not far back down the beach, fully clothed and running full speed into the sea. She is screaming and screaming.

We run toward her and soon are members in the sizeable crowd that has gathered on the sandy shore of the no longer pristine beach, eyes glued to the group of three or four men who are battling against the pounding waves, trying desperately to drag a limp body of a man toward the shore.

The crowd parts so they can lay him on the beach.

Both arms flop to the side, lifeless.

His face is an eerie purple color and his mouth is shaped like an O, gaping in a ghostly, rhythmic way, like a fish out of water.

Still the woman screams. This gaping ghost of a man must be her husband.

Someone holds her back so the lifeguards can work.

The rest of us stand there watching, shifting back and forth on nervous feet.

We watch and wait, wait and watch and shuffle our feet some more, glancing ominously at one another as the lifeguard performs CPR.

Tilt the head.

Plug the nose.

Two full breaths.

Thirty compressions.

Repeat.

Tilt the head, plug the nose, two full breaths. Thirty more compressions.

Repeat. Repeat. Repeat.

Still she screams, and the purple hue of the man's face deepens.

Or is it just that the sun has set now, that the night has come?
Tilt the head.
Plug the nose.
Two full breaths.
Thirty compressions.
Repeat. Repeat. Repeat.
At last the lifeguard shakes his head and stands, defeated.

The other, more personal encounter with death was when I was a boy. A car accident. I was in the passenger seat and my mother was driving. It was a common rear-ender in our sleepy Colorado town, although two things made the accident unique: the speed at which the person slammed into the back of us and also the twelve-foot lengths of steel rebar in the back of the pickup-truck, two cars ahead of us.

By all accounts the car that caused the accident must have been speeding along at seventy-five or eighty miles per hour, almost double the speed limit of that stretch of road. When the driver crested the hill and saw the long line of cars stopped at the stoplight ahead of him, his tires screeched for only two or three seconds before impact.

The crush of metal on metal was so forceful that it propelled our car into the back of the Buick in front of us, ramming it into the back of the pickup truck two cars ahead of us, and then shoving the pickup truck into the back of the car ahead of it. A chain reaction half a second and five car lengths long.

I remember the surreal, out-of-body feeling when I stepped out of the car, reeling in that strange and profound silence that settles in after the screech and *bam* and smashing is over, when your memory is recording everything, *everything* in absolute, specific detail. I remember what the clouds looked like. The cars that were for sale in the used-car lot next to the highway. The pale-grey color of the smashed car in front of us.

I walked up along the line of cars, surveying the wreckage, and felt myself grow woozy at the sight in the front seat of the Buick. Thankfully there wasn't anybody in the seat to begin with. Had there been, there wouldn't be much of a person left: the force of the impact had crushed the Buick forward with such astonishing force that the twelve-foot bundle of rebar in the pickup truck had been rammed straight through the passenger side of the windshield, right through the cabin of the car. It was now sticking—like a quiver-full of arrows through a bull's-eye—through the center of the passenger-seat headrest. Grey cotton stuffing was stretched and smeared over the emerging metal in a sickening tangle.

"Oh my God," I heard myself say, suddenly feeling myself on very thin existential ice.

What if we'd been one car ahead in the afternoon lineup? The rebar would have come through our windshield, through my headrest.

Through *me!*

Tell me, friend: How short was the interval of time that saved me from a face full of rebar?

Was it kindness that caused my mother to let the car in front of us merge?

Luck?

Providence?

Who knows how these things work . . .

Take away all oxygen from the brain, and ten seconds is all the time it takes until the bright and conscious world—stretched taut between memories and hopes, interspersed with friends and family, infused with scent and taste and touch and sound and sight—is subsumed beneath the dark realm of our utterly unmappable unconscious. Just four minutes after that, the intricate swirling dance of action and reaction, charge and discharge upheld by the one-hundred-billion-neuron-strong network in your brain dissolves into meaninglessness. And then, the finite alchemy that constituted *you* is ended. What was "is" not all that long ago, forevermore becomes "was."

The realization of our finitude can be a shocking and disorienting experience. Most of us tiptoe around this basic fact of existence in lots of delicate ways, keeping the skeleton in the closet behind every deadbolt we can muster. But sometimes the strangest things can summon the dread of death in unexpected ways.

One summery evening a group of friends and I are all sitting on an apartment rooftop, enjoying an impromptu dessert potluck. People have brought chocolate bars, cookies, the leftovers of a birthday cake, fresh rhubarb with honey. The conversation is easy and enjoyable as the evening descends, drifting from topic to topic—a leaf meandering down the surface of a gentle river. Someone mentions a photo they saw recently, taken by the Hubble space telescope, and then Jackie—a dear friend—confesses that she abhors looking up at the stars in the night sky.

"They make me feel frighteningly small," Jackie says, her eyes growing full. "Utterly insignificant. What am I compared to the infinite universe above and around me? What is my meager life compared to the countless eons that have elapsed since the start of it all, compared to the countless eons that will pass before the whole show winds down again into darkness?"

"It's like the psalmist says," someone else chimes in as the darkness deepens. "When I look at the night sky and see the work of your fingers— the moon and the stars you set in place—what are mere mortals that you should think about them, human beings that you should care for them?"[5]

We all sit in silence at this—gazing for a moment into the abyss— feeling the rough and tearing texture of our own finitude.

"I found out about Jackie's universal phobia on our second date," Mark, Jackie's husband laughs, trying to bring a lighter tone to the conversation. "It was early August, right in the middle of the Perseids meteor shower. I bought a nice bottle of wine, some dark chocolate, brought a warm blanket. We walked out into a field, beneath a cloudless, starlit sky. Jackie had a panic attack beneath all those stars."

"It was *terrifying!*" Jackie says, eyes wide. "I don't think I'll *ever* be able to look up at the night sky without a sense of total dread."

This sort of fear is sometimes called "the experience of the *tremendum*." It's a deep and overwhelming sense of how vast everything else is, and how very tiny we are amid the whole wide sweep of it all. "We all face the sense of our smallness and insignificance," writes psychoanalyst Irvin Yalom, "when measured against the infinite extent of the universe."[6]

But—surprisingly—the effects of the "experience of the *tremendum*" aren't all bad. If the authors and researchers in a recent article published in *Personality and Social Psychology Review* can be believed, very good things can come from being reminded of our own mortality.[7] Just passing a cemetery or being reminded in other ways of our own finitude has the capacity to make us more kind, more compassionate, more forgiving, less xenophobic, less judgmental, less arrogant. People are 40 percent more likely to help someone who is in need of help if they've just walked past a cemetery.

Did you catch that? *Forty percent* more likely to help.

Perhaps we should all make a point of walking past a cemetery on a weekly—even daily—basis.

Why this positive effect, do you think?

Is it because "Death," as Dr. Samuel Johnson—the author of the first English dictionary—once noted, "wonderfully concentrates the mind"?[8]

What he means, of course, is that *the idea of death* wonderfully concentrates the mind.

Death itself scrambles the mind—rebar tangled through grey cotton.

If the *idea of death* wonderfully concentrates the mind, perhaps this is why the Desert Mothers and Fathers—those ancient and enigmatic wise men and women—made their abodes at the edges of the civilized world, among the tombs and graves, hiding themselves there in clefts of rock. *Memento mori* is the Latin mantra: "remember your mortality," and the attempt to do precisely this is certainly why ascetics of old seem to have counted human skulls among their few possessions. Apparently gazing from time to time at the hollow eye sockets was an effective reminder that the monks themselves would one day be similarly vacant. Caravaggio and Michelangelo both depicted the fourth-century Saint Jerome as contemplating a human skull with great intentionality: maybe he'd found some pearl of great price buried deep in the darkness.

"Teach us to number our days," cried the psalmist. "That we may gain a heart of wisdom."[9]

I can't help but wonder if it is possible to track down, to ferret out the "experience of the *tremendum*." Might one *intentionally* practice "the wonderful concentration of the mind"?

People might not understand, though: living in a cemetery or walking around with a skull would undoubtedly be considered morbid (if not downright pathological) in today's world.

Where might one *find* a skull anyway?

Turns out two thousand dollars is all it takes to procure yourself a real, medical-grade human skull. Online, of course. On an otherwise uneventful Friday afternoon I have a startling conversation with one of the dealers. Most of the skulls in their inventory have been donated by individuals seeking to aid science and medicine, and thus are available for purchase only by institutions of higher learning.

"However," the saleswoman suggests after a long pause. "We do have a secondary inventory of nondonated skulls which are available for purchase by the general public."

I drop the phone.

"What!" I stammer a moment later. "What are *nondonated* skulls?"

"Undocumented skulls," the woman responds, her monotone unchanged. "Most of them are from Asia, prior to 1972. Or we've acquired them elsewhere and were unable to obtain sufficient documentation."

"Huh," I say, mulling this over. "What other means do you have for procuring human skulls?"

"I'm not at liberty to discuss our company's research and acquisition methodologies, sir," she replies.

"Uh-huh," I say. I let the silence hang. "Well, thank you for your time."

"My pleasure, sir. Be sure to call again should the need arise."

Click.

Danae forbids me to purchase a skull.

I don't argue. Besides, two thousand dollars for a *nondonated skull* is too high a price to pay in all the wrong ways.

But I'm undeterred from seeking the *tremendum*, adamant to *memento mori*. The more I read, the more I'm convinced that "keeping death daily before my eyes" just might be a very good idea. How very clarifying our finitude can be! We've all heard of Charles Dickens's Mister Scrooge, whose encounter with death transforms the greedy and miserly old man into a compassionate and selfless individual. Perhaps you've wondered how you'd live differently if you *knew* you only had six months to live. Let me be blunt: six months or sixty years—it's going to happen sooner or later. I find myself wondering how I'd live if I actually accepted the fact that I am one day going to die.

The effects, apparently, can be substantial. Saint Antony—the third-century founder of monasticism—insists upon the benefits of keeping death consciously before oneself:

> And in order that we not become negligent, it is good to carefully consider the apostle's statement: *I die daily.* (1 Corinthians 15) . . . The point of the saying is this: As we rise daily, let us suppose that we shall not survive till evening, and again, as we prepare for sleep, let us consider that we shall not awaken. By its very nature our life is uncertain, and is meted out daily by providence. If we think this way, and in this way we live—daily—we will not sin, nor will we crave anything, nor bear a grudge against anyone, nor will we lay up treasures on earth, but as people who anticipate dying each day we shall be free of possessions, and we shall forgive all things to all people.[10]

Today few of us do as Saint Antony prescribes. Instead we rail against death with everything we've got. This is why the Pulitzer prize–winning psychoanalyst Ernest Becker believes that fear of death drives almost *all* of the activity in our world. "We disguise our struggle," Becker writes, "by piling up figures in a bank book to reflect privately our sense of heroic worth. Or by having only a little better home in the neighborhood, a bigger car, brighter children. But underneath throbs the ache . . . no matter how we mask it in concerns of smaller scope."[11] And it is not just positive activity, not just the pursuit of happiness that is motivated by our fear of death. Banal means of deadening ourselves to the impending reality of death abound as well: "Modern man is drinking and drugging himself out of awareness, or he spends his time shopping, which is the same thing."[12]

❧

Curious whether the wisdom of the ages—the *intentional* embrace of mortality—might actually be onto something, I begin frequenting cemeteries. Famous and nameless, important and obscure. From Gettysburg to Edinburgh, to the little forgotten one just down the street, I make a regular habit of sitting for a while among the universal reality of human finitude.

Like today.

Today I am high atop one of the most scenic and expensive bluffs in all Montecito, California, walking toward the city's cemetery. To the north, mansion after mansion patchworks the dry land, an elaborate chessboard—visible evidence of the ingenuity, calculation, and sheer luck woven throughout the lives of the super-rich who call these estates home. Just an hour and a half from Los Angeles, the kings and queens of today's world—movie stars, rock stars, corporate multimillionaires or billionaires—describe Montecito as their "weekend getaway." The parking lots are full of Rolls Royces, Lamborghinis, Maseratis. Diamonds outnumber the stars, and the bling shines brighter than the heavens. Even a gardener might end up lucky here—the recipient of an extra Rolex—a small token of thanks for his diligent labor.

Moments later I round a corner and enter the immaculate cemetery, meandering my way up the palm tree–lined pathway to the crest of the cemetery hill and a concrete bench that rests there. I sit down on it, surrounded by the crosses and tombstones, pillars and monuments, gazing out at the expansive Pacific as it glistens blue-gold in the late afternoon's radiance.

Down on the beach I watch as an old woman walks hand-in-hand with her young granddaughter, who is splashing delightedly in the gentle waves.

How very small we all are indeed, inching our way along the boundaries of enormity.

Despite the quiet beauty of the visual scene, the soundscape is dissonant and unnerving. One of our culture's recent billionaires—you would know his name if I said it—has been constructing a temple to his prowess on a property close to the cemetery. The work interrupts my contemplation of death, the sound of jackhammers and saws piercing the air.

The mansion is an extraordinary monument to human ingenuity, an undertaking of almost epic proportions. The billionaire assembled the property through the purchase of three contiguous estates. After the three preexisting mansions had been demolished and the disparate properties unified, a single monolithic structure—larger than all the others combined—is now being erected in the center of the expansive compound.

All told the project is rumored to cost more than $250 million.

Isn't this the way of the world: the stronger overtake the weaker, build something bigger, better, bolder?

Remind me, if you would, for I seem to have forgotten here among these graves: What is the point of all that?

I glance to my right at a curious sight: a tombstone worn and weathered, now illegible, and cracked in half. Whose story did it tell when it was a younger slab, full and complete? Now the top rests haphazardly against the jagged bottom. There is no one to pay for its repair.

No one who cares enough to fix it.

I can't help but wonder—as I gaze through these gravestones, amid all the jackhammering and sawing and shouting of the construction crews hard at work on the billionaire's estate—whether everything we build is just destined to become rubble in another's ambition.

What was it the philosopher Bertrand Russell said? "Someday [even] the solar system will lie in ruins . . ."[13]

As will your recently constructed mansion, Mr. Billionaire. Cracked in half with no one to pay for its repair, and no one who cares enough to fix it.

This is a sobering thought. An open-handed slap to the face, in fact. For all the power and wealth here, for all the cultural influence and clout these culture-makers possess with their red carpets and private jets, they will all—*we* will all—one day be six feet under.

"Death," Becker notes, "is man's peculiar and greatest anxiety."[14]

I must agree, sitting here as I am in my sunny cemetery, utterly powerless before the *tremendum*.

Walking down from the cemetery I come face to face with the most obvious liability of contemplating death, what the cynic philosophers of old embodied in their very lives: the bone-deep conviction that life itself is utterly, completely meaningless. I become a grumpy, petulant cynic. I feel like lounging around all day doing nothing, much like Diogenes of Sinope—the founder of cynicism itself—is depicted in Raphael's Vatican fresco *The School of Athens*. Some of the greatest philosophical minds are pictured there—Aristotle, Plato, Pythagoras, Heraclitus—conversing and discussing and pursuing the philosophical life, searching adamantly for truth and beauty and goodness. And then there's Diogenes: lounging in rags on the floor. "What's the point?" Diogenes seems to be saying. "Someday it will all lie in ruins, even the Acropolis itself."

Wasn't the author of Ecclesiastes a cynic at heart as well? "Meaningless! Meaningless!" he shouted. "Everything is meaningless!"[15]

I mention all this to a pastor friend named Monica one afternoon over coffee, and I'm unprepared for her gentle rebuke.

"But that's just the half of it!" she says. "You haven't pressed deeply enough into the fact of your mortality yet."

I am surprised by this. I thought frequenting cemeteries was deep enough.

"Not at all," Monica insists. "Floundering in meaninglessness is not the goal of the contemplation of death. The point is to keep pressing into it, keep cultivating a deepening perspective on your own finitude until you move through and beyond meaninglessness into a place of humble joy. Humble joy, expectant gratitude, active hope and patient waiting. That is the point. That is the ecosystem you're trying to cultivate. That is where you'll echo Jesus' prayer, even in the face of death, 'Thy will be done.'"

"Humble joy, expectant gratitude, active hope, patient waiting," I echo, the words striking my soul like a gong. "These are the point?"

"Yes," Monica replies, nodding. "Cynicism is a tempting, seductive route. But it's the easy way out."

∾

"I've never had a request like this before," Leonard, the manager of a local university cemetery says over the phone. "Certainly sounds interesting."

This is the most positive response I've received to an idea that started after Monica's rebuke: digging a grave by hand.

"Why don't you come next Tuesday," Leonard says. "We'll let you dig in an open space on our property."

I arrive at eight o'clock on a cloudy morning the next Tuesday and knock on Leonard's door. He welcomes me into an office that has plaques and certificates from the American Cemetery Association on the walls. And old black-and-white photographs of the cemetery's early days, with women in black dresses and men in stiff suits managing horse-drawn buggies and wagons.

"You'll have to sign a liability waiver," Leonard says once I've sat down. "The university is fully supportive of your—ahem—*research*, but you'll still need to waive all liability before we can allow you to get to work."

Fifteen minutes later I'm standing out next to a plot that has been staked out: 96" x 39".

"Dig down to the depth of a shovel," Doug—one of the cemetery groundsmen—tells me. "That's about how far we typically go."

"How long does it take with a backhoe?" I ask.

"About twenty minutes," Doug laughs. "Mark and I have a bet as to how long it's actually going to take you to do this."

Mark is the other groundsman, a newer employee wearing a university cap, who still seems a little embarrassed to be working at a cemetery.

"How long do you think it'll take me?" I ask Mark.

"It's definitely going to take you all day," Mark says with a wide grin.

"And you?" I ask, looking at Doug.

"You'll be back tomorrow to finish," Doug answers. "The hardpan under this section is at least two feet thick. Full of rocks and roots and hard as cement. I put a sprinkler on it for you yesterday, but still. You've got your work cut out for you.

"Good luck," Doug says, and both he and Mark walk away, leaving me staring at the ground.

❧

Fourteen hundred and five shovelfuls.

That's how many it takes to dig a grave, in case you were wondering.

All told, it took six hours to complete it, counting a brief stop for lunch and at least a half hour of sitting with *two* feet in the grave, trying to summon the courage to continue staring the *tremendum* right in the face.

"I'm impressed," Doug admits once he's emerged from his office and is kneeling beside the grave. I'm standing in it chest deep—the depth of a shovel—looking up at him. Mark is there as well.

"The hardpan wasn't as hard as I feared," I say, looking up at Doug. "Thanks for putting the sprinkler on it."

"No problem," Doug says. "Can you believe they only used to pay the grave diggers two dollars per day to do this? That was back in the 1920s. Two dollars was a lot more back then, but still. Not all that much for a hard day's labor."

Mark chimes in as well. "The guy who drove the hearse got paid five dollars a day."

"Sounds a bit unfair," I say, wiping the sweat from my brow.

"Of course it was unfair," Doug agrees. "That's just the way it is. The guy who does the least gets paid the most!"

"Ain't that the way it always goes?" Mark asks, laughing.

"Sure is," Doug says. "I'll be back." Doug walks away with his head hanging low, leaving Mark and me standing there together, staring at the open grave.

"So, now," Mark starts, searching for words, "*why* exactly are you doing this? It is flat out weird, you know."

"Yeah, I know," I say, looking down into the grave. Now it's my turn to search for words. "It's hard to explain. I'm trying to come to grips with my own mortality, I guess. That's the best way I know to describe it."

Mark nods, a thread of understanding connecting us. "I've only been working here for a month, but I can't stop thinking about it."

"What's that?"

"The fact that I'm going to be down there someday. That we're *all* going to be down there someday. And the whole world will just keep on going about its business above us, like we were never even here."

We stand there for a few minutes in silence, looking down into the bottom of the fresh grave, contemplating this reality.

A fresh gust of Wind blows through the cemetery, loosing a cloud of fire-colored leaves from the towering maples that rise high above us. The leaves fall in a beautiful and heartaching sort of way from their lofty perches, some spinning, some swinging, all falling inevitably down toward their final end.

Two leaves land at the bottom of the grave, vivid and shocking as a burning bush there against the pale and colorless soil.

Cemeteries can be some of the most poisonous places on the planet.

This is rather ironic, in fact, as cemeteries weren't always poisonous places. The irony is that they've not become poisonous because of the corpses decomposing beneath the surface. In fact, cemeteries would be incredibly fertile places if corpses were actually *allowed* to decompose. Instead, the places we bury our dead now contain some of the highest concentrations of formaldehyde found anywhere outside laboratories. Our vain attempts to protect the bodies of our loved ones from the essential and natural process of decay—like so many of our "ingenious" modern ideas—hijacks a life-sustaining natural process. Instead of the elements that constituted us being returned again to the dirt from which we sprung, a whole chemical pharmacy is employed that results in dead trees, toxic soil, poisoned aquifers, just to name a few of the maladies.

Contrast this misguided attempt to forestall decay with the beautiful tale of Roger and Mary Williams, the founders of Rhode Island. When Roger and Mary died and were buried on their farm, an apple tree was planted near their grave. Decades later, when the good citizens of Rhode Island tried to exhume the Williamses' bodies to rebury them with honor in a more prestigious cemetery, not even the Williamses' bones remained. What did remain, however, were the living roots of the apple tree in the obvious *shape of their bodies.* Blindly searching for nutrients the roots of the tree had traced the path laid out through the Williamses' bones. Dead humans had been transmuted into living tree, and the nutrients that had for a while resided in the Williamses' bodies were given back, drawn up again into the sunlight and wind in the life of the tree.[16]

Or consider the early Christian Saint Phocas, a man of the soil who was—at least in my judgment—certainly worthy of heaven. Because of his Christian faith, Saint Phocas asked the Roman soldiers sent to execute him to carry out their deed in the center of his garden and then place his body in the grave he had prepared there. His purpose: ensuring that his body would be returned to the ground and—through its decomposition—replenish the earth that had sustained his life for so many years in that place.[17]

When I go the way of all the world, I beg you, please: use no formaldehyde. Do not confine my material aspects to a box of metal or plastic, and for God's sake, do not pump my casket full of nitrogen in a fruitless attempt to obstruct the beautiful inevitability of my return to dust.

Bury me instead in a simple pine box, fourteen hundred and five shovelfuls deep.

Plant an apple tree near my head and a plum tree at my feet for good measure. Then, once a few seasons have passed and the carbon atoms that constituted my neocortex have blossomed and fruited into apples, and the calcium from the bones in my toes has metamorphosed into stone fruit, stretch a hammock between the trees on a pleasant autumn day and enjoy as much fruit as you'd like—all of it on me.

And then I shall at last be nourishing to another in the most elemental sense.

✐

But wait.

Does this seem anticlimactic?

There's an alternate ending to the story, you know, though sometimes I fear it's too good to be true.

Do not judge me harshly, brothers and sisters, when I secretly and in confidence confess to you that in my darkest moments I worry that the resurrection may be only a myth. Some find it easy to believe. Others impossible. I vacillate between the two. Some days it is easy for me—perforated with inevitability like a prism with light. "Of course the resurrection is real," I say confidently. And I mean it.

But on other days?

On other days it is not so easy at all. On those days I worry that the resurrection is just a story we've told ourselves again and again down through the centuries since Christ, hoping to assuage the deep and gnawing fear we all have—that throbbing ache—the gut-wrenching worry that when the show ends, it—well—it *ends*.

To those who might chastise me for my "lack of faith," let me point out that I seem to be in good company.

Didn't the apostles themselves find it difficult to believe at first, when they'd heard about Jesus' resurrection?

Saint Peter—"the Rock" on whom the church would be built—sprinted to the grave to see for himself if the rumors the women were telling were true.

And what about Doubting Thomas?

I often find echoes of Doubting Thomas's bold audacity in my own heart: "Unless I see in his hands the mark of the nails, and place my finger into the mark of the nails, and place my hand into his side, I will never believe."[18]

Was he angry when he said this?

Weeping?

Both?

Even after eye-witnessing all of Jesus' miracles and healings, after walking countless miles with the One rumored to be the Son of God and hearing him teach and walk on water and enact the Kingdom of God as it had never been enacted before, that rag-tag bunch of fishermen and tax collectors still found that the *literal* resurrection stretched the boundaries of credibility.

How might Thomas or Peter or any of the others have *known* it could *actually* happen without *seeing* it for themselves?

And frankly—forgive me, but I must ask it—how might we?

"Lord, haste the day, when my faith shall be sight." Horatio Spafford wrote that line in 1873, a few weeks after learning that all four of his young daughters had been killed in a shipping accident while crossing the Atlantic. Swallowed whole by the deep. Vanished without a trace into the *tremendum*.

His wife had been on the vessel as well, and after her rescue, sent him a single life-altering telegram that began with six harrowing words: "Saved alone. What shall I do?"[19]

Standing at the edge of a fourteen-hundred-and-five-shovelful-deep grave, I find the same words resonating within me: Lord, haste the day, when my flickering and feeble faith shall at long last be sight!

We are like ocean foam, muses Annie Dillard. Or clouds springing up, taking shape, and then dissipating in the sky. Or like sand blown on and forgotten. She has trouble choosing between the ever-fleeting metaphors in her tremendous book, *For the Time Being*.[20]

Whatever image strikes you most, we are not permanent, you and I. We are evanescent at best, cursory, vanishing. Lilies in the field[21]—here today and gone, *gone* tomorrow.

Snowflakes, all of us. One hundred billion in the storm. Forgotten by June.

Or hazelnuts. Or fiery-colored leaves spinning and shifting in their slow descent toward the ground.

"Blessed are those who believe without seeing" Jesus said.[22]

And here is my reply: "Yes, Lord! But in your mercy, *help thou mine unbelief!*"[23]

These are the sort of thoughts that consume me as I lie here at the bottom of the grave I've dug.

I cross my arms above my chest and close my eyes, letting the world above disappear into darkness, feeling the coolness of the soil behind and around me.

And I wait.

And I pray.

And I sing. The *Kyrie.* The Doxology.

Observe well your place in this world, O Mortal. We are strong and able—yes—living and moving and having our being above ground for seventy years or by reason of strength (and with a little help from medical technology) eighty or even ninety.

But who for all of their struggles can add a single hour to their life?

Observe well your place in this world, O Human. Take note and do not forget it. *Memento mori.*

But let's say it *is* true—the resurrection, I mean.

Just imagine with me for a moment, if you will, what it might be like to wake up after slipping into that last sleep?

How will it seem, to find your consciousness adhering once again, I wonder? To know that again you *are*, when you once—very recently, in fact—were not.

What will you think?

Will there be birds singing nearby? I believe so.

And the Wind. Will it be rushing?

It must be so.

And all the rest—all the dear ones we've known and loved?

Who can tell? Who can judge? Not I, I know.

But let us hope that all people, redeemed and restored and sanctified, may yet be citizens in the Kingdom of God.

What about all things? What about my beloved dog, Elliott? Perhaps he will be the one to wake me, pressing his wet nose into my face, hungry as always and eager for a romp in the woods, just like on Saturdays?

Do not quote me on this, nor judge me for it, I beg you. Judge not the words of a man lying in an open grave. Let him hope, won't you?

I doubt I'll spring up out of the grave and start turning cartwheels. I suspect I'll be too surprised to do or say much of anything for a good while.

Maybe I'll just lie there for a few years on the bed or on the beach or on the mountaintop—wherever it is that I'll finally find myself awoken—and let myself wander back over the decades I've known in this life. Recalling the moments and memories, the faces and friends. Anticipating the Feast to come, the continuation of all those conversations that ended just as they were starting to get good, all the jokes that were truncated just as the punch line was about to dawn like a smile.

Perhaps I'll wiggle my fingers and my toes, delighted simply to be able to *move* again.

Then roll my head back and forth a few times.

Then stretch my arms up over my head and breathe in a deep and full and wide Breath before rolling over onto my side and push myself up into *the* Great Awakening.

Perhaps then I'll finally see that the grave is no full stop but merely an ellipses, an intimation, a harbinger: that the point is yet to come. And then, my dear friends, I'll *believe* for myself, and not in any abstract and hypothetical way, for then I'll *know* that the grave was in fact no prison but rather just a cocoon, a place of metamorphosis from which we've emerged with form altered and hope restored and found that—glory of glories—the Wind is billowing beneath us and above us, and all around us, indeed even *through* us.

I take my time down here, in the bottom of this grave, thinking toward that day. Longing to know what it will be like and yet utterly overwhelmed by the limitations of my humanity, my dirt-ness, my humus-ness.

"Ashes to ashes, dust to dust" is how one burial litany puts it.[24] Echoing Genesis, of course: "then the LORD God formed the man of dust from the ground and breathed into his nostrils the breath of life, and the man became a living creature."[25]

That is all we are, you and me: a little bit of dust. A little bit of Breath.

Humble joy. Expectant gratitude. Active hope. Patient waiting. This is the point of the contemplation of death. This is the gift of the *tremendum*, the pearl of great price it has to offer, if we are able to gaze long enough into the abyss.

I am beginning to see this now, even if only through a glass darkly.

I look past the sides of this earthy grave and watch as the clouds swell and shrink far above, coming into existence for a while and then vanishing.

The shadows creep up toward the mouth of the grave as the day grows long, as the night approaches.

I do what I must do, here at the bottom of this grave.

What we all must do in the end.

I wait.

And I watch.

And I pray.

O God, make speed to save us. O Lord, make haste to help us.

SECTION II

Depth with God

CHAPTER 8

Guilty as Diagnosed:
The Practice of Confession

Search me, God, and know my heart;
*   test me and know my anxious thoughts.*
See if there is any offensive way in me,
*   and lead me in the way everlasting.*

—PSALM 139:23–24 NIV

Bless the LORD, O my soul,
*   and forget not all his benefits,*
who forgives all your iniquity,
*   who heals all your diseases,*
who redeems your life from the pit,
*   who crowns you with steadfast love and mercy,*
who satisfies you with good. . . .
as far as the east is from the west,
*   so far does he remove our transgressions from us.*
As a father shows compassion to his children,
*   so the LORD shows compassion to those who fear him.*

—PSALM 103:2–5, 12–13 ESV

*To confess your sins to God is not to tell him anything he doesn't
already know. Until you confess them, however, they are the abyss
between you. When you confess them, they become the bridge.*

—FREDERICK BUECHNER[1]

*It sometimes happens that men who preach most vehemently
about evil and the punishment of evil, so that they seem to have
practically nothing else on their minds except sin, are really
unconscious haters of other men. They think the world does
not appreciate them, and this is their way of getting even.*

—THOMAS MERTON[2]

As a boy I loved playing with LEGOs. I would spend hours and hours
on the floor of my room with thousands of tiny pieces spread out
all around me, building everything from airplanes to tractors to sky-
scrapers. One afternoon I grew tired of bringing order out of chaos and
decided to do something else. But I didn't really feel like going about the
monumental task of picking up all the countless little pieces, and instead
hit upon the seemingly brilliant idea of shoving the whole mess underneath my bed. It would have taken several minutes to pick everything up
piece by piece, but by turning a handy book on edge and using it like a
shovel, I made the entire pile disappear in thirty seconds flat.

There was just one problem: in my zeal to make the mess disappear,
I somehow completely missed the fact that a plate containing my half-
eaten ham sandwich got shoved under the bed as well.

Within three days I knew something was wrong, and my room filled
up with the pungent odor of rotting meat.

"Whew!" my mother said as she walked past my room. She opened
the door and peered in. "What's that *smell?*"

"I don't know," I answered honestly, looking around for the culprit.

She looked at me strangely for a moment, mumbled something about
not being ready for puberty, and latched the door shut.

But by the fourth day she was demanding that I help her identify the source of the smell. There we were, together on our hands and knees, using the long handle of a broom to scrape out everything from beneath my bed.

Personalities can change over time, but there are some ways they stay the same. I'm sad to say that I still have a strong affinity for sweeping things under the bed rather than dealing with them in the light of day. The little voice in my head at these crucial moments is astonishingly seductive and compelling, chanting that *no one will know* if I take the easy road toward keeping up appearances. From time to time it even convinces me that I'm *such a good actor,* if I just *pretend* that everything is as it should be, it just might actually end up *being* that way.

Whenever I listen to this voice, the same inevitable course ensues. Things might be fine for a while. But then decomposition happens. Things *rot* when they're left alone in the darkness. Soon they begin to reek.

Then there's only one thing to do: get down on your knees and use the broom to pull everything out from under the bed into the light so that you can actually deal with it.

This is of course why every addiction recovery organization under the sun from Alcoholics Anonymous to Narcotics Anonymous to Overeaters Anonymous insists that acknowledging something under the bed has started to reek is the first step toward health.

The practice of confession is exactly this: using the long handle of the broom on a regular basis to pull out as much of the pile as you can reach. It isn't about shame or regret or anything of that sort.

Rather, it's about getting things put right.

And getting rid of that awful smell.

In one of his most famous essays, the Trappist monk Thomas Merton observes that "It is no accident that Hitler believed firmly in the unforgiveableness of sin."[3] Tragically, Merton argues, it was Hitler's absolute conviction that sin was utterly unforgivable that caused him to seek the annihilation of the Jews. The logic goes like this: once Hitler had scapegoated the Jews as irreparably "sinful," there was—in his mind—nothing left to be done but try to eradicate an entire race of people. In fact, much of Nazi propaganda sought to inculcate in the German public a belief of absolute "evil of the Jews." Gas chambers, warfare, and annihilation are the only logical conclusion once we allow ourselves to believe the lie that any person or group of people is the "absolute enemy," beyond every possibility of reconciliation or healing.

The mind-set that focuses on the annihilation of others is what is required by what Merton calls the "blood-drinking gods." But it doesn't have to be this way:

> From such blood-drinking gods the human race was once liberated, with great toil and terrible sorrow, by the death of a God Who delivered Himself to the Cross and suffered the pathological cruelty of His own creatures out of pity for them. In conquering death He opened their eyes to the reality of a love which asks no questions about worthiness, a love which overcomes hatred and destroys death.[4]

Viewed not from the perspective of these "blood-drinking gods" but instead through the crucified and risen Christ, sin is no longer cause for eradication of the sinner but rather becomes a motive for God's compassion.

Sin, as Saint Augustine taught, "is its own punishment,"[5] and it is precisely this punishment—death in all its forms—that God is at work to heal people from. If Merton is right, God is not some bloodthirsty maniac just itching to blast us all to hell but is instead the God of the psalmist, "who heals all your diseases."[6]

Doesn't this seem like the character of God the church's saints and mystics speak of? Isn't this the kind of God we see in Christ, Christ who came to heal and make well and set at liberty?[7] Isn't the notion of a God dead set on obliterating his enemies actually a caricature of hell, rather than the logic of heaven? Isn't it the logic of hell to suggest that holiness must be protected by killing, while it is the hope of heaven—thanks be to God—that righteousness and holiness and peace will at last come to creation through the power of the healing God?

Confession taught me this.

"Father, I need your help," I say, leaning forward intently into the bright overhead light of the priest's office. "There's something I have to know."

"Yes?" the priest replies, leaning forward as well. Concern is etched on his face.

But I stall, searching for words. This is the first time I've stepped foot inside this storied old Anglican church. I'd e-mailed the priest out of the blue about a week ago, and now that I'm actually meeting with him, I find I'm hesitant to speak what's on my mind, apprehensive about the response I'll receive.

The priest senses my hesitation, and waits patiently for me to formulate my question. "Go on," he urges at last.

"Does God *loathe* me?" I blurt out at last.

The question takes the priest by surprise. He leans back in his chair.

"No," the priest says. "No, I don't believe God loathes you at all." There is absolute sincerity in the priest's tone, for which I'm glad. I'd been worried he might laugh at the question. Instead he touches fingertips to fingertips, in a prayer-like posture, hallowing the moment. "But tell me more," he continues. "What is behind your question? What's driving it?"

"I don't know," I say honestly. "I'm just worried that God does. That I might be abhorrent to God."

"Can you say what it is that makes you feel this way?" the priest asks. "Can you identify the source of this feeling?"

I shake my head. "No, not really. It's just a general sense. A deep weightiness in my chest, the gnawing tension at the back of my head that God is just an angry God."

The priest nods as I'm speaking, listening attentively, and falls silent for several moments before responding, considering. "This is one of the aspects of my work that grieves me most, that causes me the most—" He takes off his glasses and wipes them on his black cassock, and I wonder for a moment if his eyes are moist. "What shall I say—the most hesitation."

"I know, I—" I start to speak, instantly wishing I hadn't asked the question, but the priest cuts me off.

"On the one hand, we must not be too hasty to boldly declare 'What God Thinks' or 'How God Feels' about anything. After all, who can fathom the mind of God? To do so glibly is egregious, and more often than not the people who are foolish enough to do so are precisely the people who should be keeping their mouths shut."

I nod and smile, recalling several such regrettable "pronouncements" made in God's name.

"On the other hand, though, the belief that the Creator God can have anything but love for his own creatures is just as egregious, and perhaps far more damaging in the long run."

All at once the priest stands up. "Give me a moment," he says. He walks over to the corner desk and opens a drawer. I see him pull out a card of some sort, but from this angle, I can't see what it is.

"Are you familiar with Saint Thomas Aquinas?" the priest asks as he returns. "The thirteenth-century author, theologian, philosopher?" He sits and places what I can now see is a postcard facedown on the table between us. There is writing on the back, but I can't make it out.

I nod. "I know of him. I've not read a lot of his work, but I have a general idea of who he was."

"He makes an interesting statement about how God relates to the creation," the priest says, looking up to the ceiling, trying to recall the words. "Something like, 'the being of every creature depends on God, so that not for a moment could it subsist, but would fall into nothingness were it not kept in being by God.'[8] And so the inverse is true as well. If God wanted to destroy the universe, he wouldn't have to *do* anything except stop holding the universe in existence." The priest looks back at me with a questioning expression. "Does that make any sense to you?"

I blink, trying to interpret what he's said. "I think so," I say. "You're basically saying that God could very easily destroy the whole show if he wanted to. It would be easy, in fact."

"Well, that's one way to look at it," the priest responds, frowning a little. "But another way to look at what Aquinas is getting at is that the reason creation continues existing at all is because God *wants* it to. It's not that God just hasn't yet acted to destroy it, but rather that God is—even at this very moment—actively engaged in keeping the whole thing afloat, keeping everything *in being*. Not because God *has to*, but because as the Creator and Sustainer of it all, God *wants* to."

I feel my mouth fall open in astonishment, for the idea of God *wanting* creation to continue existing, and by derivation, the thought that the Creator wants *me* to continue existing, is a potent reminder of Father Solomon's words during my first meeting with him at the monastery.

How many times must I hear this and from how many people before it begins to sink in? God wants me to exist. That's why I'm here!

The priest continues. "And Aquinas—of course—is getting this straight from what God said in Genesis about creation: that it is '*Tov Meod—very good*.' And if we believe that God is omniscient—that the fall in general and your sins in particular are not at all a surprise—then we must hear God's pronouncement of *Tov Meod* not just as a one-time statement at the start of it all before things got off track, but rather a proclamation over *all space and all time*."

"Huh," I say, sitting back and contemplating the priest's words. "I've believed for so long that God is just waiting to pull the plug on the whole thing, that God just might be an irate old man, biding his time until he can at last burn us all in an eternal fire."

"Yes," the priest says, nodding. "Sadly, that image of God—or something like it—is all too common in people's minds today. It's a tragedy, really. A mockery of who God has revealed himself to be."

"But how do we know God isn't that way? How can we be sure?"

"Because we look at Christ," the priest answers matter-of-factly. "Christ the Healer. Christ who 'came not for the healthy, but for the sick.' Christ who helped the lame walk, the blind see, the deaf hear. Christ who refused to stone the woman caught in adultery. Christ who 'proclaim[s] the year of the Lord's favor.' Christ who even as he was being crucified prayed that God the Father would forgive the people who were nailing him to the cross because 'they do not know what they are doing.'[9] When we look to Christ we see that God is Healer, not an angry executioner."

"Then why do people go on and on so much about God's wrath?" I ask. "For some people, it's like that's the most important thing about

God. They know who God hates and are practically licking their chops in anticipation of the 'hell that's prepared for them.'[10] And usually—or should I say ironically—it just so happens that God seems to hate the very same people they themselves hate. But what you just quoted from Saint Aquinas almost makes it sound like God's wrath is a myth."

The priest nods, thinking carefully. "To your first point, anybody 'licking their chops' at the thought of another person burning in hell hasn't taken the first step toward understanding Jesus' command to love your enemies. Secondly, I am in no way suggesting, and nor was Saint Aquinas for that matter, that God's wrath is a myth. God's wrath is undeniably real. If God is good and just and loving, then he must be set against that which is not good and not just and not loving. God's wrath burns against whatever damages and destroys what he loves."

I frown, and the priest can see that I'm not following.

"Let me change tack," the priest says. He leans forward again and drops his voice to almost a whisper. "I have a friend, a friend whose daughter Lilly is very, *very* sick." The priest pauses here, the silence ratcheting up the tension in the room. "Lilly is six years old, and will most likely not live to see her seventh birthday, given the rate at which the cancer is eating away at her tiny body."

I nod silently, picturing Lilly in a hospital bed, hairless and weak, when she should be out running in the sun like other kids her age.

"Now this friend of mine, Lilly's father," the priest continues. "He loves his little girl very, very much." He pauses for a moment here, composing himself, before he's able to speak again. "The sight of his daughter in pain, the sight of her struggling against the cancer, the sight of her literally dying right before his eyes . . . It rips him apart." A single, shining tear rolls down the face of the priest, getting lost in his beard.

I nod again, taking it all in.

"And the *cancer* . . ." The priest spits out this word like a curse. "Lilly's father *hates* cancer. He hates it with an absolute, burning passion. This is what I mean by saying God's love and God's wrath are one and the same. Lilly's father's hatred of the cancer is one and the same as his love for Lilly. They are intertwined, interwoven, mutually reinforcing.

It is because the father loves Lilly that he hates the cancer—because the cancer is *antithetical* to the daughter whom he loves. It is killing her. He hates the cancer because he loves Lilly. In fact we could even say that the more he loves Lilly the more he hates the cancer."

"Oh," I say in surprise, as something altogether new slides into place for me. No. It is more than that. An entire mental framework has just been upended, and with this upending, something distant and confusing and terrifying has snapped into never-before-experienced clarity and hope.

"Oh," I repeat myself, followed quickly by a sigh of relief. "That makes so much more sense when you put it like that."

"I'm glad," the priest says.

Then I start talking fast, trying to tease out the implications of what I'm hearing. "So sin is like cancer, eating us alive, diminishing what we're made to be. It's a cancer of the mind, a cancer of the heart, a cancer of the soul. And it has spread out like a tumor throughout our whole selves. And, like the Bible says, 'the wages of sin,' like the effects of untreated cancer, 'is death.'[11]" I end with the intonation of a question, wanting to be sure I'm on the right track.

The priest nods. "Yes, that's the right way to put it, I think."

I continue. "And God—like Lilly's father—he *hates* sin, hates the cancer that is eating us alive. He loves us and so he hates whatever it is that is killing us. He doesn't hate *us*, though. He loves us. He loves us and hates cancer, hates cancer because he loves us."

"Precisely," the priest nods. "God *never* loathes you. God loves. God desires for you to live. God wants you to flourish. God wants you to thrive. That's why God made you. That's why God keeps you in existence from moment to moment."

The priest falls silent for a moment before continuing. "It holds together, doesn't it, given our experience of ourselves: that we all have the capacity within us for both great good and great evil? The cancer hasn't spread everywhere yet; it hasn't metastasized throughout everything. And so we are each of us a strange combination of extraordinary goodness, uniqueness, and beauty. We live. We love. We create. We yearn. We long. We hope. And yet at the same time there is something deadly and death-dealing lurking within each of us as well, a dark and seething force that prefers death to life, darkness to light."

"I know what you mean," I say, thinking of the many reasons I have come to this place for confession.

"And it is the work of God to increase the good that is in us, and cut out—like a cancer—the death and darkness, the evil that lurks within us."

"A refining fire," I add, letting the words hang in the air, hearing them for the first time as a hopeful phrase, instead of a dark and ominous one.

"Here," the priest says, finally lifting the postcard from the table. "I want you to have this." He turns it over and hands it to me, and as he does so, the image at the center of the postcard catches in the overhead light in a flash of radiance.

It is Rembrandt's *The Return of the Prodigal Son*, and in the context of the conversation we've been having, Jesus' parable and Rembrandt's painting bring tears to my eyes.

"Kenneth Clark called it the greatest picture ever painted," the priest says.

"I can see why." I wipe a tear away.

I am awed by Rembrandt's evocative portrayal of the scene: the kneeling, thread-bare, and exhausted younger son; the calloused, aloof, indignant older brother; the wide-armed, embracing, weeping father.

"Look closer," the priest says. "Rembrandt painted the father blind."

I press the postcard up closer to my face, studying it in the light. Sure enough, Rembrandt's genius captures perfectly the indistinct, half-eyed stare of a blind old man. "But why?" I ask. "It seems a strange way to portray God."

"Does it?" the priest muses. "An open-armed love who does not care—who cannot see, in fact—what state we've finally returned in, an always-open-armed welcome that rejoices overwhelmingly at the simple fact that we are home?"

"Well, when you put it that way," I say, the tears stinging my eyes again.

"Henri Nouwen once said of this painting that 'All of the Gospel is there. All of my own life is there. All of the lives of my friends is there.'"[12]

I nod. "It's breathtaking."

"Read what is on the back."

I turn the postcard over, and find George Herbert's poem "Love (III)" and read it out loud.

> Love bade me welcome: yet my soul drew back,
>   Guilty of dust and sin.
> But quick-ey'd Love, observing me grow slack
>   From my first entrance in
> Drew nearer to me, sweetly questioning
>   If I lack'd anything.
>
> "A guest," I answered, "worthy to be here":
>   Love said, "You shall be he."
> "I, the unkind, ungrateful? Ah, my dear,
>   I cannot look on thee."
> Love took my hand, and smiling did reply,
>   "Who made the eyes but I?"
>
> "Truth, Lord, but I have marr'd them; let my shame
>   Go where it doth deserve."
> "And know you not," says Love, "who bore the blame?"
>   "My dear, then I will serve."
> "You must sit down," says Love, "and taste my meat."
>   "So I did sit and eat."[13]

"Keep that with you," the priest says. "Especially in the confessional. May it be an icon for you—a window through which you catch a glimpse of the heart of God, whose desire is to refine and to heal, to dispel the forces of death and evil, of cancer and darkness, to bring us into everlasting life."

I turn the postcard back over and let the image of the embracing father etch itself into my mind. "Yes," I say aloud. "This is who God is."

The priest stands. "Now, if you're ready," he starts, "perhaps we'll make our way down to the confessional?"

I nod and follow the priest down into the high and lofty sanctuary, the smell of kerosene and dust and old wood mingling together with the muffled sounds of the busy city outside: diesel trucks, crying gulls, shouting people, and honking horns. Even in the jumble and chaos of the city it is possible to find stillness. A homeless woman is sleeping in one of the pews, and I can't help but believe that this is exactly as it should be—the weak and weary of our world finding shelter in *the* Sanctuary.

Isn't that what has brought me here too?

I glance down at the Rembrandt postcard.

Isn't that what brought the younger son back also?

I enter one side of the confessional, a small triangular-shaped room with two chambers with a little window connecting them, each with soundproof walls and ceiling. The priest enters the other. The space in which I'm now standing is only a few feet square: I could touch each wall without having to stretch. There is a padded spot for kneeling along one wall, immediately next to the screen through which I will make my confession in the priest's hearing. Instantly I see that kneeling there will bring me to eye level with the crucifix. This is an enormously intimidating thought that almost causes me to turn and flee—staring at the crucified Christ has always seemed gruesome to me, an evocative reminder of our human capacity for brutality. I focus instead on the little booklet labeled "The Sacrament of Reconciliation" that rests on the tiny desktop beneath the crucifix.

Suddenly it feels warm and stuffy in the tiny room, hot, in fact.

I take a deep breath in and out. "Remember what this is about," I say to myself, my voice sounding muffled and quiet in the confessional. "Reconciliation and life. Healing and health. God hates cancer. Not you."

I kneel down before the crucifix, the icon of the crucified Son of

God, and, just beneath it, prop up Rembrandt's radiant painting of *The Return of the Prodigal Son* against the wall.

I open up "The Sacrament of Reconciliation" booklet and begin reading. "Forgive me, Father," I say, "for I have sinned."

But I can go no further.

For I have glanced up from the booklet and suddenly seen how the shadow of the crucifix falls on Rembrandt's *The Return of the Prodigal Son*, how the open arms of Christ *are* the open arms of the blind father, how they are both reaching out to embrace me, too, as I kneel here before them.

Are not the words of the younger son my words too?

"Forgive me, Father," I try again. "For I have sinned."

But that is all I can say. My shoulders shake as I kneel there weeping, using the long broom to pull out everything I can reach from beneath the bed, into the light of day, before the Light of the World. And I can feel the arms of the blind father embracing me, holding me close, willing that I should be healed.

After a long while the priest clears his throat in the room next to me, and begins reading the conclusion of the booklet.

> The Lord is full of compassion and mercy,
> Slow to anger and of great kindness.
> He will not always accuse us,
> Nor will he keep his anger for ever.
> He has not dealt with us according to our sins,
> Nor rewarded us according to our wickedness.
> As a father cares for his children
> So does the Lord care for those who fear him.
> For he himself knows whereof we are made:
> He remembers that we are but dust.

"Amen," I say, wiping my nose on my arm.
The priest continues.

Dear brother in Christ,
God is steadfast in love and infinite in mercy,
healing the sick and forgiving the sinful.
The Lord has put away from you all your sins.[14]

"Amen," I say again. "May it be so."

"Pray for me too," the priest asks, concluding the sacrament. "For I am a sinner also."

"I will, Father," I tell him.

Though the liturgy has now officially ended, I stay there kneeling before the crucifix, before *The Return of the Prodigal Son*, allowing the two images to meld into one, feeling as though a great and crushing weight has been lifted from my shoulders.

"Yes," I say to myself. "This is who God is."

I find such extraordinary and unexpected life in the regular practice of confession at a local Anglican church that I actually go to the three pastors of the Baptist church where I'm a member and tell them we need to have a confessional in our own sanctuary.

"I'd be happy to build it," I say. "I'll cover the costs as well. I just think it would be an enormous help to our congregation. It was to me. People are carrying enormous and unnecessary weight around. They need a place—a safe place—to actually go and find relief."

"What about in home groups and small groups?" Pastor Monica suggests. "We're trying to encourage people to confess to one another there, during those smaller meetings."

"Maybe that will work," I say. "But the kind of comfortability and intimacy required to enable people to do that takes a lot of time to develop. I'm not very comfortable revealing the darkest parts of my life to many people. It was much better for me to speak those things aloud in the privacy and confidentiality of the confessional. That's why we need a confessional in our sanctuary."

"Well," Pastor Tim says, furrowing his brow a bit, "I hear you loudly that we should offer a place and time for confession, but I just don't really see how we can build a confessional in our sanctuary. First of all, where would it go?"

"What about right on top of the baptismal?" I suggest. "We could even build in a trap door. Think of the symbolism: you make your confession and the pastor yanks on a cord and—*plunk!*—washed clean!"

Fortunately my pastors are kind and patient enough to laugh at this.

"I think you're right, though, Michael," Pastor Monica says at last, bringing the conversation back around. "People *are* carrying great burdens. We all are. And we need a safe place to go and speak them and let the words of love and absolution and healing wash over us."

"Yes," I say. "Yes, that's it exactly."

Though we don't end up building a confessional in our church, the pastors all make themselves available during the weekends of Lent to stand alongside people as they speak their confessions to God. And do you know what? *Every* time slot is filled. In fact they have to add even more slots to accommodate all of the people who want to come and make their confession, to acknowledge the ways of death and darkness that they all-too-often choose, to name the cancer for what it is, and then to let the words of forgiveness and absolution wash over them like a healing bath.

"It was astonishing," Pastor Tim tells me the week after Easter, over coffee. "We didn't really expect that there would be such a response. I mean, this is Vancouver, and our church is mostly made up of twenty- or thirtysomething hipsters. Who would have thought people would *want* to go to confession?"

I nod and smile.

Who would have thought . . . ?

CHAPTER 9

Is Anybody Listening?:
The Practice of Listening Prayer

Through a truth glimpsed fleetingly in a state of prayer [God] calls to us.

—THERESA OF AVILA[1]

The real value of persistent prayer is not so much that we get what we want as that we become the person we should be.

—PHILIP YANCEY[2]

To pray means to open your hands before God. It means slowly relaxing the tension which squeezes your hands together and accepting your existence with an increasing readiness, not as a possession to defend, but as a gift to receive. Above all, therefore, prayer is a way of life which allows you to find a stillness in the midst of the world where you open your hands to God's promises, and find hope for yourself, your fellowman, and the whole community in which you live.

—HENRI NOUWEN[3]

Prayer is not the unthinking mumbling of meaningless words, but
the opening of our hearts to the Eternal Love that is the source of
all creation. Prayer is the response of the heart to God who is Love.
Prayer is the opening of one's heart to peace, to the peace of God, the
opening of one's mind and one's heart to the Spirit of God. Prayer is
the desire that we might be filled with this spirit of love and of justice
and of peace. It is the offering of ourselves to God, who is Love, that
we might become the poor instruments of his love, that we might
radiate throughout our land and to everyone we know the peace, the
compassion, the sweetness, the tenderness and the mercy of God.

—JEAN VANIER[4]

I t's never wise to debate someone wielding surgical instruments.
I learn this while flat on my back in the chair of a dental hygienist—
a loquacious and evidently evangelistic woman in her late forties whose
missionary strategy (who put her up to it, do you think?) includes preach-
ing while her razor-sharp curette is wedged between her captive audience's
teeth. Throughout the cleaning she's recounting with evident flair the
depth and passion of her personal relationship with God. As we near the
end of the cleaning, her subject shifts to the efficacy of her prayer life. Even
her blue surgical mask doesn't restrain her enthusiasm. The one time I try
to get a word in edgewise I find her deflecting my tongue with the little
dime-sized mirror, turning what I thought was a well-positioned response
into nothing but babble.

"No, no, honey," she says, applying a little more pressure. "I'm working here. Just keep your mouth open and listen."

"Righ—," I submit.

"So like I was saying," she continues, "I was so stumped and troubled
by this idea that God was so very complicated, so very far *beyond* me. I
just wasn't understanding anything I read or heard, and I was finding it
very distressing. I just wanted a God I could *understand*. A God I could
relate to."

"Hmm," I say, nodding slightly.

"And that's when my dear friend Janice introduced me to this little booklet, and once I'd read it, everything became pure as perfume, clear as crystal. I realized that things were so much simpler than I'd originally made them out to be. I came to see that God wasn't nearly as complicated as I had been led—or I should say *deceived*—into thinking."

"Huh," I grunt, trying to indicate that I'm listening. But the spit gathering in the back of my throat morphs my best attempt at affirmation into a sort of gurgling sound.

"Here, honey." She offers me that gasping little sucker-tube to spit in. "Just use this."

"That's very interesting," I say, speaking as quickly as I can before the razor point gets shoved back in my mouth.

"Interesting indeed," she says, pushing my shoulder back into the chair. It's obvious that this is *her* show, and I'm not going to steal it. "And liberating too. I felt freedom and empowerment like I'd never known before." She raises her razor again, and I open my mouth without another word. "And do you know what happened the very next day?"

"Wha—," I attempt to ask.

"I used my very last dollar to try to buy a Coca-Cola. It was hot and I was thirsty. Ready for some refreshment." She stops cleaning my teeth for a moment and looks me straight in the eye—a very disorienting feeling given the fact that her head is rotated ninety degrees from mine. "That stupid vending machine ate my dollar. Stole it right out of my hand. No Coca-Cola. Nothing. There I am, kicking and hitting the thing and nothing is happening, nothing at all. I almost broke my hand smacking the side of that stupid thing. When all of a sudden I remember that I've got *God* on my side now."

"Yea—," I gurgle.

"So I begin to pray," she says. Her smile is evident despite her mask. "I start to pray and tell God what I needed right then and there and then—*wham!*—out pops my ice-cold bottle of Coca-Cola. Some people say that prayer doesn't work at all, and I'd like to ask them, each and every single one of 'em, what they've to say about *that*."

Her timing is perfect, for just as she finishes her story the teeth cleaning is over. She pushes the button with her toe that sends the electric chair whirring, bringing me back to upright.

What do *I* have to say about this?

"That's amazing," I venture.

"Amazing indeed," she says exultantly. "Amazing indeed. Did you ever think God could answer your prayers, *just like that*?" She snaps as she speaks, a quick and sharp sound—*lickety split*.

"I don't know," I answer with a shrug. "Who knows how God works?"

"Now, Michael," she says, pulling down her blue mask and looking me square in the face. "God is *not* mysterious. We can all know exactly how God works. I'd be happy to provide you with a copy of the very same pamphlet that so radically changed my life. A donation of five dollars is all that is required, and I can personally guarantee you that your questions will be answered, and not only that—God will start hearing your prayers as well."

I haven't been back to the dentist in a while, but ever since I've referred to this approach to God, this style of prayer, as "vending-machine prayer." In this method, if you just pray *the right way*—and there have been countless profiteers promoting their own versions of *the* way to pray—God will surely give you whatever you ask for.

Or maybe prayer is like this: A woman I know—Margaret is her name—recently moved into a new fourth-floor apartment. She had been living in a moldy basement-suite for years, and this fourth-floor setup—although still a bit rough around the edges—was a substantial change for the better. With its high ceilings, wood floors, and abundant windows facing west toward the downtown skyline, Margaret couldn't be happier.

There was only one minor drawback to the place, which she sadly discovered *after* moving in: there was no doorbell.

"How are people supposed to let me know when they're here?" Margaret complained to her new landlord.

"That's not my problem," he snapped back. "And don't even *think* about asking me to install one for you. Do you have any idea how much that would cost in a building this old?"

"People could always throw rocks at my window, I guess," Margaret said thoughtfully.

"That's what security deposits are for," came the retort.

For about a month or so people simply stood on the street below Margaret's fourth-floor window and shouted up at her, until she either heard their calls and buzzed them in or—hoarse and defeated—they departed.

One day en route back to her doorbell-less apartment Margaret happened upon a snapped-in-half fishing pole on the side of the road. Being the resourceful woman she is, the fishing pole metamorphosed in Margaret's mind from a piece of roadside debris into a possible solution for her pressing social problem.

An hour later Margaret returned home armed with the pole, a coil of fishing line, and a bright shiny new bell. With some exemplary McGyvering, Margaret rigged up a durable hinge off a nearby gutter, dropped the fishing line down from her fourth-floor window, mounted the half-a-fishing pole next to the entryway door, and connected the whole setup to the new silver bell, just outside her window.

Voilà!—she had a functional doorbell.

"And it only cost me $5.75," Margaret beamed to her landlord. "Perhaps I can subtract it from next month's rent?"

People started stopping by more often just so they could ring the thing.

Sadly Margaret isn't home when I stop by. But I stand there on the street anyway, outside the locked entrance to the building, pulling and pulling and pulling on the fishing line, hearing the delightful ringing of the shiny bell, way up high.

Wondering what I am doing, and why a fishing pole has been mounted to the outside of the apartment building, a passerby stops to watch. It's an old man with downturned lips and the collar of his jacket pulled up against the world. I nod a hello and keep on ringing and ringing, wearing a contented smile on my face.

Perhaps the note of the bell hit this old man the wrong way, but soon his face sours to a mean glare.

"Why do you keep ringing if no one answers?" he demands.

"Maybe she's asleep," I explain. "If so I need to keep on ringing for a while longer yet, and try to wake her."

With a shake of his head the man mumbles something and disappears around the corner.

As he walks away my face sours too. I can't help but wonder: Is this what prayer is like? We just keep hauling on the fishing line, hoping Someone might hear us? Must we all be like the old widow Jesus told of in Luke 18? Who kept on nagging the judge, nagging the judge, nagging the judge until at last he heard her case?

Is *this* what prayer is like?

I am off the west coast of Scotland, on the ancient isle of Iona, walking toward the centuries-old stone structure that is the abbey, and my thoughts are full of vending machines and fishing lines. It is after dark, and although summer is nigh, a terrific gale has blown itself up from the Atlantic, shifting what was a pleasant afternoon into an uproar of chaos in less than an hour. I lean into the wind and rain and ocean spray as I walk on toward the abbey, trying to keep from being blown over backward. I'm en route to the Taizé service that is scheduled in the abbey church this evening, and I don't really know what I'm getting myself into.

Taizé is an enigma to me—I know very little about it. What I do know is that Taizé is a form of sung prayer that puts virtually no emphasis on spontaneous creativity nor individual facility with words. It isn't at all about one's ability to find the right words or concepts to throw at God, nor even about doctrine or theological acumen.

Instead Taizé is a community's sung meditation on short passages arising from the Scriptures (especially the Psalms) interspersed with increasing periods of silence. The idea is that there is an extraordinary *depth* to this kind of prayer, that there are *layers of meaning* into which we might be drawn given enough time and intent.

"It's like the prayer equivalent to the slow-food movement," the kind-looking woman with the German accent and dreadlocks explained to me earlier in the day. "Utterly opposed to the fast-food, drive-through–style religiosity that has become so trivializingly common."

Before I had a chance to respond, Lady Dreadlocks walked away, continuing to invite others to that evening's Taizé service.

And here I am: trudging through the storm toward the abbey church. Despite my waterproof pants and rain jacket, I am sodden by the time I push through the old wooden doors. As I catch a glimpse of what lies therein, a net of yearning closes over me and welcomes me inside. It's like I've stepped back centuries, and the place I'm entering is still permeated with evident but subtle holiness, the kind of holiness that makes you want to lower your voice and slip off your shoes *just because it's the right thing to do*. Here the omnipresence of God is more than just an abstract theological idea, but in fact a *felt* reality: quickened pulse, shortness of breath, hope rising up in that low place just behind the sternum.

The abbey church is huge—cavernous, even—like the caves our hunter-gatherer ancestors might have stumbled into out of the storms that raged in their distant pasts. Though this great cave moans and creaks beneath the onslaught of the storm, I feel safe in its quiet strength. I reach out and touch the stone wall, feeling its cool girth beneath my hands. Storm or no, this place is solid. It will keep.

Light and life have gathered together in a small cluster toward the nave. A constellation of candles glows warmly on and around the altar, illuminating from below the crucifix that presides there. On the stone floor beneath the altar a square grid of cushions has been laid out to welcome this evening's Taizé participants. Half the cushions are already in use, people sitting with legs crossed, eyes closed, and hands in a posture of open receptivity.

I make my way silently to one of the cushions, slip off my shoes, and settle myself onto the floor. I slow my breathing and wait.

The leader—Lady-Dreadlocks herself—begins by explaining the simplicity Taizé invites us into.

"Tonight there are no song books, no flyers, no pieces of paper to shuffle around," she says. "Just us. Just our voices. Just the yearning we all bring to this place and this moment. There is the strong stone of this building as well, above and below and around us, and the warm light of the candles and the Light of the World on the altar. Heed the invitation that is being offered to you. An invitation to listen, to join in, to sit silently, to lift your own voice in prayer with the others gathered here from around the world. If you don't know the words to a song or even the language in which it is being sung, just listen as others sing and then—when you're ready—join in with us. Add your own unique voice into the melody we are offering here tonight."

She falls silent for about a minute and then begins.

The first refrain arises from Psalm 104:

> *Bless the Lord, my soul*
> *And bless God's holy name*
> *Bless the Lord, my soul*
> *Who leads me into life*

She sings the refrain once, her strong, resonant voice filling the empty space of the abbey church, softening every now and again beneath the storm's roar but then reemerging and filling the void again.

The second time through several others join in, and the sung prayer grows stronger, their voices filling the space with living harmony. On the third time around most of the others begin to sing as well, and so do I, feeling a great thrill as my own voice finds its place alongside the twenty or so other pilgrims who have gathered here in symphony at the edge of the world.

The simplicity of the song catches me by surprise. There are no verses, no bridge, no quippy modifications. We sing the refrain again, and again, and again, until I stop counting and find myself sinking down into the deeper layers of the prayer.

Counting the number of repetitions isn't really the point—it's too quantitative. This is a church, not a gym.

Taizé—I am starting to see—is about *qualitative* prayer. Through the repetition I feel myself slipping into an experiential intimacy with God unlike anything I've experienced in the untold volumes of theological texts I've read, in the countless hours of attentive listening to didactic sermons. Something else is going on here. Something deep and abiding and powerful.

The comparison to the slow-food movement suddenly makes great sense: this isn't about how many billions of hamburgers have been served but rather like rolling a good wine around the mouth for a while, savoring it, letting its complexity affectively engage and delight and warm.

With a feeling like I've just set down a great weight, I see that this kind of prayer doesn't have an agenda, doesn't have a point. It's not about trying to coerce God into something, or wake God up, or pound on the side of the vending machine until what you want finally pops out below. It's about *being*, and being in the presence with the Other.

Coming to prayer in order to accomplish something is like hiking to Yosemite's Bridal Veil Falls just to get your heart rate up instead of—well—hiking to Yosemite's Bridal Veil Falls simply because it is eminently worth hiking to, worth being in the presence of.

Maybe that's the point of this kind of prayer. Just being there. Not accomplishing anything. Not executing anything. Not checking prayer off the to-do list. But being affected by it. Shaped by it. Becoming different because of it.

As we continue praying, singing this rhythmic refrain, the words become a steady heartbeat, a long and enduring crash of waves on the shores of my consciousness, a gentle and insistent invitation to soften a little into something a little less cold and rigid, something a little more fluid and alive.

Later (*How long was it?* I wonder—*Minutes? Hours?*), at the appropriate time the song naturally concludes and we all fall silent.

And that's when I hear it.

The great stone cavern around us has been joining in song with us: the mighty stone catching our voices and harmonizing with them, echoing and reverberating. Our human praise has mingled with the elements themselves, inviting them to join us in this dance of prayer.

At last even the stone's resonance passes into silence, and we all rest in this quiet space, here at the center of the storm.

But the silence feels taut. Active. A leaning-forward kind of attentiveness. A hold-your-breath kind of waiting, as though we're all expecting the silence to break open like an egg so that something brand-new might spread its wings and fly.

I bring all this—the Iona Taizé service, the vending-machine model of prayer, and a huge knot of fishing line—and heap it all in a tangle before Father Solomon.

After a long silence Father Solomon leans forward in his chair. "It is little wonder that you found so much life in the Taizé service. These other kinds of prayer—the vending machine and the fishing line, as you call them—these put far too much emphasis on what you are *saying* or *doing* in prayer. They make prayer about your efforts to get God's attention, instead of emphasizing a posture of listening and receptivity to whatever God might be saying to you."

"But isn't that exactly what prayer *is*?" I ask. "Talking to God?"

"That's just the minor half of it," Father Solomon says with furrowed brows. "You think prayer is only about talking *to* God, 'let[ting] your requests be made known to God,'[5] as the apostle Paul says. And this is—of course—one aspect of prayer. We call it petitionary prayer. But I wonder if I might persuade you to experiment with your prepositions a little bit. Perhaps discover whether a few slight adjustments might not have a significant impact."

"Tinker with my prepositions?" I respond, uncertain.

"Yes," Father Solomon says, smiling. "Rather than talking *to* God, or talking *at* God, what if we were to use the word *with* instead?"

"Oh," I say after a momentary frown. "You mean treat prayer as more of a conversation rather than just a chance for me to rant before a divine audience?"

"Exactly," Father Solomon answers, nodding. Then he falls silent for a moment. "Of course, within this 'conversation' you must always keep in mind that God is the Creator and you are the creature. This is no mere chat between equals. We must always remember whom we are listening to, with whom we are conversing. Awe is paramount. Humility foremost. Reverence essential. Even Moses took off his shoes when he realized in whose presence he stood."

"You're saying I should pray barefoot?" I ask with a smile.

"Perhaps!" Father Solomon laughs but then continues. "More than just *thinking* about prayer as a conversation, what might it look like for you to actually *practice* prayer as a conversation, perhaps even emphasizing listening and silence over the all-too-common monologue?"

"Leave it to a monk to emphasize silence." I laugh. But I'm wondering if Father Solomon might be onto something. Hadn't the periods of silence in the Taizé prayer been exceptionally rich, a fitting balance to songs and harmony?

"Silence might be a very good place for you to begin," Father Solomon says, letting his words hang in the air for several seconds before continuing. "Think about it. Even at a human level so many of us are so very hasty to speak, to make our own thoughts and perspectives known, without perhaps actually knowing much at all about what we're saying. I have had conversations with a great many people who report hardly ever feeling like they are heard, whether by fellow students or spouses, or even their so-called friends. Most people today seem to have entirely forgotten how to listen—or perhaps they never even learned how in the first place. Now everybody is shouting all the time, trying harder and harder to get themselves heard above the noise. Is it any wonder that the 'still small voice'[6] of God is often drowned out amidst such cacophony?"

"Does God *speak* to you as you pray?" I ask. "I've heard of people hearing God speak, but frankly, I've often thought of that as a little strange. You know. People who say they've heard the voice of God sometimes strike me as just reaching for a divine backing to their own agenda."

"It is good of you to be wary," Father Solomon responds, nodding. "All too often people claiming to have a 'word from the Lord' may only have their own ego to thank for what they think they've 'heard.' But at the same time, one mustn't be too hasty in coming to conclusions about these things. God *does* speak. Our whole faith is built upon the belief that this is the case. And in answer to your previous question, yes: God does speak to me. But not yet with anything simple as words."

I frown. "What does that mean?"

"In my experience—and it is *my* experience, mind you, your prayers may be very different—God speaks through a language 'too deep for words,'[7] as Saint Paul put it. Do you really think the ineffable, infinite God would speak only through these feeble human constructions we call words?" Father Solomon laughs, though not unkindly.

But I'm missing the joke, and just blink a few times. "This is all new to me, Father Solomon. Of *course* I think speech means words. What else can it mean?"

"My dear man," Father Solomon says. "Words are good, yes, but they're not all they're thought to be. They are useful tools, to be sure. But their realm of usefulness does not encapsulate the whole of human existence." Father Solomon stops to pull on his beard for a moment, and adjusts his glasses. "Think of it this way. Words are like the pinnacle of an enormous iceberg, an iceberg of human emotion and longing and thought and experience. In one sense words are the highest point: the culmination of culture and experience and history. They are life rarefied and elevated and distilled into articulacy. But in another sense the tippy-top of the iceberg is just that—the tip. By nature it is a very small fraction of all that actually exists beneath it, all that supports it. Thus the pinnacle is a gross oversimplification, a dumbing down of all the rest, of everything that supports it."

"So if God doesn't 'speak' to you using words, how do you know that something is being said—that something is being communicated?"

"Well," Father Solomon replies, leaning forward, "I *listen*. I listen and I *wait*. I try to notice what is happening inside of me, way down in the places too deep for words, at the seat of my true self, through the currents of consolation and the desolation I discern there. I've found it very helpful to rise early—while it is still dark—and light a candle, and sit in the presence of the light, letting myself thaw a little in its warmth. I'll read a short passage of Scripture and then—rather than putting it on the dissecting table to analyze it and apply rationality to it—I allow it to soak into my life for a while like water into a dry sponge."

"I like that picture," I say, wanting to begin practicing this kind of prayer. "If I was to try this, to begin attempting this kind of prayer, how long should I start with? Five minutes maybe?"

"Why not try starting with twenty or even thirty minutes?" Father Solomon challenges.

"Twenty minutes!" I exclaim. The thought of sitting silently for that long is almost laughable. "From dawn until dusk there isn't a single moment of my day that isn't full of to-do lists and errands and responsibilities and noise. You might as well ask me to stand on my head for twenty or thirty minutes."

"It will seem less insurmountable, more attainable the more you practice it," Father Solomon says with a smile. "And besides? Who ever said prayer would be easy?"

What I encounter this morning as I wake early to pray is exhaustion coupled with a deep and unsettled dread. I am weary and overwhelmed and feeling deep in my core the demands and stresses of life as they crush down upon me. It has been a heavy week: New atrocities abroad even as old wars still fester. More jaw-dropping, random violence in my own country. A highly visible shame and agony deep in a friend's family, forever changing their lives. The death of an elderly acquaintance. The anniversary of a beloved cousin's death. Flooding in my home state—hundreds missing, billions in damages. Bills and bills and more bills, piling up unopened on my desk. Money rushing out faster than it comes in. And a bad night's sleep to boot: hours of tossing and turning beneath anxiety-ridden dreams, laced aggravatingly with the emergency sirens that seemed to be driving in circles around my house. All this tangles in my subconscious and magnifies the doubts and fears that lurk there naturally.

And it's only Wednesday.

So let me be blunt: after the week I've had I have nothing to say to

God this morning—no words at all. Language feels feeble, shot through with haughtiness, the structures of sentences far too flimsy to carry the great weight of the world and the smaller but just as overwhelming weight of my own life at this particular moment.

I'm leaning heavily this morning on Father Solomon's suggestion that just sitting and listening might be more than enough, for I haven't the strength anymore to ring God's bell, don't have the wherewithall to attempt getting the Coke can to drop through any of my usual means.

And here I am: weary and tired and full of anxiety, settling myself precariously into my green rocking chair. I grab a book of matches and a honey-smelling beeswax candle, switch off the reading light, and plunge myself into darkness.

I just sit there for a while. Scared and alone and overwhelmed. Listening to the sound of the storm as it thunders and gales around me.

I remain like this for several minutes, listening to all that the darkness has to say, recalling the dismal and unsettling dreams of the previous night, feeling the weight of everything that I must face in the hours of the coming day.

Then I strike the match, and hold its warm life close to my face, watching the flicker of ocean blue as it tapers into a bright yellow wreathed in ocher. I touch it to the wick, letting the first flame spread its light and warmth and life, coaxing it to multiply and double its force despite the darkness.

As the candle catches, the words of Scripture well up into my mind and I hear—at least I *think* I hear—something abiding and true and too deep for words: *"Light has come into the world, and darkness has not overcome it."*[8]

It isn't much, I grant you.

But it is enough.

It is enough this morning to just sit here—in the midst of the raging of the storm—to just sit here silently for twenty or thirty minutes in the presence of this light. It is enough to be without words, and to listen.

It is enough to be.

∽

This regular practice of listening prayer has planted a new metaphor in me, a far more accurate one than the fishing line or the vending machine could ever be. I'm convinced now that prayer is like a midnight ocean skinny dip.

Let me explain.

This comes from direct experience.

It is well after midnight when I step out of the darkness of the forest onto the moonlit borderland between this tiny island and the endless sea. A beach is a feeble place, an uncertain realm where the solid ground on which we stand descends out of reach beneath the unfathomable mystery of the deep.

I slip off my trunks and stand there on the borderland naked and cold, feeling small and exposed and vulnerable. This must be how Adam and Eve felt before they happened upon the fig tree: small and exposed and vulnerable.

But tell me, friend: Isn't this the way it always is?

Where might we flee to hide from the omnipresent one? What camouflage is strong enough to dull the piercing vision of the one "unto whom all hearts are open, all desires known, and from whom no Secrets are hid"?[9]

So here we stand, and here I stand, small and exposed and vulnerable, here on the verge, wondering if I have faith enough to embrace my finitude instead of always trying to rail against it.

Wondering, too, if I have it in me to wade into the depths.

I inch forward and toe-touch the infinite.

C. S. Lewis's phrase comes to mind again, the hearty cry of Aslan's country: "Further up and further in!"

Somewhere from out at sea a bell begins ringing, even as the waves knock-knock-knock against my shins.

Both are insistent. Persistent. Beckoning.

Wait a minute. Who is trying to get whose attention here on this beachhead of prayer, this verge between humanity and divinity, this borderland between what I am and what I am not? All along I thought it was *me* trying to somehow get God's attention, but now I can't help but wonder if it isn't the other way around.

A great surge of longing and hope wells up within me, warm and bright as a flame.

I raise up my hands and wade out into the sea and find that—despite all my fears and all my doubts and all my striving—I am held and lifted up.

Buoyed, in fact.

Afloat.

Yes: this is what prayer is like.

And I am beginning to hear.

CHAPTER 10

Taste and Become: The Practices of *Lectio Divina* and Regular Eucharist

To know much and taste nothing—of what use is that?

—SAINT BONAVENTURE[1]

It is the very nature of language to form rather than inform. When language is personal, which it is at its best, it reveals; and revelation is always formative—we don't know more, we become more.

—EUGENE PETERSON[2]

Lectio is meeting with a friend, a very special Friend who is God; listening to him, really listening; and responding, in intimate prayer and in the way we take that Word with us and let it shape our lives.

—M. BASIL PENNINGTON[3]

Saber *and* sabor *[are] rooted in the Latin* sapio *or* sapere, *meaning to taste, to have a flavor, as well as to understand.* Sapientia, *later translated into English as wisdom, means to have knowledge or wisdom of the world, but also to taste things in the world. Likewise, the word* sapiens *means being wise, and it is also derived from* sapere, *to taste and/or to know.*

—ANGEL F. MÉNDEZ MONTOYA[4]

B efore I mention anything at all about these two spiritual practices, I must confess two things to you.

The first is this: I am a computer scientist by training. In its normal course my mind likes gliding smoothly along the tracks provided by formulas, logic, and sequence. I believe in the power of human rationality, and when I first swallowed Descartes's dictum "I think therefore I am" hook, line, and sinker, it was all too easy to affirm this human capacity as the foremost method for parsing the universe.

But the second confession is this: my faith in the unassailable superiority of human rationality is getting a little shaky. I find myself wondering if Saint Thomas Aquinas—perhaps the greatest systematic theologian of all time—might not have been weeping with joy after his mystical experience of God, even as he waved off his most substantial work—the *Summa Theologiae*—as "nothing but straw."[5]

Don't you find it to be the case that so much goes beyond what our rationality can grasp and describe? That we are left standing like children on the seashore, squinting up at the sky as our kite reached the end of its string and *just kept on going*? Though I used to look with suspicion upon mystery, I find myself *drawn* to it now, intoxicated by the ineffable, yearning for something overwhelmingly inexplicable and humblingly grand.

Not that I'm denying the validity of rationality. Of course not. There's too much evidence to the contrary.

All I'm suggesting is that rationality has its appropriate space and that that space is limited. All I'm saying is that there is—I hope—something more to being human than just our minds, however powerful they may or may not be.

I tell this to Danae, and she looks straight at me for a moment, lost in thought.

"*Eat This Book*," she says at last.

"Sorry?" I ask, eyebrows raised.

"That's the title," she says with a laugh. "It's called *Eat This Book*. You'll like it. It's right in line with the Taizé service at Iona, and what you've been experiencing in listening prayer, right in line with what you're describing now about feeling invited by the Holy beyond rationality."

I spend several hours with *Eat This Book*,[6] and Danae's recommendation is spot on: Eugene Peterson's project helps me bring to articulacy something I now know I've been missing for a long, long time but haven't quite known how to name.

Most of us—myself included—typically approach the things we read in one of two ways. Either we "skim" it or we "scavenge" it. By "skim" I mean the way I read things when I'm pressed for time and need to just get it done. Amid my harried frenzy I browse. I glance. I leaf. My eyes flit across the page, dart over the pixels, sprint over the sentences. If I'm lucky perhaps I'll remember what I read a few hours later, but by the time a week has gone by, it's lost in the dim and feeble recesses of my memory. At best I'm left only with a faint echo, a vague sense that "I read something about that somewhere recently . . . Now where was it . . . ?"

Alternatively, I "scavenge" the text, picking over it the way a crow picks over a landfill, searching with black and beady eye for something flashy or noteworthy that I can pull out from the rubble and carry with me, something that might impress others or wow them with my ability to clamp down on what shimmers. This posture assumes a certain objectivity, as I survey everything from a great height, looking it over with an expression of cold calculation on my beaked face. Like a lawyer scanning a legal brief, picking up factoid here or a statistic there that might somehow prove useful in the battle to come.

When I'm really on top of my game (when I've had enough coffee), I'm able to combine these two approaches together, so that I skim and scavenge all at once. I survey the whole landscape in just a few minutes and fly on with prizes glinting between talons.

This affinity for skimming and scavenging reinforces an all-too-prevalent belief many of us have about ourselves: that it is *good* to be an "objective consumer," that we only need to depart our position of relative objectivity when something shiny enough catches our eye, and then return quickly thereafter to that same objective safety.

But here's the thing: such a consumptive, distant, and objective approach really does a number on things like depth and intimacy and meaning.

Viewed from a great enough distance, all the people you love most in this world are really just rounding errors amid the 7.2 billion other humans. So are you, by the way. Everyone living today isn't even a tenth the total number who have been. Viewed this way, the Sistine Chapel becomes "just a painted room," Beethoven's Fifth is "just a mess of dark lines on a white page." And frankly, our whole world is "just a pale blue dot," fading into the obscure black background.

Meaning is found not in scavenging or skimming, not from an increasingly "objective" distance but instead by *diving into the depths of the thing*, by *Selah!*-ing, by diminishing the distance to intimacy, by increasing attentiveness and allowing the Holy to shape and form us rather than keeping it at a calculated distance.

In this way *Lectio Divina* is to reading Scripture what that sung Taizé service at Iona was for me to prayer: an antidote of sorts. A different way of approaching the Holy than my skimming and my scavenging, a different way than my vending-machine prayers and infinite fishing line. Both Taizé and *Lectio Divina* are about affective experience of and engagement with the holy, rather than just *cognitive analysis*. Neither are antirational, but their approach invites us to encounter the Holy with more than just analysis.

And this is what Eugene Peterson is on about in *Eat This Book*. As opposed to our frenzied and objective skimming and scavenging, Peterson draws from deep within the Christian tradition and suggests that we must learn not to *read* our holy texts, but instead to *feast* on them—to savor them. To slow down and sit with the text, giving twenty minutes to twenty words or even two, instead of trying to blaze through four or five whole chapters in the same amount of time, skimming and scavenging as we go. In *Lectio Divina* the reader comes to the text hungry and full of desire. Not looking for shiny ideas but instead yearning to be nourished and fed. This kind of reading "enters our souls as food enters our stomachs, spreads through our blood, and becomes holiness and love and wisdom."[7]

Let me put it this way: in *Lectio Divina* we come to Holy Text not to be informed, but to be formed. Not to coolly observe, but to taste and become.

Perhaps the most moving time of *Lectio* during my Sacred Year comes the day I receive word that Kim, a friend and mentor of mine, will soon die from the ovarian cancer she has been fighting for years. I learn this from her husband, Ken, as he announces their decision to abandon further experimental treatments and transition consciously into the gut-wrenching process of saying good-bye.

Perhaps Kim will make it until Thanksgiving. But Christmas is doubtful.

During my time of *Lectio Divina* soon after learning about Kim's approaching death, I sit and chew on the scene from John 11 in which Lazarus had already died and been buried. He had been in the tomb four days by the time Jesus at last arrived on the scene, long enough for the decay to begin, long enough to firmly establish in everyone's minds the utter certainty that the situation was beyond hope.

Lazarus was dead.

Buried.

Gone.

I read the section of John's gospel once, twice, and then a third time, just to be sure I've bitten it all off, so that I might chew on it for a while and let the texture and consistency of it become apparent to me, soak down deep and nourish me.

I put down the Holy Text and begin to ruminate on the scene, letting the whole thing roll around my consciousness, letting the agony of it all and the despair of death and the whole crushing weight of losing someone you love weigh heavy down on me.

This is what *Lectio Divina* is about: reading, yes, but not reading for information, for quick facts, for easy answers, but reading instead for formation and transformation by entering into the depths of the text. Looking perhaps for a word or a phrase that "strikes a chord" in my heart of hearts, listening for a word or a phrase that piques a strong emotion or solicits a strong memory. And then *Lectio Divina* invites me to take that word or that phrase with me throughout the day—as though I'm tucking that word or phrase into my pockets next to the hazelnut—so that it might act like a link, bringing me back into the time of *Lectio Divina*, remind me of what happened there in that quiet space and of the nourishment encountered therein.

For me this means that every time I put my hand into my pocket and feel the hazelnut, I repeat that word or phrase from the morning's *Lectio* and thus keep coming back to it throughout the day. Amid the pain and sorrow of the slow and now inevitable approach of Kim's death, I will take that word or that phrase and keep on trying to hear it, keep chewing on it, keep searching for solace and comfort and hope this tiny portion of Holy Text might provide.

A particular phrase of John's gospel comes to me on this heavy day, striking a resounding chord within my own deep sadness. It is this: "take away the stone."[8]

These are Jesus' words, of course, spoken outside Lazarus's tomb. And they are as unthinkable and shocking to me here and now as they must have been to all those who had gathered in Jesus' day.

Martha objected immediately. "Lord, by this time there will be an odor . . ."[9] A valid concern, and her point is clear even if you have to read between the lines to see it, echoing her earlier tearful statement to Jesus outside the town: Jesus was *too late*. Lazarus was *already* dead. And death had been put where it must be put: away. Buried. Behind the closed tomb, behind the stone.

Of course Jesus knew this. Martha told him this already, and he could see clearly enough that the tomb had been sealed.

Yet there Jesus stood, weeping with those who wept, mourning the loss of a friend as we all do. Mourning the reality of this life that ends universally in death.

Yet Jesus said it all the same: "Take away the stone."

As I continue to chew on the scene this morning in my time of *Lectio*, the oddity of it, the inanity of it, the shock of Jesus' words hitting me again, things begin moving laterally, branching out like neurons or a trees' roots. The prophet Ezekiel's phrase, about the God who "will remove the heart of stone and give a heart of flesh,"[10] comes into my consciousness.

Isn't this just another implication of the phrase "Take away the stone"? Or how about the stone Moses struck with his staff, and how having been struck away the stone then unleashed the flow of life-giving water for the Israelites in the desert? Then of course there is the stone that Mary will later find already rolled away from Jesus' tomb on the first day of the week.

"Take away the stone," said Jesus.

Mustn't it be this way? Mustn't stone and death be rolled away if life is to come again?

Take away the stone of death and disorder and chaos, *take away the stone* of idolatry and ideology and isolation, *take away the stone* of addiction and poverty and cancer, *take away the stone* of the *nihilo* itself that threatens to swallow all life into its destruction and chaos.

Take away the stone so that fullness of life might flourish and flow where once there was only the sickening stench of rot and the crush of darkness and oppression and death.

Take away the stone.

Words worth chewing on and mulling over, indeed.

But this time of *Lectio Divina* doesn't end for me there.

As my objectivity diminishes to intimacy I find myself *inside* the scene, *in front of* the tomb, standing there with all the rest of the characters depicted in the Scriptures. Through the power of my God-given imagination I have been invited *inside* the scene, and my senses are all alive with the power and potency of the narrative. I smell the dust of the road and feel it grind between my teeth. I am here, standing beside Mary, beside Martha, too, hearing the sisters weep in the gut-wrenching way that only death can shake the human frame.

And I am weeping too—here in my imagination, here outside of Lazarus's tomb. I weep for Lazarus, yes, and for my cancer-riddled friend and her family who are even now preparing the stone that will mark her grave. I weep for us all who will one day find ourselves fourteen hundred and five shovelfuls beneath the surface of the world, bound and imprisoned in the stony darkness of death.

In my mind's eye, in my mind's ear, in my mind's participation and imaginative engagement with the Holy Text, I hear the stone being rolled away from the tomb even as I see Christ praying, even as the Son of Man is there with his hands and face lifted toward the heavens, thanking his Father for hearing him, praying that we might all believe that he was sent to us by the Father.

Then I watch as Jesus turns toward the darkness of the tomb and calls out in a voice so loud it makes me start even here, even now, half a world away and two thousand years later: "Lazarus, come out!"[11]

We all fall silent, watching and waiting before the darkness of the tomb.

A gasp moves through the crowd and we all back away, astonished and full of hope.

This is the kind of intimate insight into Holy Text a "skimming" or "scavenging" approach simply doesn't permit. It isn't informative but rather formative. I came away from it changed. Not just more knowledgeable.

The phrase "Take away the stone" keeps on coming back to me in the hours and days that follow, accompanied by a deep and potent longing. A deep and potent longing not for an *idea* but for an entirely new kind of reality. A reality where death and darkness and all the chains that bind us are at last thrown asunder.

Two weeks before Christmas I receive word that Kim has died.

I sit on the couch and weep, holding tight to the hazelnut from my pocket. Letting the holy phrase "Take away the stone" resound through me.

Maybe it is the effect of *Lectio Divina*, or maybe that afternoon I spent lying in an open grave, or the task of having to say good-bye to more and more people whom I've loved in this life and the thought of the inescapable final good-bye beyond which there is only a question mark and hope.

Whatever the reason, I start attending a local church's Eucharist service regularly. Two, occasionally even three times a week.

This is something I've never done before.

For most of my life Eucharist has just been an idea. An occasional act,

like getting my teeth cleaned or having a physical exam. Important—
yeah, yeah—but I can take it or leave it. If it's just a reminder, can't I
find other ways of remembering without it? Until now I've held the
body and the blood of Christ at arm's length and surveyed or scavenged
it, debated or argued about it with others and occasionally submitted
myself to it.

Lectio and Taizé are casting the Eucharist itself in a different light:
maybe this, too, is less about information and more about formation?
Less about knowing and more about becoming?

The Eucharist services at the local parish are on Wednesdays, Fridays,
and Sundays, with the weekday services being held in the tiny side chapel while the main Sunday service happens in the larger space.

There aren't many of us here as I settle myself down into the pews on
a snowy Wednesday evening. And I'm well under half the average age
of the other congregants. I look like a brown barrel floating on a grey
sea. All the rest are wrinkled and alone, widows or widowers who spend
as much time fighting with squealing hearing aids as they do saying the
prayers. But I find their presence deeply comforting, even if the subtle
smell of mothballs permeates the space by the end of the service.

Their presence is comforting, yes, but also sobering and poignant.
How many graves have they all stood beside? Nearing life's end they
come here day in and day out to stand or kneel as best they're able on
creaking knees and popping hips, looking up toward heaven in the hope
that the God who made them and gave them life in the first place might
be able and willing to say, "Take away the stone" once they themselves
are gone and buried.

This evening I'm sitting next to a kind widow named Miriam whom
I've gotten to know a little during the previous weeks. I've grown fond of
the strange combination of grandmotherly wisdom and brutal honesty
she offers to all who will listen.

"I used to be like you," Miriam told me when I first met her. "I was
young and thought I could circumscribe the globe if I tried hard enough,
thought I might conquer the world. Sooner or later the blur of all those
months and years and decades takes *you* for a ride."

I smiled and nodded at this kind old lady, listening to what she was saying but not really letting it sink in.

"Don't disregard me so glibly," Miriam said, grabbing my hand hard. "Listen. You, too, will end up like me one day: frail and old and knowing that you need life and nourishment to come from somewhere else, that your ability to find it for yourself is long past. You, too, will one day realize that you must lean on someone greater than yourself, someone more enduring. It is a terrifying thing to have to realize. And yet somehow good too." Her voice trailed off then, as she stared off into the distance, remembering something that brought tears to her eyes.

Tonight, when the order of the service directs the priest to stand up and say, "Behold, Christ our Passover Lamb is sacrificed," Miriam reaches across the space between us and grabs my hand again in a bony vice grip. As the *snap* of the wafer breaking in half echoes through the chapel, she increases the pressure.

The priest invites us forward and, once the others have stood to make their way, I try to stand and do likewise. But Miriam won't let go of my hand. Instead she pulls me in close so that I can hear her whisper. "This is what I told you when we first met," she says loud enough for all to hear. "We must all find a source of life and nourishment beyond ourselves, from someone greater, someone more enduring than we are. This mystery is the only hope we have."

At last Miriam lets go of my hand and motions for me to go forward.

I nod and stand and make my way to kneel before the altar. Miriam comes and kneels beside me, beside all the rest of us.

"This is the body of Christ," the priest says as he presses the piece of bread into my hand.

"Amen," I say, bringing the bread of life to my lips.

"And this is the blood of Christ," the priest says as he lifts the chalice toward my lips.

From the corner of my eye I see Miriam wiping away a tear.

Saint Peter's words come to mind as I return to my seat, mingling with the words of the weeping Miriam: "Lord, to whom shall we go?"[12] We have circumscribed the globe and conquered the world and find ourselves here yet again, kneeling and in need of nourishment from somewhere else, realizing we must lean on someone greater, someone more enduring than we are.

∽

"Perhaps the best thing to say," a famous and well-respected theologian once told me, "is that the Eucharist works in our lives the way digestion works in our bodies. It is foundational and essential. Indeed, we are alive because of it. While we may consciously know that we are eating, the *knowing* that we are eating isn't where the life comes from. Life comes through the eating itself. What is actually happening is subrational, but we mustn't therefore despise it. After all, rationality *depends* upon it. And this is itself warrant for continuing to 'take and eat, take and drink.' After all, our very existence depends not upon our rationalizations about 'taking and eating' but by our *actually* doing so. And if we abandon the Sacrament itself in order to ponder and reflect upon it, we do so at great peril. Something like malnourishment will appear at first, and if it is not soon remedied, life itself will come under threat."

"So we live and move and have our being atop a great mystery," I say, trying to summarize this venerable theologian's words.

He nods and smiles. "Precisely."

∽

For all my love of logic and rationality, for all my belief in the power of ideas and notions and human cognition, I am becoming more and more comfortable with the idea of being alive and sustained by mystery.

Maybe that's why the Orthodox church calls the sacraments the *Holy Mysteries*.

I like that.

It's as Miriam said: these mysteries are the only hope we have.

CHAPTER 11

Resonant Loneliness: The Practice of Still, Silent Solitude

I have often said that the sole cause of man's unhappiness is that he does not know how to stay quietly in his room.

—BLAISE PASCAL[1]

For many, silence is threatening. They don't know what to do with it. If they leave the noise of the city behind and come upon a place where no cars are roaring, no ships are tooting, no trains rumbling, where there is no hum of radio or television, where no records or tapes are playing, they feel their entire body gripped by an intense unrest. They feel like a fish which has been set on dry land. They have lost their bearings. . . . If they are forced to sit in a room without [a] constant flow of sound, they grow very nervous. . . . There was a time when silence was normal and a lot of racket disturbed us. But today, noise is the normal fare, and silence, strange as it may seem, has become the real disturbance. It is not hard to understand, therefore, that people who experience silence in this way will have difficulty with prayer.

—HENRI NOUWEN[2]

Be still, and know that I am God.

—PSALM 46:10 ESV

D on't even get me started on Twitter.

Despite the success of its IPO, the whole thing reminds me of the crow's nest in the tree just outside my bedroom window. Every morning at approximately 4:30 a.m., a whole murder of crows ("murder," I just learned, is the proper name for a collection of crows) decides to start off their day with an hour-long chorus of caw-caw-cawing. It hasn't failed to rouse me yet, nor has it failed to start my day off with a low-grade, seething sort of anger. Sure, the conversation of crows can be an intriguing, even beautiful thing, like that one especially raucous morning when I looked out the window and saw that the crows were trying to defend their nest from a bald eagle who'd decided to perch threateningly nearby.

But usually, the whole murder just sits there caw-caw-cawing for the apparent joy of it. But from my perspective, it's not beautiful. It's not interesting. It's not informative.

It's just noise. Distracting, bothersome, grating, agitating.

Like I said, Twitter often reminds me of a whole murder of crows. Most people don't tweet anything beautiful or interesting or informative. They just caw for the apparent joy of it. And they caw and they caw and they caw.

And then, if the volume gets loud enough, we call it a "trend."

God have mercy.

As an antidote, behold the story of Elijah.[3]

There was once a man named Elijah whose heart was set on God. Elijah toiled to help others in his city flee the ways of madness that had infected their life together and thereby find the narrow path toward life and God. But as is so often the case, the people of Elijah's city would not listen. They preferred cheating to honesty, darkness to light, death to life, and so they sought to kill Elijah.

So Elijah fled.

He fled from the city and into the mountains, and once in the mountains he found a cave, and once in the cave, despite being weary and exhausted, he found a modicum of peace and safety.

Perhaps God will speak to me here, Elijah thought to himself as he went to sleep that first night.

And so God would.

But first Elijah had to wait.

And wait.

And wait.

And then, after Elijah had waited a very long time, a great storm billowed up around the mountain. Stronger than a hurricane the winds shook the mountain to its very depths, and the stone walls of the cave groaned under the buffeting winds.

But Elijah knew this was not the Lord.

So he continued waiting.

Then there came an earthquake, and when the stone walls of the cave began reverberating like a bell Elijah feared for his very life, crying out to God that the cave might not collapse and bury him alive.

But Elijah did not flee the cave.

He continued waiting.

Then there came a mighty forest fire that engulfed all the trees on all the hills surrounding the mountain and the cave. Elijah pressed his tunic up against his mouth so he would not choke on the ash and smoke.

Still Elijah continued waiting.

And then, in the night after the fire, after the earthquake, after the storm, while Elijah slept in the darkness of the cave, there came a fragile and eternal silence, a quiet whisper, a surreal kiss on the lips of his soul.

At this Elijah knew he was at last in the presence of God Almighty. He again covered his face with his tunic, this time as a sign of humility, and went to the mouth of the cave to hear what it was that God would say to him.

I'm drawn to stone architecture for all the reasons I'm not a big fan of plastic: in our world of quick and easy mediocrity, permanence is a rare and beautiful thing indeed. Although the forces of sun and water, summer and winter are strong enough to erode even stone, it is one of the longest-lasting materials we have to work with in our world. We make our castles and tombstones out of the stuff, hoping they might last a few centuries or more, until the elements wear even these mighty monuments down to sand.

Thanks to stone, the Hermit's Cell—or the foundation of it anyway—still exists on the isle of Iona, right where it has been for hundreds of years.

I stumble upon this contemplative circle one afternoon while exploring the island, having wandered down the southwest side of the hill called Dùn Ì. The austere beauty of the cell's decayed impermanence calls to me in a ghostly sort of way, arresting me in my tracks, its intentionality and beauty and bold declaration of all the human effort arrayed against our transience echoing down through the centuries.

With the cell now nothing but a circle of foundation rocks approximately fifteen feet across, I must imagine it as it might have looked when it was originally built. The stones are now all upright on one another, rough-hewn timbers emerging from the foundation at regular intervals, supporting the roof of thick, thatched grasses that provides simple but adequate shelter from all but the fiercest of Ionan storms. The small entrance, just two feet wide, opens to the south, where exposure to the feeble sun of these northern latitudes would have been the greatest. A brisk wind is blowing. The fragrant smell of wood smoke and the sound of the cracking and popping of a small fire waft out to me from inside.

Sensing my approach, the hermit who built this cell emerges in the doorway, and a look of shocked surprise spreads across both our faces at this unanticipated meeting. My rain jacket and jeans are doubtless just as strange to him as his woolen, smoky (and awfully pungent) habit is to me.

We nod cautiously at one another, acknowledging the shared desire to learn more of silence and solitude, the shared question that has led us both to this secluded place, on a secluded island, at the very edge of the world.

Realizing I've intruded on the hermit's solitude, I turn to depart back across the centuries. But the hermit nods as I go, making the sign of the cross over me as I continue on my way. Back in the present moment I blink a few times, enter the remains of the cell myself, and, unslinging my backpack, turn a full 360 degrees to survey my surroundings.

There isn't another person in sight.

Just the stone.

The wind.

The sun.

The sea.

The sky.

I am alone in silence.

I sit down, delighted to have finally arrived, but find that I'm able to last less than ten minutes.

Then I'm up and fidgety, nervous and unhinged at having been still for so long, away from people for so long. "I should get back," I say to myself. "They're probably worried about me back at the abbey."

But I know this is not true. Why should they worry? I haven't even been gone an hour.

With great effort, I silence the nervous caw-caw-cawing of my ego and sit back down again in the sun-warmed grass at the center of the Hermit's Cell. I think of Elijah, try to focus on waiting.

The next hour is one of the most difficult I have ever passed in this life, an ironic fact considering I don't really *do* anything at all in that hour. At the end of it I am physically, emotionally, and mentally exhausted.

Why was it so hard?

Perhaps it is that I am a writer and a public speaker. An activist, even. I make my way in the world by what I say and what I do. I am (relatively) young. I am (sometimes) thoughtful. I am (more or less) a people person. Stillness, silence, and solitude, therefore, terrify me, because I define and construct my sense of self by what I say and by what I do, by the ways I exert influence on the community around me. It is this web of action and interaction that provides me with my sense of *who I am.*

To be without speech, to be without action, to be without others with whom I'm interacting is thus to be laid bare, to be stripped naked in an incredibly vulnerable way, to have to face head-on an ethereal abyss full of unanswerable questions I try with all my words and thoughts and actions and relationships to somehow cover over and deny.

Of course I'm not alone in my fear of stillness and silence and solitude. Our culture is literally obsessed with trying to obliterate all three. Nationwide 4G networks and ubiquitous wi-fi and Facebook's endless news feed are just today's iterations of the nearly universal human tendency to avoid stillness, silence, and solitude. You needn't experience a single moment of silence in the day if you don't want to. The alarm app on your phone will play your favorite song to rouse you from your slumber, a company out of Rhode Island makes a waterproof wireless speaker system so you can catch up on the news while you shower, state-of-the-art in-home stereo systems not only know what room you're in but can even predict the "mood" of music you'd like to listen to while you're making breakfast based on current weather and past listening habits.

But who has time for a sit-down breakfast anyway? Just grab the iPod and Bluetooth it to your car's smart-stereo en route to the drive-through coffee shop where you forgo the bagel and bark at the barista to double the espresso. Then it's meetings, meetings, meetings, followed by dead-lines and even more pressure from the higher-ups, who are all jumping up and down on your head. If you even *get* a lunch break you might head to the gym, where the bass beat of the music is designed to increase your heartbeat and news channels on the flat-screen TVs flash a different story every fifteen and a half seconds and the ticker tape at the bottom of the screen seems more like a hamster on a carnival Ferris wheel every time you look at it. And then it's just more of the same throughout the afternoon and into the evening. When at last we collapse into our beds it is to the sound of the stereo once again, that will automatically switch itself off once it knows we're asleep.

We are a culture of nervous fidgeters, an entire society succumbing to ADHD (diagnosed or not). And what's more astonishing, this ailment is something we have cultivated in ourselves. As Stephen Nachmanovitch points out in his excellent book *Free Play*:

> "Fidget" comes from an Old Norse word that means "to desire eagerly." Fidgeting and boredom are the symptoms of fear of emptiness, which we try to fill up with whatever we can lay our hands on. We are taught to be bored, to seek easy entertainment, to ardently desire the ephemeral.

There are multi-billion-dollar industries—television, alcohol, tobacco, drugs—based on feeding this fear of emptiness. They provide opportunities for our eyes and brains to fidget and forget. Shorter and shorter attention spans are inculcated in us by the rhythms of society, which become increasingly nervous and jittery, which shorten our attention spans further—another vicious circle.[4]

Isn't all the caw-caw-cawing we exert so much energy toward really just an attempt to convince one another (and ourselves, too, of course) how important, intelligent, witty, powerful we are? Isn't it all a flawed attempt at manufacturing meaning in our lives? On and on the viscous circle continues, a never-ending ticker tape Ferris wheel that's whirling so fast that even if you can hang on, it will make you sick to do so. If you don't believe me, try stepping out of the carnival for an hour. Or even fifteen minutes, if you can. In a quiet room, without movement, without thought, without intention. See how much you feel the nervousness reeling in your soul.

The first time I tried to do it—a long while before I even thought of going to Iona—I was a wreck after a minute and thirty seconds: wide-eyed and twitchy as any crack addict in need of a fix, any Twitter junkie in need of another 140 characters.

Perhaps silence and stillness and solitude are so very terrifying to us to the precise degree that we have bought into the lie that we must manufacture our own identities, create our own significance, define our own existences. To do this is to ground our sense of well-being on the illusion that we are in control, that we are powerful and able enough to overcome the insignificance and transience that marks human life. Perhaps we then fear silence, stillness, and solitude for the same reasons we fear the hospital bed and the nursing home and the cemetery, for they cast in startling clarity how feeble and frail we all actually are. These are places of "obsolescence" in our society, where we relegate the "insignificant," "unproductive," "unimportant" from our midst, "getting them out of our way" so the rest of us can keep on with our busy attempts to shore up our egos, to keep upright our feeble sense of significance. We are a culture gone insane (literally: "not healthy").

Insane as I am, when I first came across Belden Lane's suggestion that "certain truths can be learned, it seems, only as one is sufficiently emptied, frightened, or confused,"[5] I scoffed at his suggestion, assuring myself that the only "truths" that interested me were the sort that could be learned when one was full, confident, and clear-sighted. In short, the only truths my insane ego was interested in were truths it could control.

But pressing on into Lane's book, *The Solace of Fierce Landscapes*, I found myself drawn to the *via negativa* of Christianity like someone aching from lack of water. This apophatic (not ap*ath*etic, but ap*oph*atic, i.e., without the use of images / words / thoughts, that is, emphasizing silence) tradition maintains that there is much we must learn about ourselves and about God in stillness, silence, and solitude. The *via negativa* teaches that while perfectly "natural," in fact all our murderous caw-caw-cawing leads us *away* from the peace, the love, the stability we so earnestly long for.

The archetypes of the *via negativa* are the desert mothers and fathers of the fourth century. These courageous women and men fled the ceaseless caw-caw-cawing of the city for the desert regions of Egypt. They are the prototypical hermits and ascetics, the original monks and nuns, and thus great sources of eternal and enduring wisdom, a wisdom I need desperately to hear amidst my modern frenzy.

Reading the desert mothers and fathers is what sent me searching for a cave of my own.

It is a dark and stormy night just off the coast of British Columbia on Galiano Island, almost seven months exactly since I was at the Hermit's Cell on Iona. The usually contradictory weather reports are calling unanimously for the January storm to intensify over the next twenty-four hours. It is utterly, definitely, absolutely dark. It has been for hours now, the pale winter sun having succumbed long ago to the thick darkness that marathons on and on into the depths of the northern night.

"Are you sure you want to do this tonight?" my friend Loren asks, though I can hardly hear him over the smacking of the rain on the windshield. Loren has kindly ventured out into the storm to meet me at the Sturdies Bay Terminal upon my arrival at Galiano Island on the late ferry. Loren is driving carefully now—more carefully than I've ever seen him, in fact—along the winding road that curves like a spine through the length of the island. We can hardly see twenty feet ahead of us on the road for all the torrential rain.

"You could always stay the night at our house and head up to the cave tomorrow, once the storm clears off a little. After breakfast."

Loren's offer of hospitality is more than a little appealing. I've spent numerous evenings at his idyllic "farmhouse by the sea," sitting around the radiant cast-iron stove he and Mary Ruth keep burning all winter long, sipping wine and discussing theology and philosophy. The hike into the cave took more than an hour even on the fair-weather day months ago when I first set off to find it. How long might it take in the darkness of night? How long in this storm? And do I really want to start off a weeklong silent retreat in a cave, soaked through? The offer of a dry bed and a hot breakfast (Loren's legendary crepes, perhaps?) is almost enough to sway me from the course I've set.

"No thanks," I say at last, shaking my head. There's never an easy time to find silence, never an easy road to stillness or solitude. Trudging uphill through a storm in the darkness of night in search of the elusive "still point" in an island cave is more or less what the venture into silence always requires.

"I think I'll try to make it to the cave tonight," I continue. "I need the cave more than I need comfort. If I can't find it I'll make my way back down the ridge and take you up on your offer."

In the green glow of the dashboard lights, I see Loren smile. After all, he's the one who told me where to find the cave in the first place. "Good," he says with a nod. "I was hoping you'd say that."

Loren has never been one for chitchat, so we fall into a comfortable silence as we drive on toward the trailhead. This leaves me to ponder an evocative section of Thomas Merton's *New Seeds of Contemplation* I was reading on the ferry. It's a shocking critique of how I live most of my life:

There are men dedicated to God whose lives are full of restlessness and who have no real desire to be alone. They admit that exterior solitude is good, in theory, but they insist [as pretense] that it is far better to preserve interior solitude while living in the midst of others. In practice, their lives are devoured by activities and strangled with attachments. Interior solitude is impossible for them. They fear it. They do everything they can to escape it. What is worse, they try to draw everyone else into activities as senseless and as devouring as their own. They are great promoters of useless work. They love to organize meetings and banquets and conferences and lectures. They print circulars, write letters, talk for hours on the telephone in order that they may gather a hundred people together in a large room where they will all fill the air with smoke and make a great deal of noise and roar at one another and clap their hands and stagger home at last patting one another on the back with the assurance that they have all done great things to spread the Kingdom of God.[6]

When we arrive at the trailhead Loren lets me out of the car and waits until I've hoisted my backpack up onto my shoulders and closed the trunk. He rolls down the window as I prepare to set off into the night.

"The basement door will be unlocked," he calls above the rain. "Just use one of the bedrooms down there if you must."

I shout a thank-you.

Then Loren rolls up the window and drives away, and I set out into the storm, hoping to find shelter in a cave.

Just to be clear: I don't have a *thing* for caves.

In fact, I'm quite claustrophobic. So I hike with a growing sense of fear, a heightened sense of trepidation. It takes me almost two hours to reach the cave, the path literally flowing with streams from the unending rain.

When I at last arrive at the mouth of the cave, I have to stop for a moment outside and steady my resolve against the swelling terror. This is more than just claustrophobia. I am on the threshold of my doubts and fears about my own insignificance, my own finitude, my own inability to sustain meaning in my life.

The mouth of the cave is low—so low I have to stoop down to slide into it—and only about the size of a large garbage-can lid. I kneel down beside it, patting the knee-high slab of sandstone that forms the roof of the cave, wondering if it will hold for another week.

"It's held for this long," I say aloud.

And with a great heave, I slide down into the darkness.

Athanasius—the biographer of the third- and fourth-century hermit Saint Antony—writes that the founder of Western monasticism lived in monastic solitude and discipline for something like eighty years. The effects of this discipline were substantial, and when Saint Antony emerged from his "Inner Mountain," Athanasius writes that it was evident to all who saw him that he had reached a place of "utter equilibrium, like one guided by reason and steadfast in that which accords with nature."[7] Later on, Antony is described as being different from other people, namely in the great "stability of character and purity of the soul,"[8] which I take to mean his obvious lack of frenzy, the imperturbability, the external peace that he radiated to all around him. It was as though, in the language of Paul, Saint Antony's time in solitude, silence, and stillness had "rooted and established [him] in love."[9]

How can this be?

Though a week's retreat in a cave is but a drop in the bucket compared to Antony's eighty plus years of asceticism, there in the cave I found myself in a head-on confrontation with the nagging question that subconsciously energizes so much of my frenzy. It is the basic binary question at the bottom of all human existence, the question we must all face: Am I my own God? Or, as Augustine puts it, "are any of us skillful enough to fashion ourselves?"[10] I know what Christianity says I *ought* to believe, but of course knowing what one should do and actually living it are very different. How do I live my days? What is the tenor of my life?

The question hit me on the second night like a smack, and I found myself hyperventilating, hardly able to stave off the encroaching panic. For if the answer to that binary question is the former—that I *am* my own god—then I'd better get on up out of this cave and back to the city so I can ramp up my frenzied pursuit of significance through words and influence and wealth and power, for that is the only means I have to secure meaning in my very finite days.

But if the latter—if I am a creature made and beloved by a Creator—then everything is different.

If this is the case, then this cave, and even the coffin in which I will one day rest under fourteen hundred and five shovelfuls is not a place of cold isolation and absolute loneliness. Instead it is like a womb. Dark, yes, but not the harsh darkness of an empty and meaningless universe. Instead it is warm, and is in fact the place where life is miraculously formed and transformed, where God is at work to weave us more fully into the people we've been created to be. Both the cave and the tomb can be seen as a cocoon, into which we crawl as our old, exhausted selves and from which—by the grace of God—we emerge as something new and unexpected, alive and vibrant. Revived. If this is the case then I am held, even here in this silence, even here in this stillness, even here in this solitude. I am held and I am loved and I am rooted and established in love.

And if this is true then even here in all this darkness I am not now, and nor will I ever be, alone.

At this the panic vanishes like a mist in the wind, and a calm—unlike anything I've ever experienced before—wraps itself around me. This calm soaks in deep, well past my ego, down, down, down into the subconscious, past even that into the bedrock of my soul. And then I know that it is precisely here, at the very core of my being, that the eternal silence, the quiet whisper, the still small voice of God must be heeded.

In the midnight darkness of the cave, by the light of a single, flickering candle, I sing and sing and sing again a song I learned at the Taizé service on Iona, a song from deep in the history of the Christian faith, a song of two simple words that seems to me to be the perfect articulation not only of our condition but also of our hope: *Kyrie Eleison.*

Lord have mercy.

~

On the afternoon of the third day, I hear a questioning voice, calling from outside the cave. "Hello?"

It is Loren, and I'm delighted that he has come for a visit.

"Hello!" I cry, my voice echoing throughout the cave. I put down my book and scramble out. "Welcome!" I say with obvious enthusiasm. Given that this is the longest I've ever gone without seeing or speaking to anyone, I'm delighted by the human contact.

"I wonder," Loren muses with a wry smile, "what exactly is the proper etiquette when approaching someone else's cave?"

I laugh and invite him in for tea. "The kettle is still hot," I say, motioning back into the darkness of the cave.

"No, no." Loren is quick to wave me off. "I don't want to interrupt you. I just wanted to be sure you actually made it here the other night in that storm and didn't get lost or fall off the edge of a cliff or something like that."

"I'm fine," I say with a wide grin. "It's a bit lonely here, of course, but very good as well."

"What have you been learning?" he asks.

"That silence and stillness and solitude are as hard as they are beautiful."

"Indeed," Loren says with a smile. "Indeed they are."

After another moment, he adds, "Well, keep on."

And he disappears again into the forest.

~

There exists here another strange and beautiful tension, a necessary dance between solitude and community. They inform one another, keep one another in balance. Dietrich Bonhoeffer puts it this way:

> Each taken by itself has profound pitfalls and perils. Those who want
> community without solitude plunge into the void of words and feelings,

and those who seek solitude without community perish in the bottomless pit of vanity, self-infatuation and despair.

Whoever cannot be alone should be aware of community. Whoever cannot stand being in community should beware of being alone.[11]

Not surprisingly, we find this balance, this healthy tension, this "utter equilibrium" between these two poles of solitude and community in the life of Jesus. A surprising event occurs in the life of Christ as recorded in the first chapter of Mark's gospel. Jesus and his followers had departed from the Sea of Galilee and gone into the neighboring town of Capernaum where Jesus had healed people of a variety of ailments. Jesus' fame had spread so quickly that the "whole city was gathered together at the door"[12] of the place where Jesus was staying.

But then, early the next morning, Jesus up and left. It was still dark, Mark tells us, when the King of kings got up and went out to an *"eremon topon,"*[13] a desert place, a lonely place, a silent place, in search of quiet in which to pray. Can you picture Jesus there at the edge of the desert? Quiet? Listening? Like Elijah, coming to the mouth of a cave with his tunic covering his face in humility, turning his face toward the rising sun and awaiting the still, small voice of God.

Early in the morning Jesus up and left. He went away from the people who were dear to him, away from the crowds that had gathered to see him work miracles, away from the expectations and the demands and the pressures of the people closest to him. And there, in that still point, in that quiet, desert, lonely place, Jesus learned that the work he had been doing in Capernaum was finished.

But the carnival masters were quick to notice that their lion—the main attraction, after all—had gone AWOL, and they were hot on Jesus' trail.

"Everyone is looking for you,"[14] said Simon and the others who had come to track Jesus down. In my mind I picture them wringing their hands in dismay, dusty and breathless, anxious brows knit high as they glanced nervously at one another with looks that said it all: "bring Jesus back . . . the show must go on."

But in his *eremon topon* Jesus had heard another thing entirely. "Let us go on to the next towns," Jesus responded. "For that is why I came out."[15]

Is it too much to suggest that even Jesus had to get away and clear his head enough to hear the Father speak? That he had to step out of the madness of the competing demands that pressed in upon him in the crush of the crowd in order to reorient himself, in order to hear the voice of the Father, in order to be sure that he only did "what he sees the Father doing"?[16]

What pearl of great price might be unearthed in the still point? What might we find there in the still silence of solitude? What Jesus and Elijah both found, of course. For if we are willing to go there, to ignore the storm and the earthquake and the blaze and shut down the worried caw-caw-cawing of our fears and frenzies, we just might hear the eternal whisper, the thin silence, the still small voice of God, and know the "I AM GOD" who whispers to us that we are held by a love greater than we can even hope to imagine, that we needn't try to fashion or uphold ourselves by our own strength. That, like Jesus, we are being invited to "only do what we see the Father doing," that we are being invited to participate in this love, to join the great and joyful dance that is as extravagant as it is unnecessary, as beautiful as it is good.

After making my way down the mountain from my cave, I decide to stop for a few minutes at one of Galiano Island's stony, east-facing beaches. In the distance I can see Vancouver—the great city—gleaming and bright in the sunlight. Soon I will be back in the thick of it, having traversed again across the ocean of silence and stillness and solitude that has insulated me here for the past seven days. In two hours I'll be back at my desk, absorbed again into the busyness and work and community.

A longing for a memento of the cave grips me, a desire for some vivid and evocative reminder to bring me back—even if only in my imagination—to the silence and stillness and solitude I found here in the cleft of rock, back into the warm presence of God.

Then I see it—a delightfully smooth, black stone. I stoop and pick it up, feeling its cool weight in my palm. It's about the size of a half-dollar, black as the midnight darkness of the cave, smooth as sea glass.

Abbot Agatho carried around a stone in his mouth for *three years*, "until he learned to be silent."[17]

Wiping the seaweed from the black stone on my shirt sleeve, I open my mouth and place it on the flat of my tongue, testing it. It is cold and salty, and it fits. It is appropriate, feeling right.

I keep it hidden now—my stone of silence—in the top drawer of my desk.

Often, when I'm feeling the caw-caw-cawing of my ego in an especially frenetic sort of way, when I feel the weight of my existence beginning to shift off the true ground of being and onto the weak foundation I all too often try to fashion out of my words and influence and power, I'll pull out that stone of silence, place it again on the flat of my tongue, and sit there for a while, hazelnut in hand.

Listening.

I wait for the storm to pass, for the earthquake to subside, for the fire to burn itself out so that at last I might emerge from the cave and listen for whatever the still, small voice of God might have to say.

CHAPTER 12

A Deep, Deep Breath:
The Practice of Sabbath

There are more important things to do than hurry.

—ROBERT FARRAR CAPON[1]

You have made us and drawn us to yourself, and
our heart is unquiet until it rests in you.

—SAINT AUGUSTINE[2]

Perhaps the most radical sociopolitical invention of the past four thousand
years was the Sabbath. The practice of the Sabbath . . . recognizes that we
need space and time reserved from the rushing and pressures of everyday
life, reserved for going inside ourselves, for rest, review, and revelation.

—STEPHEN NACHMANOVITCH[3]

E arly one autumn morning I set out for a run in Vancouver. Although it is Saturday I have an extraordinary amount of work to push through today, the result of chronic overcommitment mingled danger-ously with mismanaged expectations. But before I start slogging through it all, I just need some fresh air; need to try and clear the fog of stress so I can see a little better, think a little clearer.

Though it rained last night the clouds have retreated for sunrise, piling up around the North Shore mountains like a crumpled grey blanket. The run is delightful at the start, with the city shining the way it sometimes does in that crisp, early morning light and the air just cool enough to make my inhale spark a little. I am filled with life, feeling it course through my veins like liquid fire as I run.

I make my way through a small, forested park, past a glassy-smooth inlet with silent sailboats at anchor, and then along streets lined with bakeries and coffee shops just beginning to waft their weekend fragrances into the morning air. In my exultation I stop paying attention to my course, and after a few absentminded turns I find myself crossing an unfamiliar bridge and then running along one unfamiliar street after another.

I take a right turn, hoping it will bring me back around to the waterfront in the direction I need to go, but instead I find myself directed toward a large industrial park with chain-link fences and razor wire.

Stopping to survey my surroundings I glance up and suddenly realize how dark and expansive the blanket of clouds has become along the North Shore mountains—an ominous indication that the weather is about to shift for the worse.

And fast.

I turn and begin retracing my steps as best I'm able, running fast despite the distance I've already come, eager to make it home before the storm breaks over me. I dash down a side street in hope of a shortcut, only to find myself dumped out onto yet another unfamiliar street leading in the wrong direction.

That's when it begins to pour. And I mean *pour* as it can only do in the Pacific Northwest: unrelenting torrents of water heaved up out of the Pacific Ocean and pummeled straight back down again onto the city. Within a few minutes it is raining so hard that I can hardly see half a block in front of me. The streets begin to fill with water, dirty creeks lofting random bits of garbage up on their shoulders while cigarette butts float like confetti down the submerged sidewalks.

The temperature drops dramatically, and I feel the warmth begin leaking out of my body.

I run faster, hoping to generate a little more heat, hoping I can find my way home.

I run and I run and I run through the unrelenting storm.

If asked, could you define what an *idol* is?

Someone once asked me, and I've been replaying this question over in my mind ever since. As far as I can make out, an idol is something—anything other than God—that we have elevated so much that it is believed to be the source and sustainer of our life and well-being. There are lots of idols in our world—money, power, fame, influence, airbags, national security, economic independence, medical science. All of these can be good things when they're in their proper places. But they keep on wanting to crawl up on little altars and demand our allegiance and our sacrifice.

I'll tell you about another idol, one that stands at the center of my Colorado hometown. It's an impressive piece of bronze artwork, meticulously crafted and nearly ten feet tall. The artist titled the piece *The Self Made Man*, and it is one of the most significant pieces of commissioned artwork in that minimalist western town. The statue stands in a small square, just off Main Street, close to the old library. It is a perfect encapsulation of the "American dream": a strong and ardent man is frozen in midswing, raising his hammer high against the heavens, defying the gods, chiseling himself into existence out of a block of hard stone.

A whole chorus of mantras parade through my head whenever I recall this idol: "Pull yourself up by your bootstraps!" "Be all you can be!" "Define your own future!" On and on and on the liturgies run, conditioning allegiance to the idol. The longer I dwell in its presence, the more the sense of urgency rises, increasing the conviction that if I do not keep swinging my hammer, I'll sink back down into the vice-grip of insignificance.

I've worshiped this idol for a long time, believed the rhetoric that flows from it. For most of my life I've believed that not only was it within my power but in fact it was my God-given responsibility to fashion myself into something strong and powerful and effective, using whatever hammers I could find to form myself into someone possessed with as much wealth and strength and power and influence as possible. "Think of the good you will do in the world then!" I've often told myself. "Think of the impact you'll have!"

But here's the thing: I've grown weary of all the blood and sweat and tears I've sacrificed before this idol, all the years I've struggled under the great weight of trying to fashion myself out of stone. It is strange, isn't it? Most people in the long course of human history—some one hundred billion of us, great blizzard that we are—have struggled to have enough to eat, adequate shelter, sufficient clothing. Yet here I am, with more than enough clothes in my closet, more than enough food in the cupboards, a leak-proof roof over my head. And I am still tossing and turning about existential questions like whether or not my life has enough "meaning" in it, whether I'm *doing* enough for the good of the world, whether I am—as one prominent pastor put it—"wasting my life." Perhaps this stems from the subconscious perception that everyone around me is doing great and extraordinary things, far more impressive than I myself am: starting non-profit organizations, mentoring at-risk youth, making millions and giving it all away. I'm flat-out weary from the ever-present fear that I'm falling behind, that I'm not getting ahead, that I'm not doing enough, not producing enough, not swinging the hammer high enough or hard enough.

I confide all this to a dear friend over a pint at a local pub. Bruce listens and nods as he sips his ale, agreeing. "What you've described is one of the dominant narratives in our culture," Bruce muses. "One of the defining pictures of how we see ourselves. We think we're our own creators, that we must *make* ourselves from raw material."

"Yes, that's it, isn't it?" I say, realization sparking in my mind. "That's exactly what that statue means: we think we're our own makers. To be a self-made person means you must be your own creator. We must craft ourselves—*ex nihilo*: out of nothing. We have to keep on swinging the hammer, chiseling ourselves into existence. If we stop, we'll just sink back down into nothingness."

Bruce nods. "No wonder so many of us live such frenetic, stressed-out lives—it's hard to ever stop and rest, ever to be at peace when we think failure is constantly threatening, with the weight of nonbeing always clutching us about our legs and dragging us down. We must constantly toil. Toil or drown. There's always something more we should be doing, something someone else is doing if we aren't."

These two images—slogging through a frigid storm and chiseling myself out of stone—capture the essence of how I feel most days. Most minutes, in fact. I'm either sprinting or feeling stuck, feeling stuck or sprinting. The good days are the running days, when I'm sprinting my way through my to-do lists and checking things off one by one. But if I'm not sprinting I'm probably in it *up to here*, just keeping my nose above the surface, convinced that at any moment a huge wave just might crash over me and send me choking, sinking down forever into nothingness.

Before beginning to keep Sabbath regularly, the idea of taking a whole day off in God's name struck me as a quaint ritual, and one that was promoted either by people who are fundamentally negligent or else legalistic.

Sabbath seemed either like a direct affront to my usefulness, my autonomy, my upward mobility, the good work I was trying to do in the world or else yet another crushing weight that I might have to hoist up on my shoulders and start carrying around.

Maybe this is why I almost threw Norman Wirzba's book, *Living the Sabbath,* across the room at his insistence that "Sabbath observance [is] one of our most honest and practical indicators of authentic religious faith. The extent and depth of our Sabbath commitment is the measure of how far we have progressed in our discipleship and friendship with God."[4]

"Excuse me?" I wanted to shout at Wirzba. "I'm doing *all kinds* of stuff for God, thank you very much. Aren't my actions and commitments in the world a far better indication of my 'authentic religious faith' than being *lazy* in God's name?"

The day after my beer with Bruce is fairly typical—typical in the sense that I'm spending it swinging my hammer, toiling and panting as I run through the storm, strained to the breaking point, tired and overworked.

During a lunch-break-turned-apple-on-the-run frenzy, I bite too deeply into the apple's core and the familiar but almost missed taste of the seed stops me in my tracks. The memory of my first hour-long apple contemplation comes rushing back to me, and with it the startling stillness and silence and solitude of the Galiano cave.

Might *this* be what Sabbath is?

A *Selah!* built right into the rhythm of the week? An *eremon topon*—just like Jesus' in Mark 1—into which we might enter regularly?

One thing this Sacred Year is beginning to show me is how each of these spiritual practices can work like an antidote to some of the more poisonous aspects of our culture today. They are refreshing and life giving, whereas so often the habits and methods I've developed in my frenzied, stressed-out life are deadly poisons. The spiritual practices work like balm on wounds, healing even if painful at first.

Thus silence counteracts noise. And contemplation counteracts commodification.

Might Sabbath counteract the idol of the self-made man?

No wonder I mocked Sabbath at first: idols always die hard.

Marva Dawn defines the Sabbath as a day in which we cease doing anything that feels "obligatory" and instead focus on resting, embracing, and feasting.[5] It is a day for delight. For sleeping in. For making love. For eating delicious meals and leaving the dishes until tomorrow. For taking long walks. For sitting in front of the wood fire and reading a novel. No chores. No obligations. No homework. No e-mail. No bills. Nothing at all that feels like work, nothing that seems to be oriented toward productivity or achievement. In short: no swinging of the hammer, whatever form it takes.

At first Sabbath is strange—not *having* to do anything. It feels like the first day of vacation, when you don't know what to do with yourself, and you're both exhausted and jittery all at the same time.

But after a few months of keeping Sabbath, it has become a dear friend. In the presence of Sabbath the very texture of time seems to be different.

The minutes become longer, fuller, more luxurious somehow. I stop mincing minutes, glancing out of addiction at my wristwatch or smartphone, wondering how I'm going to finish everything I must. On Sabbath I experience the world in a different way. The light seems brighter, the smells stronger, the Wind more obviously whispering.

It is the expansiveness of time and the deep enjoyment possible therein that makes holiness palpable on Sabbath. For instead of Sabbath being a *holy place*, Rabbi Abraham Joshua Heschel points out that Sabbath is instead *holy time*. This, Heschel insists, is directly in line with the biblical narrative, for the first thing God declared holy was *time*, not *space*:

> There is no reference in the record of creation to any object in space that would be endowed with the quality of holiness. . . .
>
> The mythical mind would expect that, after heaven and earth have been established, God would create a holy place—a holy mountain or a holy spring—whereupon a sanctuary is to be established. Yet it seems as if to the Bible it is *holiness in time*, the Sabbath, which comes first.[6]

I wish you could have been here with us in *holy time* this past Sabbath. It was one of the richest and most refreshing I've known in a long while. Days later even the memory of it is enough to fill me with warmth and hope as I am sitting here at my desk, working.

This is what it was like.

I limped into the final stretch of that long and arduous week, barely crossing the finish line. A full schedule of speaking had kept me on the road four out of five days, bouncing from hotel room to hotel room, 4:00 a.m. wake-up call after 4:00 a.m. wake-up call. I'd been in three different cities, spoken in front of thousands of people, and after each event, engaged in countless conversations with many wonderful people. Added on top of all that, my return flight home was delayed and then canceled due to weather, lengthening the trip even more.

And that was just the speaking.

Editorial deadlines were hounding me, articles I promised to write were pressing in with special urgency, and the list of urgent repairs around the house was growing by the inch while I struggled to cross things off by the millimeter.

I felt that I didn't have a moment to lose, that I simply couldn't stop working, that I didn't have time to rest.

That is usually the indicator that I *must* stop, that I *must* keep Sabbath, or risk losing myself completely in the storm, under the torrent and pace and demands of my life that are roaring out of control. I've learned to name that crushing urge to keep working for what it is: a temptation to kneel before the idol of the self-made man.

At last Sabbath is come. The sun is almost set. The house has been tidied, some food prepared, and wine poured into a specially designated Sabbath chalice hand-thrown for us by a dear friend. In a few moments—in keeping with the Jewish tradition—Danae and I will officially begin the Sabbath by lighting two candles. Arising from the two Sabbath accounts in Exodus 20 and Deuteronomy 5, one candle is for the word *remember* and the other is for the word *observe*.

The candles are in the center of the table, next to the chalice. An oil lamp that my mother threw decades ago is also there, waiting to be lit.

Good food, good wine, candlelight, lamplight; these are the essential ingredients for establishing the *atmosphere* of Sabbath. For Sabbath, you see, is not just another thing on the to-do list, but an *ethos*, a particular way of being in the world.

At last Danae and I come to the table and sit down together. Once here, we slip off the manacles we must wear all week—those accursed things called wristwatches by which we mince and dissect the minutes into little chunks of maximized efficiency. Slipping them off literally feels like setting down a hundred-pound load of the harried life. We turn off our cell phones, too, and put away our wallets.

These may seem like simple, insignificant acts, but taken together they form a ritual: a ritual putting aside all these methods of productivity, consumerism, and influence. Thus we let go our hammers. All these things—wristwatches, smartphones, credit cards, cash—go into our "Sabbath box," a simple mash-up I made not long ago out of scrap pieces of pallet wood. They won't be allowed out until Sabbath is over.

We turn off the lights, light the candles, and pray a liturgy to mark the arrival of the Sabbath Bride. Then we feast, and *know* we are feasting.

And this is just the beginning—dear friends of ours are arriving from out of town. Friends of the rare type that we do not feel we need to "entertain," but instead with whom we can truly be ourselves, friends with whom we've shared much life and sorrow and hope, friends who live on another continent and whom we're able to see only once in a very great while.

They arrive late but we stay up talking well past midnight, drinking wine, listening to music, eating dessert, drinking deeply of the refreshing goodness of old and established friendship. Precisely what the Sabbath is meant to be about.

The next day begins after a long sleep-in with a delightful collaboration on a blueberry pancake feast for breakfast. With no wristwatches to truncate the meal, the conversation ranges and flows, spreading out luxuriously. One hour? Two? Who's counting? We sit and we feast and we talk as long as feels right.

For there are no plans on Sabbath, nothing "required." It is a day of rejoicing, of freedom, of flexibility. Of feasting and delighting and embracing.

After breakfast we embark on a leisurely walk along a wooded trail through a local city park, tracing our meandering way along a gently flowing river. As we saunter along together, the gentle feeling of warm wonder begins to overtake me, astonishment at the good gift of friendship, of the extraordinary beauty of the world that I did not make, of the body that I have been given which is able to see and touch and hear and taste and smell it all. The crushing feeling that I am a self-made man is evaporating, and I am remembering that I am merely a creature. A creature who has been created to live and move and have my being in the creation founded, established, and upheld by a Creator God.

"This is good," I say to my friend after a moment of comfortable silence. "Very good indeed."

"That it is," he agrees, inhaling deeply the rich smell of the forest.

As we circle back toward home, the four of us break unexpectedly through the trees out into an old apple orchard. The sight and sweet smell of the fruit stops us all in our tracks, and we simply stare at the unexpected bounty laid out before us. There are at least twenty apple trees, each with boughs so overburdened with ripe fruit that they are literally touching the ground.

"Do you think we can take some of the apples home?" Danae asks aloud.

Suddenly an older woman wearing a straw hat steps out from behind one of the trees, an apple in each hand. She places them into one of the two large bushel baskets at her feet. "Of course you can!" she says, smiling broadly. "These trees are public property, but hardly anybody knows about them. They're one of this area's best kept secrets. That's why there's so much excess fruit."

"More people should come and pick!" I chime in, stepping toward the nearest tree. "Look at all the fruit that is just rotting on the ground."

"I've told countless people," the woman says, her face falling a little. "But nobody has time to come and enjoy places like this anymore. We're all so busy we miss the freely available goodness that is all around us."

"How true that is," we all agree.

"Take as many as you can," the woman says. "Some of the trees are better than others, though, so be sure to sample a few as you go along!"

The four of us spend the next thirty minutes gathering as much fruit as we can from an orchard that we did not plant, that we have never worked, that we did not even expect to find. At the end of it we've stuffed every pocket and backpack and all other available space with fruit, and still the boughs hang to the ground with excess.

"There's so much," I say in amazement. "The whole neighborhood could come and pick enough apples to carry us through the winter, and we wouldn't even pick half of them."

My friend smiles as he bites into yet another apple. "It's like that verse in Isaiah: 'you who have no money, come, buy and eat . . . without money and without cost . . . Listen, listen to me, and eat what is good, and you will delight in the richest of fare.'"[7]

Luxurious time.

Old friendships.

Unearned abundance.

This is what Sabbath is about.

Rabbi Heschel speaks of the Sabbath as a "homeland."[8]

The more I keep Sabbath, the more I yearn to be a native there.

Over the months of regular Sabbath keeping in the Sacred Year, an astonishing thing begins to happen: the ice-cold image of myself as a "self-made man" begins to thaw a little. Sabbath spreads out through my psyche, like spring coming into a wintry landscape, like water being soaked up into a dry sponge. And like the life-giving revitalization that it is, the echoes and reverberations of Sabbath-keeping began spreading out across the rest of my hours, across the rest of my days, changing and altering the texture of ordinary time itself. The cutthroat sense of having to fashion myself out of stone has begun to loosen a little. A different image is underlying the work that I'm doing, that of seeking to be faithful to the calling of the Creator who is making and sustaining all things in existence. Of course I slip back into my frenzy now and then. Like this afternoon when I literally felt my blood pressure rise and the anxiety creep up the back of my neck.

But as the blood pressure rises so do I, walking to the kitchen to grab an apple from the Sabbath orchard. An apple received as a gift, not one that has been earned.

I press it against my nose and inhale deeply, the sweet, spicy flavor of the semiwild fruit reminding me midweek of the Sabbath's excess. I don't have an hour to enjoy this particular apple, but even five minutes will serve as a sort of course correction, a reminder of my limited place in an abundant and extravagant creation.

"Thanks be to God," I say through a juicy bite. "Maker of heaven and earth, great Giver of every gift therein."

Shortly after my friend Bruce and I part ways from the pub, he sends me an e-mail with a subject line of "A Different Way." There is an image attached, a photo he'd taken on a recent trip to Chartres Cathedral in France, of a centuries-old sculpture on one of the entryways. In the sculpture there is a human being—someone just like you, just like me—who is encased in stone. But instead of holding the hammer high against heaven, with chisel pressed tightly against the *nihilo* that binds about the waist, in this sculpture the human is being *welcomed* into existence by the creator God.

This is the power of the antidote of Sabbath: to remind us that life is a gift, that the world is a gift, that we are most emphatically (and most joyously!) *not* our own gods, that we are *not* responsible for fashioning ourselves out of stone.

More than an hour after slogging through the Vancouver torrent, at last I see a familiar street. I turn down it and keep running, confident I'm headed in the right direction now, but daunted by the distance I must cover to return home.

I finally make it there, almost two and a half hours after I departed, more than an hour of which I've been sloshing my way through the downpour. I am soaked. My fingers look like bleached prunes, and I'm walking on shoes that double as brimming buckets. My teeth are chattering, and I'm more than a little hypothermic, convulsing uncontrollably.

"Where have you been?" Danae asks, leaping up from the couch when I push open the front door.

"L—lost," I stammer.

Danae embraces me for a moment, but then holds me at arm's length. "You're *freezing!*"

Too cold to speak, I just nod.

"Quick," she says. "Go get in the shower. I'll make you some tea."

I nod again, strip off my sodden clothes, and climb toward the shower. Though weary and heavy laden, at last, I am home.

CHAPTER 13

Into the Wild: The Practice of Wilderness

The answer must be, I think, that beauty and grace are performed whether or not we will or sense them. The least we can do is try to be there.

—ANNIE DILLARD[1]

Wilderness is not a luxury but a necessity of the human spirit, as vital to our lives as water and good bread.

—EDWARD ABBEY[2]

Wonder is the only adequate launching pad for exploring a spirituality of creation, keeping us open-eyed, expectant, alive to life that is always more than we can account for, that always exceeds our calculations, that is always beyond anything we can make.

—EUGENE PETERSON[3]

Love all of God's creation, the whole and every grain of sand of it. Love every leaf, every ray of God's light. Love the animals, love the plants, love everything. If you love everything, you will perceive the divine mystery in things. Once you perceive it, you will begin to comprehend it better every day. And you will come at last to love the whole world with an all-embracing love.

—FYODOR DOSTOYEVSKY[4]

I was speaking recently with an old friend, an avid outdoorsman, a renaissance man of astonishing skill and deep adoration for all things good and true and beautiful. We were talking about James Cameron's award-winning movie *Avatar*, and our conversation meandered over the film for quite a while, covering everything from the beauty of the visual effects to the epic (if somewhat familiar) arc of the story, the memorable adaptation of archetypical characters.

When the conversation began to taper off, I thought I might as well bring it to a definitive close. "I wish our world was as beautiful as the world in *Avatar*."

My friend scoffed and sat silently for several stunned moments, pondering my statement with an astonished expression.

"You fool," the wise old man spoke in a gentle rebuke. "Our world *is* as beautiful. You're just too asleep to see it."

I am asleep, in fact, on the deck of a friend's sailboat, anchored in a quiet cove in the Southern Gulf Islands of British Columbia. I am mummified in my sleeping bag, oblivious to the sea dew that is soaking me and everything else on deck that has been bathed in great and shining droplets of water. The gentle, rocking dance of the sailboat at its anchor lulled me into a deep sleep hours ago, and now I am somewhere else, expeditioning dreamland.

"Michael!" a voice says from close by.

"Huh?" My response is sluggish.

"Michael!" The voice is more insistent now, and a hand shakes me awake. My eyes snap open, and for a brief and terrifying moment I feel I'm falling from the side of the boat, fated to drown in my mummy bag. I shout and flail, tearing at the drawstring cord about my neck.

"Whoa!" David says, laughing and leaping away so that I don't inadvertently send him flying into the sea.

Relieved to find that I'm still on deck, I fumble for my glasses, feeling my heart pounding in my chest.

I'm not one to appreciate being startled awake in the middle of the night.

"What is it?" I hiss.

David smiles. Despite the darkness, I can see his face in uncanny detail, as though lit from some unexpected source of light.

"Look," David says, pointing past me, high up into the sky.

"What?" I ask, spinning around to look behind me.

I gasp.

"No *way!*" I hear my feeble statement, realizing instantly how shallow and inept words are before the mystery I'm seeing. The skin along the back of my neck bristles with awe.

Beautiful as the thick-as-sand stars had been hours earlier when I'd lain awake watching them in wide-mouthed wonder, this new and larger beauty to which David had woken me—the aurora borealis—surmounts even the beauty of the stars. I understand now why one Inuit tribe insisted that the aurora were messengers from on high, to which all people must first listen and then—if they even dare to respond at all—may speak only in a whisper.[5]

David and I sit on the bow of the sailboat with our necks craned heavenward for the duration of the aurora's presence. For the next half hour the greens and purples swirl together in a vibrant dance, even as they flicker and pulse like a dragonfly's incandescent wings. For years I have wanted to witness this, but I had given up hope considering how rare it is to see them this far south—especially during the short summer nights. This inimitable appearance—I find out later—is the result of an exceptional solar flare, a singular event, and not likely to be repeated anytime soon.

"I almost slept right through it," David says, once the aurora begins to fade.

"So did I," I respond in the gathering darkness. "I'm so glad you woke me. I would have missed it entirely if you hadn't."

Early in her Pulitzer prize–winning book *Pilgrim at Tinker Creek*, Annie Dillard details a glorious compulsion she had of hiding pennies along her childhood sidewalk in Pittsburgh. "I would cradle it at the roots of a sycamore," she explains, "or a hole left by a chipped-off piece of sidewalk." The young Dillard would then draw chalk-arrows on the cement, and write "SURPRISE AHEAD" for the next person contemplative enough to pay heed to a child's scribblings.

"But," Dillard later reflects, "who gets excited by a mere penny?"

It's an urgent question.

Canada just nixed the penny completely, and America may well follow. Pennies just don't make financial sense anymore: the little copper coins cost more to make than they're worth, and so—at least according to the economists—we're better off without them.

How long will it be until the nickel is obsolete? And the dime as well? Why not the dollar too?

"It is a dire poverty indeed," Dillard concludes, "when a man is so malnourished and fatigued that he won't stoop to pick up a penny. But if you cultivate a healthy poverty and simplicity, so that finding a penny will literally make your day, then, since the world is in fact planted in pennies, you have with your poverty bought a lifetime of days. It's that simple. What you see is what you get."[6]

Whoever has ears to hear, let them hear: *what you see is what you get.*

But we—sad fools—most of us are too asleep to see much of anything, so mummified in our slumber that we neither hear nor see much at all. We suffer from a dire poverty indeed, missing all the natural glory that surrounds us.

Richard Louv has coined a term for our condition: "nature deficit disorder."[7] He insists that the implications are substantial and worrisome. In his rather ominously titled book *Last Child in the Woods*, Louv explores the breadth and complex implications of our increasing separation from the natural world. The bottom line is this: some of our most prevalent and debilitating conditions—among them, ADHD, depression, schizophrenia, and a substantial number of additional ailments besides—may actually be in some way derived from the basic fact that we are spending less and less time in the presence of nature. The ailments named have all shown significant signs of improvement as a result of even relatively short amounts of time in nature.

Louv isn't saying anything new, of course. Haven't the wisest among us always known that a walk in the woods was good for the soul? Henry David Thoreau insisted on the "necessary tonic of wilderness,"[8] and Muir once wrote to a friend, "I am well again, I came to life in the cool winds and crystal waters of the mountains . . ."[9]

And it isn't just men who claim this either. Anne Frank believed in nature's healing abilities as well, noting some fifty years before the term *attention deficit disorder* even came into existence that "the best remedy for those who are afraid, lonely or unhappy is to go outside, somewhere where they can be quiet, alone with the heavens, nature and God. Because only then does one feel that all is as it should be and that God wishes to see people happy, amidst the simple beauty of nature. . . . I firmly believe that nature brings solace in all troubles."[10]

Having almost snored through one of the world's most extraordinary natural phenomena, I've been doing my best to take Louv and Dillard and Thoreau and Muir and Frank at their word by plunging as often as I can, wide-eyed and open-eared, into the wild.

Doing so has brought up an interesting question: What do we mean by *wild* or *wilderness* anyway?

Trying to track down a definition of wilderness is like following a snow leopard through a blizzard. What shall we say? Is wilderness only *untouched* land? A virgin forest, or a vast plane of barren tundra close to the Arctic Circle? If so, there isn't much wilderness left (if there's any), and it is accessible to very few. Or perhaps it is wild if it is relatively unmarred by humans? Deserts could therefore be wilderness, so long as the winds have sufficiently erased the trails of any nomadic peoples that still meander there. Or how about the other 70 percent of the earth's surface area? Does the middle of the Pacific Ocean count as wilderness? It could, if it weren't for the Great Pacific Trash Vortex that swirls between Alaska and Hawaii—definitely an indication of human blight.

Having once endured a hurricane on Long Island, the philosopher David Abram explores the question "what is the 'wild'?" in his book *The Spell of the Sensuous.* Without power, telecommunications, or even accessible roadways, the only option in the storm's aftermath was for people to take to the streets and walk, and encounter one another in all the newly discovered wilderness of their city:

> In the absence of automobiles and their loud engines, the rhythms of crickets and birdsong became clearly audible. Flocks were migrating south for winter, and many of us found ourselves simply listening, with new and childlike curiosity, to the ripples of song in the still-standing trees and the fields. And at night the sky was studded with stars! . . . For those few days and nights our town became a community aware of its place in an encompassing cosmos. Even our noses seemed to come awake, the fresh smells from the ocean somehow more vibrant and salty. The breakdown of our technologies had forced a return to our senses, and hence to the natural landscape in which those senses are so profoundly embedded.[11]

Given the proper conditions it seems wilderness can even be found on Long Island.

If it can be found there, perhaps the better question is—if we have ears to hear it and eyes to see it—where *can't* wilderness be found?

Perhaps that seems a little slippery to you—after all, if *wilderness* can be found just about anywhere, then it might not seem like a very useful word at all.

Here's the definition I'm working with when I say I'm seeking to plunge regularly into wilderness: Wilderness is any place that cracks open the illusion that we live and move and have our being in a purely human world. It is any place that punches through the smoggy horizons of efficiency and calculation and utility and gives our hearts a shove sufficient to make them float a little more lightly, even if they don't quite get airborne. It's any place where the constant pressure of *never enough* vanishes like the specter it is amid the overwhelming and fragile abundance of the world that surrounds us. We are in wilderness whenever we feel a sort of interconnectedness with and kinship to the nonhuman world, what Thomas Merton calls "a dimension of primordial familiarity which is simple and primitive and religious and poor."[12] When it suddenly makes crystalline sense why Saint Francis of Assisi sang of "brother sun and sister moon."[13]

But it took a hurricane to open the eyes and ears of Abram and his neighbors to the wilderness all around them.

Must we all await a hurricane to shake us from our stupor?

Perhaps there is a better way. Perhaps we'd better all become contemplatives just as soon as we can. If *what you see is what you get*, maybe becoming contemplatives is just the thing we must all do, for that is its meaning, after all: *Contemplari*: (Lat.) To gaze at attentively.

How we think about and relate to the world around us—philosophers and theologians use the fancy word *metanarrative* to describe this—is a lot like the lens on a camera: it affects, frames, and in fact *changes* everything that is viewed through it. The most common lens in use today depicts the world around us as a pile of natural "resources," raw material with which we as human beings may do whatever we want. The whole world is coal, fit for firing the furnaces of our ever-expanding economy.

That's one way to frame the world, and like any camera lens, it has both its advantages and disadvantages.

But not so very long ago the lens in most people's heads was quite different, and through *that* lens the world looked more like a nursery, more like a *womb*, in fact, specifically created by the divine for the well-being of human beings. And longer ago than that the world seemed like a garden, more beautiful and delightful and surprising than useful.

Looking through this sort of lens was easier as a boy.

One afternoon many years ago, feeling the approaching thunderstorm's siren song deep down in my gut, I threw open the front door of our house and lay down in the center of our street, face lifted toward the coming storm. My childhood cul-de-sac was quiet and serene, relatively traffic-free. As far as I was concerned, I'd just hit upon the best-in-class front-row seat for the spectacle unfolding in the summer sky above. As the epicenter of the storm approached, the interval between the flash and the accompanying boom diminished to instantaneous. Each bolt ripped across the sky, blinding me for an instant and leaving visual echoes etched on my retinas for long seconds afterward.

I'd counted close to thirty searing flashes before the heavens burst open and the rain began flooding down around me, bringing its sweet and gentle fragrance, mingled beautifully with the street's warmth. I laid there for quite a while, watching and listening and *feeling* the storm's life and vitality and presence as the rain fell and the air all around me danced with living fire.

Midway through the storm the front door of my house burst open.

"Michael!" my mother called.

"Yeah?" I shouted back as nonchalantly as I could from my dripping-wet front-row seat. Another flash. A quick boom.

"Come in here right now!" she shouted.

I couldn't tell if she was just worried or actually angry. I paused a moment, hoping for one last bolt before I responded.

"Do you hear me?" Definitely angry. "You're going to get struck by lightning!"

"Aww, Mom!" I said, slowly pushing myself up from the fragrant street. "Do I have to?"

"Yes!" She stamped her foot. "Get back in here right now!"

Just then a flash closer than all the rest—close enough to make my hair stand on end and leave the air smelling acrid and burnt—struck a nearby tree with a shock so loud it felt like I'd been punched in the sternum even as the windows of every house on the street chattered like loose teeth. Tree limbs thicker than my waist came tumbling down to the ground, but I didn't learn this until after the storm had passed, for at that moment I was sprinting—utterly breathless and yet utterly alive—back into the safety of my home.

It was a close call. And that's the point. That's exactly what I needed then, and what I need now, in fact, as I crawl on my belly toward the edge of the cliff, eager to survey the wilderness from my perch high up in it all. To the south a passenger ferry bound for the mainland slips out of view around an island, leaving me alone at this crossroads of earth and sky and sea. I am more than a hundred feet up, sitting on the thin shelf that will be my abode for the next twenty-four hours. I am here to listen and wait, to see if I can hear again the pulsing heart of the wilderness, hoping to discern something amid all this ripe expanse. Above me an airborne murder of crows reels and dives on the brisk wind, undoubtedly enjoying themselves, while the arbutus tree that has somehow found a toehold on this cliff spreads its green fingers out wide into the same delightful breeze. The waves crashing on the boulders below sound distant and almost artificial from this great height. The wind messengers the fragrant, briny spray straight up the side of the cliff, depositing it on my threshold, letting me taste the sea.

I breathe in a great breath, and then exhale and feel my soul stretch and groan the way I do when I've been sitting at my desk for too long, relieved and delighted to have been freed from the confines of requirement.

I am not needed here, not obligated to anything except joy and delight and life.

Suddenly a shadow moves beneath the surface of the sea, directly below my perch, and then a moment later, a plump adult seal emerges, sliding quick as a specter onto the sandstone boulders, then inch-worming along after the momentum has subsided. Then the seal stares back to the underwater world it has just departed, as though anticipating the arrival of another. This second shadow isn't far behind, though it is merely half the size of the first. It seems tentative, swimming quickly toward the other seal, but veering to the side at the last possible moment, circling round again. After several passes the first seal utters a sharp cry that—given how intently I'm contemplating what's happening—echoes up the canyon walls and startles me witless.

On the next pass the smaller seal—the pup—comes splashing out of the sea onto the rock beside its mother. It moves lithely, inching quickly along with obvious delight and enthusiasm. The pup snuggles up to its mother and then—anchoring its head against its mother's stomach—wriggles its bottom half around so that it is lying perpendicular, their two bodies forming a T atop the boulder.

The pup whimpers a little, nudges its mother's side, and after an all-too-human sigh, the mother obligingly rolls over onto her side and allows the pup to nurse.

I am baffled. Rocked. Blown over by an everyday hurricane.

"Of course they nurse," I say under my breath. "They're mammals." Every seal in the world has been likewise nursed. But the cognitive abstraction that seals are mammals, and that they therefore nurse their young, had in no way prepared me for the intimate beauty and quotidian glory of the wild scene unfolding below me.

I've heard that a human mother may experience some of the most transcendental moments of unity in the nursing of her child. Are such moments the exclusive territory of human beings? Lying there on my stomach, watching the mother seal sigh again in what I can only describe as obvious contentment, I am not so sure.

"Simple and primitive and religious and poor," writes Merton.

Yes. Exactly.

Speaking of uniquely human traits, don't ever let anyone tell you that human beings are the only creatures capable of *intending*. Or *delighting* for that matter. Just this morning I find myself plunged deep into an unexpected wilderness—right in my own backyard. A housemate set up a new bird bath a few weeks ago, but this particular raven has something else in mind besides mere washing up.

For the full half hour I sit there contemplating, this raven flies back and forth from its source, all the while carrying various pieces of food to soak and soften in the bird bath: stale bread, a few broken crackers, almonds. The almonds are what help me see that this is an *intended, planned* endeavor. Of this I have little doubt, for the raven *drops the almonds off first*, perceiving somehow that they need to soak the longest in order to soften. Only once there are three or four almonds in the birdbath does the raven change its fare, shuttling the more quickly softened bread and crackers to the bird bath, submerging each for several seconds beneath the surface before gobbling each in turn. The raven has to jump up and down several times on a particularly large piece of bread in order to get it to go under. Thirty seconds later, once the bread is adequately sodden, the raven hops back up onto the edge of the bird bath and devours the delicacy in three quick bites.

After five or six such rounds the raven dips its beak into the bath and extracts the soaked almonds, one at a time. After it has swallowed the last one, it caw-caw-caws loudly, flapping its wings and blinking its shiny, camera-shutter-fast eye.

Don't tell me it isn't relatively pleased with itself. It is possible to smile with a beak, you know. And smile it does.

I have to wonder: Why doesn't the raven just eat the food wherever it finds it, and avoid the additional effort, the extra wing-work, the delayed gratification of a more sumptuous, soaked meal? But then again, why don't I eat *my* food raw?

The answer: *preference.*

Last week I paid ten bucks at my favorite Middle Eastern restaurant for an appetizer of roasted almonds and flatbread drenched in olive oil.

The raven gets its fare for free.

Who got the better deal? Who was more delighted by the meal?

"We doused the burning bush," Dillard writes elsewhere. "And cannot rekindle it; we are lighting matches in vain under every green tree. Did the wind use to cry, and the hills shout forth praise? Now speech has perished from among the lifeless things of earth, and living things say very little to very few."[14]

I used to think it strange that Saint Francis preached to the birds and the animals and the trees. But I'm no longer convinced. Perhaps he was more contemplative than I have yet learned to be. Did he use a different lens? Or maybe he heard or saw something the rest of us are—lamentably—snoring through.

Is that why Saint Francis forswore shoes?

Had he seen the Sacred Bush of the world, burning all around?

It is nearing midnight as Danae and I depart our ridge-line cabin with two of our dear friends and begin flashlighting our way down the dark forest path toward the secluded cove. We've heard rumors of a rare and resplendent reality, an "algal bloom" of phytoplankton—the ocean's version of fireflies. These tiny phosphorescent, bioluminescent creatures light up the sea with teal fire and turn waves into ribbons of living blue. We're venturing out into the darkness to try to learn for ourselves if the rumors just might be true.

There are a few high-altitude clouds shining silver in the light from the three-quarter moon, and I can just see it through the silhouetted trees, descending toward the western horizon. A light breeze is blowing, still fragrant with the smell of sun-warmed forest floor and the rich fragrance of the sea. Always the delicious smell of the sea on this island.

As we emerge from the forest into the pebbly beach of the cove, I'm delighted to see that the moon is low enough to be completely hidden by the rocky outcropping along the cove's western edge. Darkness is necessary for the mystery and magic we're after tonight—the glow of the phytoplankton is a skittish thing, easily spooked and obscured by too much ambient light, too much "noise."

Despite the frigidity of the water I strip off my shoes and socks, roll up my jeans, and walk straight into the water, discovering instantly that the rumors are real. I let out a cry of delight, surprising the others who think that I've stepped on something sharp. But I hardly notice. I am waylaid by wonder, arrested by awe. All the world around me fades into background as the mystery I'm wading into engulfs me completely.

The phytoplankton are in full bloom, each step farther into the pitch-black water sending out a burst after blue-green burst of water-flame. I'm wading knee-deep through the liquid Milky Way, the heavens above reflected exponentially off the surface of the shimmering depths below. A small fish senses my footsteps and flees in a flash, leaving a comet-tail of glowing blue-green behind. This first fish spooks another, and then another, and the message flickers like lightning through the rest of the school, and all at once—BOOM!—the underwater fireworks begin as the whole school flees in a turbulent burst of light.

I gasp, overcome, embracing and embraced by the mystery of beauty far beyond my understanding, far beyond my deserts.

"What's wrong?" Jared asks. There is genuine concern in his voice.

"It's so beautiful," I say, searching for words and coming up short. "Glorious."

"What is?" Kelleigh asks, disbelief in her voice.

"This," I answer, spinning around, trailing my hands along the surface of the sea. Each fingertip leaves a glowing trail behind it. I write my name in the surface of the sea in a carefree, flowing cursive. "Can you believe it?"

There is a long silence from the shore.

"Are you sure the plankton are in bloom?" Danae says at last.

"What?" I cry, shocked by the question. "Of course they are." I leap and splash along the shore, proving my point. Skipping through the stars, the sea around me lighting up again, flashing forth in its subtle color.

But on the shore: only silence.

"I can't see anything," Kelleigh says.

Now the silence is mine. I have heard what she says, but I also see what I see.

Suddenly I understand. It's all a question of perspective. A question of distance. They can't see because they're too far away, standing there on the shore.

"Wade in and see for yourself," I plead. I keep on splashing, engulfed in but not consumed by the sea's fire.

I can hear them grumbling in disbelief from the shore as they peel off their shoes and socks and wade into the cold water.

"Ooh!" Kelleigh yells out as she enters.

"No way," Jared says as he, too, steps into the water, moving deeper and deeper.

"They *are* here!" Danae exclaims, splashing about.

I look over to where their voices are coming from, suddenly seeing for myself the cause of their earlier disbelief: I can't see anything but darkness. Their movements through the water don't produce any light at all, for I am too far away to see. I move closer to Danae as she scoops up a handful of sea, cupping it in her palms and swirling it a bit, panning for stars. Only once I'm close enough to hear her breathing do I actually see the light she cups in her hands.

"It's beautiful," she whispers.

I stoop low and scoop up my own palmful of liquid fire, a wide smile breaking across my face.

Thoreau was right, wasn't he? When he claimed that "the universe is wider than our view of it"?[15]

And deeper and higher and more mysterious as well.

"That it is," I say at last. "That it is indeed."

If you've ever had the chance to stand in the cavernous interior of one of the great European cathedrals, you might have noticed how much they *feel* like old-growth forests. All those enormous pillars skying up toward the heavens—just like the great girths of redwoods and cedars and Douglas fir—even as the arches of the stone ceilings branch and intertwine in static representation of their living inspirations.

With the right lens, cathedrals and wilderness both have the power to remind us—like bloodred strings tied around a finger—that we are now, and in fact always have been, on permanently holy ground. And more than that, that we and the whole world besides are rooted in, surrounded by, and upheld by a mystery and a love deeper and older and longer than we could possibly conceive. In such a place as this, at such a time as this, the only appropriate attitude is humble, reverent awe. And childlike joy at having been granted access into such a garden in the first place.

Quick! Take off your shoes!

And if you don't believe me, jump in and splash around a little. See if the whole thing doesn't flash out "like shining from shook foil,"[16] as Gerard Manley Hopkins puts it; see if it doesn't burn like one of Dillard's pennies blazing in the sun. Lie down in the rain, find your own perch on a cliff, swim out until your feet no longer touch the bottom.

Once you're there, hold it all close, and see if you can't catch a glimpse of the world rekindled, glowing there in the chalice of your open palms.

CHAPTER 14

Saunter On: The Practice of Pilgrimage

*It's a dangerous business, Frodo, going out your door. You
step into the Road, and if you don't keep your feet, there's
no knowing where you might be swept off to.*

—J. R. R. TOLKIEN[1]

Solvitur ambulando—It is solved by walking.

—SAINT AUGUSTINE[2]

*There is a day
when the road neither
comes nor goes, and the way
is not a way but a place*

—WENDELL BERRY[3]

Walking is the exact balance of spirit and humility.

—GARY SNYDER[4]

Saunter (v): to walk in a slow, relaxed manner, without hurry or effort.[5]

The smiling, white-haired woman halts my descent from Rivendell Retreat Centre with a brief chat. She has one of those kindly grandmotherish faces, and though I've seen her several times during the past few days of my retreat, we've not yet spoken. I'm on my way down to the prayer labyrinth; she's on her way up. Rivendell's labyrinth is an astonishing structure, built here on this mountaintop by volunteers years ago who were happy to engage in the backbreaking work required to replicate the labyrinth from Chartres Cathedral, half a world away.

After we introduce ourselves, she tilts her head toward the clearing where the labyrinth lies waiting. "Do you know the difference between a labyrinth and a maze?"

I stare blankly at her, combing my memory for an answer, but coming up empty. "I guess I thought they were the same thing," I say.

She shakes her head but doesn't lose her smile. "A maze has many false ways, many dead ends, many traps." She turns to look back at the Labyrinth, just visible through an opening in the trees. "A labyrinth, however, has only one course, leading toward the center, winding and illogical though it may seem."

A helpful distinction indeed.

I smile and nod at the revelatory gift Lady Wisdom has just bestowed upon me, but her generosity hasn't run its full course yet. "It's an apt metaphor for life, isn't it?" she continues. "Though it often seems like it's full of false ways, dead ends, and traps, I've come to believe this journey we find ourselves on is much more labyrinth than maze. Sooner or later, you'll find your way to the center."

She pats my arm and continues up the hill.

Saunter is a delightful word, isn't it? It has lodged itself deep in my mind, like a hot spoon into ice cream. My mind waters every time I hear it, in fact, and I am caught up in the montage it provides: I am wandering along a teal-colored Caribbean cove; or meandering, mouth hanging open in astonishment, through an old-growth forest with the trees skying upward all around me like pillars of some dusty cathedral;

or ambling through a field of golden wheat, fingertips lacing their way through the sun-warmed grain.

The word *saunter*, as Henry David Thoreau helpfully notes, probably arrived into English from the combination of two French words: *sainte* (holy) and *terre* (land).[6] Though some would disagree with him, if Thoreau is right, to *saunter* means to bless the land, or—if we flip the agency around—to move through land in a way that receives its intrinsic holiness for the blessing that it is.

If Thoreau is right, then it's more accurate to say that Moses *sauntered* toward the burning bush, isn't it?—that he moved slowly, reverently, "without hurry or effort," as he drew nigh to the Holy One.

What a gift that would have been: to walk on holy ground and *know* that the very dirt on which you stepped was holy.

Now there's an idea. Lace *that* up on your feet and see where it takes you.

After these months of my Sacred Year, there's a growing part of me that is wondering whether or not—as the psalmist put it, "The earth is the Lord's, and everything in it."[7]—*all* land might be holy? Maybe the reason we cordon off certain places and label them as holy is so that they'll serve as flags, hints, reminders that the whole wild world is holy, that time and space itself is infused with the presence of God. For if what the theologians say is true—that God is omnipresent—is there anywhere where God is not?

If all land is holy, does that mean we ought to saunter everywhere?

Maybe that's why Thích Nhất Hanh teaches that walking on water isn't the only kind of miraculous walking to be had: "walking peacefully on the Earth is the real miracle."[8]

I'm willing to bet this sage was out sauntering when this revelation came to him.

Undoubtedly you sense the obvious, if disquieting question emerging from all this: When was the last time I *sauntered* somewhere?

I cringe as you ask it, feeling that it's not exactly fair.

After all, very few of us saunter these days.

Who has the time? We're too caught up in the rush of just trying to *get there* that we don't have the presence or habit of mind to saunter, to go "in a slow, relaxed manner." Like a two-year-old screaming in the backseat, the little conductor in the engine room atop our shoulders is constantly checking the clock, tapping a foot, crying out, "Are we there yet?" We're so dead set on our destination, too frenetic to follow Moses' lead and turn left, too frenzied to notice the burning bush, too utilitarian to see ground as anything but a platform to be built upon or as raw material to be exploited for whatever the latest trend demands.

True.

The question "When was the last time you sauntered?" isn't at all fair—like asking a hippopotamus how high he can jump.

"But let's put *sauntering* on hold for a minute," you might offer, "and try an easier question: When was the last time you *walked* somewhere?"

Do I even remember?

"Sure," I'll respond, tongue in cheek and eyebrows raised. "Just this morning I walked all the way from my front door to my car."

But I know that's not what you're getting at. And besides, even counting all the walking we do en route to our cars, or from one conference room to another within our office buildings, or from one store to another down the long and brightly lit corridors of our shopping malls, the average American only walks a total of 1.4 miles *per week*!

This fact, as Bill Bryson points out, is utterly ridiculous.[9] Whether you thank God or evolution or both that you have two feet with which to explore the world instead of just a slippery stomach like a snake, surely you'd agree that the primary purpose of the human foot is *not* to press down on an accelerator.

You'd be surprised how far your feet will carry you if you're willing to give them half a chance, if you'd allow today's "course" or "flight" or "jaunt" or "errand" to broaden itself out wide enough to metamorphose from a meager, utilitarian noun into a multifaceted, kaleidoscopic verb. You'd find yourself carried over the river and through the woods straight to Lady Wisdom's house, but beyond that too. You could find yourself anywhere, in fact: high atop mountains, beside stormy seas, past foes both seen and unseen and—if you're more lucky than blind—perhaps alongside a few friends as well.

True, though you'd no longer be traveling at the speed of light nor of sound nor even of the internal combustion engine, you would instead be moving at the ho-hum, everyday-glorious speed of one foot in front of the other in front of the other, at—as one author beautifully words it—"the speed of life."[10]

To walk somewhere mindfully, contemplatively, is at least half the distance to *sauntering*, at least half the distance to allowing the process of moving between point A and B to *move you*, to *transform your soulscape* instead of merely shuffling your landscape a bit.

The last time I remember walking somewhere mindfully was a blustery day back on the isle of Iona, off the coast of Scotland. The clouds are so low and fast I wonder if I might have to duck to save my head from a close, wild one. And the sea breeze is more like a gale as it bowls over us, howling around the stonework of Iona, sounding otherworldly. Just to stay upright, we all—the other pilgrims and I—have to lean hard into the wind, trusting its ethereal substance to counteract our propensity for falling.

We take turns drafting as we make our way south, like cyclists in the Tour de France or geese, changing positions every ten minutes or so when the leader grows tired. I am surprised how much easier it is to follow someone else's lead in those conditions, stepping where they step, trusting that they know at least something about the way we are going.

This is a Tuesday, a "Pilgrimage Day" when, in all but the fiercest storms, the Iona community leads a group of fresh-off-the-ferry faithful on an eight-hour pilgrimage around the ancient isle. The group I find myself in is an interesting mix, a gangly cohort tossed up there by the sea from six different continents, more than a dozen countries, speaking at least four or five different native languages. A few are nearing octogenarian status, while others have just broken free of their teens.

Most of us are somewhere in between. We set off toward the south, the wind stepping it up a notch, testing our resolve to actually continue on the Pilgrim way.

Every so often we stop to pray through a litany together, to look back over the way we've come thus far, to look forward down the road at what might come. We stop at a crossroads (the only one on the whole isle, in fact) and there at the center, with a way stretching out before us and behind us, and to our left and our right, we are invited to think back over the many crossroads at which we've stood in life, sans map, sans compass, with only a dim sense of which way is the best way forward.

We recite old prayers as we go, short, windswept words for protection and guidance and hope. The prayers must be heard, for our Breath quickens as we go, the Wind blows on as we pray, wrapping itself around us, round and round, bringing to mind Father Solomon's instruction that "the Scriptures draw no hard lines between 'Wind' and 'Breath' and 'Spirit.'"

Eventually we make our way to the south end of the island to Saint Columba's Beach, the place where—about a millennia and a half ago— Saint Columba landed with twelve companions on this rocky, windswept keep at the edge of the known world. I stand on the beach in silence, picturing the thirteen of them: seasick and dripping, shaking with cold and fear as they tumbled out of their battered wooden boats, glad to be alive after the crossing, kissing the stony shore a hundred and one times, sauntering their way up out of the deep that had led them along the labyrinthine way.

I'm struck by how similar these two ways of living and moving and having our being are: *sauntering* and *pilgrimaging*. It seems to me that all *pilgrimaging* really means is *sauntering* in the hope of finding yourself on the Emmaus road, encountering the God who—if he exists at all—is more likely to be found *out there*, somewhere between where we have been and where we are going, with the whole jumbled mass of our questions and insecurities and hopes in tow, than in any sit-down static sort of tame religiosity. *Pilgrimaging* means living as though the journey itself is worthwhile, including the ups as well as the downs, the highs and the lows, and everything in between as well. *Pilgrimaging* means living as though there are not only experiences to be had but lessons to be learned, people to meet, and great goodness to embrace all along the way, such that Catherine of Siena's mystical musing that "all the way to heaven is heaven"[11] might just turn out to be truer than we could hope.

Christ did say, after all, "I am the Way."[12]

This means, of course, that, like sauntering, *pilgrimaging* isn't at all about efficiency. And frankly, in a world that rides so high atop the golden calf of efficiency, viewing it as the fastest way to the biggest bottom line, *pilgrimaging* is yet another potent antidote. For *pilgrimaging* is about the journey, the path, the way between here and there, between now and then. The idea isn't to *get* there. It's *to go*, and to be attentive to the process of transformation the way offers as we go. It's about what happens inside of us between the *now* and the *then*, between the *here* and the *there*.

It has been several months since Iona, since I pilgrimaged my way around that sacred isle with those other ardent seekers. Not all that long—I can still picture the view from the top of Dùn Ì when I close my eyes. Even so I know I need to pilgrimage again, to open my stony heart up to the journey instead of just bulleting everywhere all the time. That's where the idea arises to pilgrimage from my home in Vancouver out to the monastery where this whole Sacred Year first started. It's an easy enough drive—just about an hour, if you interpret the speed limits loosely.

But how long to pilgrimage there?

There's only one way to find out.

I throw a few books and some clothes in a backpack along with a little food, a camp stove, a water bottle, and some dry clothes, and head off toward the east.

Soon I realize how different these miles will be by foot instead of by tire—as substantial as the contrast between a physical place and a photograph of the same. Sure—all the photographs of Yosemite Valley *look like* Yosemite Valley. There's Half Dome, and there's *El Capitan*, and the white arch of Angel Veil Falls too. But if you've ever had the chance to be there, you know that no photograph can do the place justice.

I am fully present to each and every one of the 48.6 miles from my home to the monastery, seeing, hearing, smelling, touching, and tasting every moment in a way that makes me wonder how I could ever have driven through these miles in so unaffected a way. As the afternoon wears on I'm in my body in a visceral, poignant way, feeling each step in every one of the fifty-two bones in my feet.

Each vibrant detail along the way flutters like a bird in the net of my mind. Who would have known that highway ditches are like great caches, holding very interesting things among their ridges and valleys? I could reconstruct a whole life from the miscellany I encounter in the first half of the day. More than a full wardrobe: boxers, panties, bras, undershirts, shorts, sweaters and sweatshirts, shoes, even a couple of hats. Lots of socks too. (Why so many socks, I wonder?) Most of an apartment as well: TVs, CDs, a broken chair here, a window shade there, more than one lamp. There was a broken plate and a full complement of silverware. (The food was gone, though—what a happy roadside rodent that must have made!)

Lifetimes blinked by every few miles as well, the full list of memorials I encountered as long as a Sunday obituary page. I had no idea how many people have died along this highway. Roadside shrines of cracked and peeling crosses, faded photographs, and wilted flowers mark the places. Maybe it's the roadside shrines or the pain in my feet or the blast of wind each passing semi brings, but I'm painfully aware of my own vulnerability here on the side of the road. I'm wondering if I'd have time to jump into the cache of the ditch to avoid an absentminded driver when suddenly I hear the sound of an approaching engine accelerate in a way that seems odd—different from the other cars who have been monotonously careening past me on this bloody highway.

My eyes snap up and forward, locking onto the glinting windshield of a white van that is approaching at a sickening pace.

"Not to worry," I reassure myself. "He's just accelerating for the hill."

But then I catch sight of the driver—a young man with a dark beard and eyes wide open, staring directly at me with an eerie, wide-eyed intent. And that's when two strange things happen in the same moment. First, the man grins ominously, just as I watch him begin easing the steering wheel over, directing the white van into a direct collision course with me.

I suck in a quick breath, realizing that I'm playing an unintentional game of chicken with a van manned by someone who should be under lockdown in a psych ward.

At the last possible moment—just as I am preparing to hurl myself into the ditch—the driver lets out a deafening blast on his horn and veers back into his own lane with screeching tires and a silent, passing cackle.

⌘

Pilgrimaging includes risk. Fortunately, not everyone I meet along the way has it in for me. There are even a few saints, including a kind woman working behind the counter at a gas station.

"Why the big backpack?" she asks as I open the door. The cowbell on the door clangs loudly.

"Just some supplies," I say quickly, limping into the station. "Can I use the bathroom?"

But she doesn't answer. "Where are you going?"

"Mission," I answer. "Do I need a key?"

But she is persistent.

"Are you *walking* there?" Her penciled eyebrows peak in disbelief.

"Yup," I say, nodding.

She pops her gum several times, thinking this through.

"No," she finally answers.

"No what?" I ask, confused.

She points toward the back of the building. "No, you don't need a key."

I make my way past aisles of brightly branded high-fructose corn syrup to the bathroom.

When I emerge a couple of minutes later, the woman is wiping down the ninety-nine-cent coffee stand with a stained white rag.

"Let me get this straight," she says, putting a no-nonsense hand on her hip. "Did you say you're walking to *Mission?*" Her tone makes it sound as though I'm walking to New York City.

I nod.

"Why would *anybody* want to do that?"

I laugh, and catch a brief glimpse of myself in the door of a soft-drink cooler. "I don't know," I respond at last. "I know it would be a lot easier to drive or take the bus or the train to Mission, but . . ." I'm searching for words, now. Trying to bring into articulacy something I feel way down below the surface, but don't quite know how to say. "I feel like we learn something different depending on *how* we get where we're going, you know?"

Her eyebrows peak again, and I can tell I'm not making any sense.

"It's like what happened over there," I say, pointing now out the window back up the road, to a place I'd stopped a half hour earlier. "I stood there at that bend in the road for a full five minutes, watching two bald eagles playing—I mean it, they were *playing*—with one another, turning somersaults and loop-the-loops, 'tagging' each other with their wings, literally just exulting in their existence."

The woman nods a little, starting to see what I am getting at.

"And here's the thing," I continue. "Nobody else saw it. Just me. To everyone else those bald eagles weren't even there—obscured by the dome of their car's roof. Sure, they were going somewhere important: to jobs, to families, to obligations, I'm sure. But the joy and wonder of that one unique moment in all the history of the world—well—they could have seen it, too, if they hadn't been going so fast."

"And you saw it because you were walking," she says.

I nod.

"And now I know about it, too, because you were walking, and have the time to stop and talk with a woman in a gas station."

"Yeah," I agree, nodding again. "You're exactly right: I probably wouldn't have stopped here at all if I'd been driving. I would have just kept going, rushing on by. We would've never had this conversation."

We stand for a moment in silence, wondering at the strange,

labyrinthine way that has led us both to this unexpected conversation in a gas station.

"Do you want a cup of coffee or something?" she asks at last, breaking the silence. "It's on the house."

"Really?" I ask, surprised.

"Are you kidding?" she says with a laugh. "Anybody crazy enough to walk as far as you're walking needs all the help they can get."

Within ten minutes of my arrival at the monastery I've collapsed onto my bed in a heap of mud and wet clothes and tears. I'd gotten used to the mud and sodden clothes, as it had been raining pretty hard for the last three hours of walking. But the tears take me completely by surprise. It isn't just that my feet and legs and back and hips are aching so badly I can hardly move without groaning. The tears are flowing from the incredibly full feeling I have inside, like I've just feasted on extraordinary food without even knowing that I was famished.

According to just one of my frequent flyer accounts, I've flown almost three-quarters of a million miles, which, stacked end to end, means that I've circled the globe something like twenty-five times in about as many years.

But I can honestly say that those forty-six miles to the monastery are the most meaningful miles I've ever traversed. I don't mean that there was a single enormous, earth-shattering lesson in walking there. Instead I mean that I felt, experienced, that I *Selahed!* those miles more than any others I've traveled before.

Before I even realize what's happening, I'm out like a light.

The monastery's bells wrench me from my sleep hours later, reverberating through my guest room as though the bell were actually *inside* my room. I fumble for the light and glance at my watch.

It's 4:55 a.m., time for morning prayer, or *Lauds* as it's called. This is the first of the seven set times of prayer the *Rule of Saint Benedict* guides the monks to keep—the monastic rhythm I admire deeply, but mostly from afar. At this moment, I have a thing or two I'd like to say to the cheeky psalmist who penned the lines "rise early, before the sun is up."[13] Isn't there a counterbalance in the Proverbs? Something like "Whoever blesses his neighbor with a loud voice, rising early in the morning, will be counted as cursing."?[14]

Nevertheless, I stagger out of bed, peel off my still damp and muddy clothing, and hurriedly put on some fresh ones, wincing and sucking in jagged breaths at the pain in my legs.

Pilgrimaging means quite a bit more than just a walk in the park.

I limp from the guesthouse across the short sidewalk to the monastery church. As I pull open the heavy oak door, I'm surprised to find that the church is filled with a thick, inky darkness, punctuated here and there by small, warmly burning candles. In their faint light I find a seat amid all the empty pews in the dark and cavernous space. My heart lifts at the sound of the monks arriving, the soft sound of their habits rustling together like leaves stirred up by a quiet wind. Though I sit in the main section of the church while the monks gather in the nave, the church's natural acoustics are so perfectly designed that I can hear the monks rustling the pages of the day's lectionary from where I sit.

These same acoustics bring yet another flood of tears to my eyes as the monks begin their morning antiphons (sung responses), for the whole church resonates with a vibration that takes me instantly back to the Taizé service at Iona. I bow my head in joy, letting the sound of the prayers resound over me, around me, in me, through me. As the monks sing the set psalms, I can't help but be awestruck by the fact these same 150 prayers have guided and directed and comforted countless pilgrims down through the centuries, echoing and resounding and filling the darkness with light and hope.

What a gift to be met by them here and now, to let their poignancy and beauty and hope and longing grip me some three thousand years after they were originally composed.

What a gift, and what a mystery.

Lauds lasts an hour and a half, followed immediately by the morning Mass. And though I've had my eyes closed in deep listening for most of the prayer service, this pause between the two movements causes me to lift my head.

I'm shocked by the utter change that has overtaken the sanctuary.

As the monks sang the rain stopped outside, and dawn has made its way into the world. What was once the darkened church is now filled with a glorious, shocking light. But it's more than just light. It's color.

High above the ground, all along the eastern and southern walls of the church, the stained glass is seemingly singing with light, each tiny tile and panel radiant. I know in that moment that stained glass is *meant* to be seen after Lauds, as darkness passes away into the light in all its multifaceted, multispectrumed glory.

I sit there for a long while, overwhelmed by beauty, overtaken by longing, speechless and awestruck by the illumination that has just wrapped itself around me on this pilgrimage.

As I'm preparing to depart the monastery for the city a few hours later, Father Solomon meets me at the exit. We haven't had the chance to speak yet during my short stay here at the monastery, and I'm glad to see him.

"How was your pilgrimage here?" Father Solomon asks.

"Very good," I respond. "My legs ache, to be sure, but I've never been more grateful for any walk."

"I don't doubt that at all," Father Solomon says with wide eyes. "It's fascinating, isn't it? What happens when we slow down and attend to what's happening around us and within us? I find walking is a perfect practice to induce a spirit of contemplation."

I nod and ask something that's slowly been coming clear to me. "It takes a long time to learn to listen and to hear all that God is speaking to us, doesn't it?"

"Indeed it does," Father Solomon replies with a smile. "And that's what the spiritual life is all about—training us to intentionally watch and wait for all the ways God is at work in the world, all the ways God is at work in us, to bring us all into—as Jesus says—the *fullness* of life."

I nod, thinking back to the meandering miles that led me here. "As

I was pilgrimaging here, I couldn't help but notice what a microcosm of life pilgrimage can be: the journey begins with zeal and strength, you encounter both astonishing beauty and great difficulty along the way, you meet those who would do you well along with those who would do you harm, and you find yourself confronted by moments of both surprising difficulty as well as unanticipated joy."

Father Solomon nods, mulling over my words. "Life itself is a pilgrimage, I agree. And collaboration happens along the pilgrim way: we help one another as much as we're able, because we're all trying to find our way—trying to learn where we're going, what we're meant to be living for, whether there is any meaning in this thing we call life. Nobody can make it alone, but then again, no one is tasked with journeying alone."

"I'm thankful our pilgrim paths have crossed," I say. And I mean it.

"Me too." Father Solomon falls silent for a moment, a smile on his old face. "Peace to you on the journey, Michael," Father Solomon adds, extending his hand.

"Peace to you on yours, Father Solomon."

I've just sat down to a sticky table in a less-than-enchanting coffee shop to await the bus that will shuttle me back to the city. I'm nervously checking e-mail on my smartphone to see how far behind this three-day pilgrimage has gotten me.

I hardly notice at first when the man in a stained sweatshirt sits down at the table next to me.

But then he starts talking to me.

"Hard to believe how sunny it is all of a sudden, eh?" the man says. He is uncomfortably close to me at the adjacent table, definitely invading my space.

"Yup," I reply, doing my very best to make it obvious that I'm not at all interested in having a conversation right now. I bring my phone up closer to my face, hoping he'll catch the hint that I'm too busy to engage.

"After all that rain, the colors really pop, don't they?" the man continues, failing (or refusing) to take my hints. "Like they're punching you square in the retina."

This reference to the power of color catches my attention, especially after the experience I just had in the monastery. I look directly at him and suddenly notice that he's had a hard life. He is unwashed and unkempt, there's a large scar on the right side of his face, and his right eye is so crossed it looks like he was speaking from experience—someone probably *had* punched him square in the retina.

The man sighs, a sound billowing with loneliness. He takes a long swig of his coffee and looks back at me with one eye.

"What are you working on?" He nods at my phone.

"Nothing important," I say, putting it down. "I'm Michael." I offer a hand.

He shakes it vigorously, awkwardly, sloshing his coffee. "Virgil," he responds.

"What's your story, Virgil?" I ask, leaning back in my chair. "Are you from around here?"

"No," Virgil says, taking another swig. "From back east. Out here visiting my daughter and grandkids."

We talk a while about his family, and he laughs as any grandfather might at how quickly the grandkids are growing.

"Do you often visit them?" I ask.

"Every now and then," Virgil answers. "It's easier now that my sister's dead."

"Huh," I say, surprised. "What do you mean?"

"Well, my sister and I, well—" Virgil sucks in a quick breath. "We were the best of friends, you see. There were eight of us. I'm the baby in the family, and my sister—the one who just died—she was the one right ahead of me. She looked after me, you know, when we were kids. And so I've looked after her for the past few years, after she got sick and all." His lip begins to quiver as he says this. Virgil takes another pull on his coffee, and coughs, trying to cover the tears. I can feel the loneliness and the sorrow radiating from him like a cold heat.

"And after what happened last month—well—I'm the last one left."

"Virgil," I say, searching for words, "I'm so very sorry to hear that."

"Anyway," Virgil continues, changing the subject, "I was a bus driver for most of my life. That and a snowplower. It's important to keep the roads clear, you know."

He sips again on his coffee, obviously trying to keep his thoughts moving in a particular direction.

"Very important indeed," I agree, nodding.

"Yeah, I've been helping people get where they need to go for more years than I can count," Virgil says solemnly. "I hope at least some of them found what they were looking for."

He sighs again, the exhalation whistling through his missing teeth.

"I'm sure they did, Virgil," I say.

"Yes sir," he goes on, with a nod and a half smile. "Now that my sister is dead and my wife too—she died a couple of years ago, you know—now I can go wherever I want. No obligations, nobody to answer to, no ties holding me back. Autonomy—that's the word for it, isn't it? Total freedom? I went on a cruise last month, and next week I'm off to Mexico for a little while, and then, hopefully I'll make my way over to Europe after that."

I try my best to stitch together the great tapestry of things Virgil is saying, trying to imagine the cross-eyed widower Virgil, mai tai in hand, sitting in Cozumel or snapping photos of the Eiffel tower. I begin to share his ache.

"All of that sounds incredible," I say. But my tone is more a question than a statement.

"Nah." Virgil shakes his head. "All that mobility and autonomy and lack of restraint is crap. Complete crap. I should know. I've sought it most of my life and now that I've actually got it, it's not at all what it's cracked up to be."

Tears well up in his crisscrossed eyes and begin coursing down his wrinkled old face, disappearing in a forest of stubble.

"No?"

Virgil shakes his head. "I'd forgo autonomy in a heartbeat if it meant I had a hand to hold. My wife's. My sister's. Even my older brother's would do. It's what hell must be like, being all alone and totally free."

This sends me reeling, and the silence stretches out between us like taffy.

"I'm sorry," Virgil says at last with a meek smile. "I normally don't unload on people like that. I just—well, you know. Some days are harder than others. I just needed someone to listen for a while, I guess."

"Not a problem, Virgil. You don't need to apologize at all. I uh . . ." I'm stumbling now, searching for words.

Virgil stands and nods. With a deep breath he looks at me out of his one good eye. "Peace to you on your journey, Michael."

Without another word Virgil spins on a heel, walks out the door, and vanishes.

Two of my friends—Matt and Nancy—have a practice of late-night walks through a labyrinth someone painted long ago in our church's parking lot. I find this practice both beautiful and poignant. About an hour or so after the sun sets, they meet there in that parking lot, light several candles at the labyrinth's center, and begin again the slow, methodical saunter toward the light. It helps them reframe their days, helps remind them that as winding and circuitous as their life may seem, they are slowly, by God's grace, being drawn along the way.

Feeling lost and adrift myself one night, I text Matt to see if I might join them at the parking lot.

"Of course," comes the reply.

An hour and a half later Matt and Nancy and I are all sauntering the labyrinth together, pilgrims silently praying, listening, finding our way along.

Lady Wisdom's words come back to me as I feel the parking lot grow thin: "Sooner or later—by God's grace—you'll find yourself at the center."

Where, thanks be to God—the Light shines still.

SECTION III

Depth with Others

CHAPTER 15

Requisite Thunder:
The Practice of Gratitude

Gratitude follows grace like thunder lightning.

—Karl Barth[1]

Whoever is not thankful for little will neither be thankful for much.

—Estonian proverb[2]

*Reflect upon your present blessings—of which every man has many—
not on your past misfortunes, of which all men have some.*

—Charles Dickens[3]

As a child I would spend long and luxurious weeks on my grand-parents' small farm in rural Pennsylvania. My grandfather's love for Coca-Cola had long before earned him the nickname "Coke," and my grandmother had for so long been called "Eye" ("The Great Eye sees all," Grandpa Coke warned me gravely after a failed attempt at swiping a cookie from the jar) that I was shocked to learn that her actual name was Irene.

The farm belonging to Grandpa Coke and the Eye was a small two-acre plot, a wedding present from the Eye's parents on which the two of them had managed to eke out an existence for more than five decades. Grandpa Coke had built the house himself, brick by brick, joist by joist, working late into the night after pulling double shifts at a nearby steel mill. My father remembers the wintry night when the family took up hasty residence in the unfinished house after a falling out with the Eye's parents. My father was five years old. Grandpa Coke and the Eye and the kids—my own dad and his younger brother and sister—all huddled together in the sparse living room before the unfinished hearth, keeping the bitter cold at bay with a few inadequate blankets and a feeble fire.

Though old age had slowed them both some, the Grandpa Coke and the Eye of my memories were resilient and strong as any first-generation Americans had to be. Having gradually converted their two-acre plot into the rather productive Stony Hill Nursery, they supplemented their social security payments by selling burlapped trees and shrubs or black-plastic-potted azalea plants made known to the world by the hand-painted sign on the side of the road.

Then there were the Eye's famous dried-flower bouquets. She'd sell ten dollars' worth of flowers for twenty dollars each and had women from the surrounding counties flocking to Stony Hill Nursery on their friends' recommendations. I cracked the door to a spare bedroom one afternoon and found I could just barely squeeze into the humid fragrance of the room: countless drying lines running from wall to wall and from floor to ceiling held little bunches of subtle-smelling strawflowers upside down as they dried.

It was a modest but pleasant life for two people who knew first-hand what it meant to tighten their belts through not only the Great Depression but also the Second World War; a tiny slice of paradise for two people who'd managed to raise three children on a steelworker's salary and whatever odd jobs the Eye was able to find.

I stumbled out of bed one childhood summer morning and tiptoed down the steep wooden stairs to a kitchen full of the fine smells of a farmhouse breakfast: bacon, eggs, cheddar cheese, and cornmeal pancakes. But there was another fragrance in the air that I didn't quite recognize, something basic and underlying, present and strong and seemingly foreign.

"Morning, sweetie," the Eye said, giving me a rough peck on the cheek. The scent of her white soap mingled with cigarette smoke would stay with me for hours. "Go on and sit down next to Coke. Your breakfast will be ready soon."

"Hello, Michael," Grandpa Coke said, surreptitiously removing a metal flask from beside his coffee cup as I slid myself up onto the chair next to him. "How's Michael?"

"Sleepy," I answered through a mighty yawn.

"Sleepy?" Grandpa Coke said in mock surprise. "Here, have some coffee." With a wry grin he slid his cup across the table toward me.

"Coke!" the Eye bellowed from the stove. "Don't you dare."

"Aww, Eye," Grandpa Coke replied. "I wasn't going to let him have much." Grandpa Coke winked at me and smiled, pulling the lukewarm coffee back toward himself.

"Here you are, sweetie." Grandma Eye smiled as she brought three steaming plates over from the stove. She put them on the table before us and sat down next to Coke.

"Thank you, Grandma."

But my face fell as I looked down at the plate—it wasn't at all what I was expecting. Instead of scrambled eggs and crispy bacon, slain there on the center of my plate was a misshapen pile of yellow goo. Coke and the Eye both had the same thing on their own plates.

I looked back at the Eye, questions slugging through my sleepy mind. "Grandma, what's *that*?"

"It's gratitude," the Eye said. "Served up hot and fresh. The very best kind."

"It looks gross."

"Hey now," Grandpa Coke spoke up. "I grew this here cabbage in my own garden, right back over there. Don't you go startin' your day with an insult."

"It's cabbage?" I said, eyes widening even more. I shook my head and made a face. "I don't like cabbage."

"Now Michael," the Eye said, gripping my smooth, young hand between her calloused palms. "We start our Saturday breakfasts with cabbage as a reminder."

"A reminder of what?"

In that moment Grandma Eye and Grandpa Coke shared a look that I am only just now beginning to parse: a look of poverty endured and of hunger braved, a look grown out of a life that—while perhaps not everything they'd hoped for in the radiance of their young love—was by no means a defeat.

"It is a reminder of how much we have to be grateful for," the Eye said, still looking at her husband.

"I don't understand," I said, forking the goop around on my plate.

"It's a reminder of the great abundance we have," Grandpa Coke added, turning to face me directly. "Did you know, Michael, that there was a time when all we had to eat was cabbage?" Coke looked at me with a pained expression on his stubbly face, and swallowed hard. "Cabbage for breakfast, cabbage for lunch, cabbage for dinner. Nothing but cabbage, cabbage, and more cabbage. Now we have much more than that. Eggs and bacon and cheese. But we still eat a little cabbage every Saturday as a memento—as a reminder so that we never forget how little we once had and how great an abundance we have been entrusted with now."

"Are we still having eggs and bacon?" I said, glancing sideways at the stove.

"Of course we are," Grandma Eye said, quickly wiping her cheek. She squeezed my hand one more time before picking up her own fork. "Right after we finish our cabbage."

If ever it sank into my childhood brain at all, I think I wrote off my grandparents' cabbage-eating habits as a throwback to a bygone era, an era when people didn't have enough to eat and which—thanks be to God—I didn't have to worry about anymore. And most of us—if we have the spare funds to buy a book like *The Sacred Year*—probably aren't forced to subsist on cabbage for breakfast, cabbage for lunch, cabbage for dinner.

In our post-cabbage, "developed" and "dog-eat-dog" world, gratitude ranks quite low on a list of desirable characteristics, behind more profitable qualities like IQ, creativity, education, and the like. You know what I mean: qualities that will "help us get ahead" in this rat race we've created are the things many of us feel like we need. Amid the daily grind of modern life, stopping to be thankful for what we have already been given can in fact start to seem like a sure way to "fall behind," to "lose the edge."

"Why keep sprinting if there's nothing driving you to acquire more?" I ask Matthew, one of my closest friends, over a cup of coffee.

"Perhaps living a life infused with gratitude is how some people are able to work for the love of it, rather than out of the addiction for more money, more power, more prestige. By being grateful for what they already have, they aren't obsessed with working tooth-and-nail for more."

"I'm not sure about that," another friend says when I explore this idea with him. "Gratitude sort of feels like retirement to me. You know, something that would be nice to experience *someday*, but not something that belongs in this season of life. Maybe once I make a million, finally get my promotion, put my kids through college. Then I can afford to take time to be thankful."

I share this sentiment in many ways, but I'm also longing to know what it means to work for the love of something rather than out of the addiction to more money, more power, more prestige in the world. And besides, what if what Annie Dillard says is true—that "how we spend our days is, of course, how we spend our lives"?[4] Could it be that learning to cultivate gratitude now—today, in fact—might actually move me toward what could be called a grateful life?

And what if the opposite is true?

Might stanching the flow of gratitude as it bubbles up within us so callous our hearts and minds that we become incapable of being grateful later on? We've all met those great geriatric grumps, the men and women whose sour faces are picture-perfect reflections of their inner states, for whom the sun is too bright and the rain not wet enough.

∽

A recent study published in the *Journal of Personality and Social Psychology* highlights the marked effects a regular practice of intentional gratitude can have. Despite its less-than-inspiring title, "Counting Blessings Versus Burdens: An Experimental Investigation of Gratitude and Subjective Well-Being in Daily Life," the results of the study are fascinating. The study went like this: Three randomly selected groups of people were established. Group A was asked to spend time reflecting daily on things for which they were grateful. Things like *the beauty of the sun reflecting off the lake, kind word from a coworker, progress on an important life goal,* and so forth. Group B was asked to record a daily "objective" report of what they'd done during the day: *went to the store, went to work, made dinner,* and so forth. Group C was asked to record the negative or frustrating things that had happened to them during the day: *that idiot who cut me off, the stack of unending bills, the fight with a family member.*

Now, one thing you have to understand about academic-types. Academics have this thing about causation. While they are perfectly comfortable asserting correlation (i.e., A and B occur together) they very rarely feel confident enough about something to assert a *causal* relationship between two things (i.e., A *causes* B). If ever you hear a researcher asserting a causal relationship between two things, you must keep in mind that only a fool would go so far out on a limb unless they were *very* certain that the data they were looking at warranted such a conclusion. It is the academic equivalent of a Hail-Mary pass from the ten-yard line to a wide receiver who has three defenders on him. If it works (proves true) you'll be counted a hero. But if not—well—it's the kind of thing you can do only so many times before you're handed a pink slip.

The authors of this article believe that the intentional practice of gratitude *causes* substantial positive psychological and social change. So much so they're willing to say:

> People in the gratitude condition experienced higher levels of positive affect during the 13-day period, and it appears plausible that this effect on positive affect generally was due to the intervention's effect on gratitude per se. They were also more likely to report having helped someone

with a personal problem or offered emotional support to another, suggesting prosocial motivation as a consequence of the gratitude induction.[5]

Don't you just love academics?

Let me try to parse all that jargon. What they're basically saying is relatively simple and straightforward: practicing gratitude not only makes people feel better within and about their life, it also makes them *more willing to act kindly toward others*. Participants who recorded the things for which they were grateful not only had a higher "positive affect" rating about their life but also were more inclined to help someone else, offer emotional support, listen to someone else's problems, and the like. And through the careful construction of the research, the researchers believe they've identified a *causal* link between the practice of intentional gratitude and being a more contented, helpful, amicable person. Put simply, "the ability to notice, appreciate and savor the elements of one's life has been viewed as a crucial determinant of well-being."[6]

My practice of the Daily Examen has been going steady for months now, but rather than just mentally noting things for which I am grateful during the Examen, I've decided to apply the results from the study in the *Journal of Personality and Social Psychology* and ratchet it up a notch. This means converting a portion of my journal into a "catalog of gratitude" and taking the time to make a daily record of the things for which I am grateful. While it was challenging at first to be specific, to actually bring things for which I am grateful into concrete detail rather than just trying to summon a general feeling of goodwill and "thankfulness," I became more adept at it over time. And, while practicing certainly helped, so did the kernel of folk-wisdom advising me to "consider your life *without* the good things you enjoy," a perspective that intensified the light of gratitude on never-before-considered aspects of my life.

The effect of this actual listing of things for which I am grateful begins to have an almost immediate effect, for it shifts my consciousness in a surprising way. Instead of merely having to think *back* over the day at the day's end, I start noticing things *during* the day, *as* they are happening.

"This will end up on the list," I catch myself saying after a friend's letter arrives. "And this too," after a particularly delightful walk on a snowy day.

Perhaps that's the way the practice of daily gratitude works—almost as a kind of reverse "bucket list." It's not a hankering of things that might happen someday, but instead a hundred thunderous bloodred threads tied around our fingers, all of them reminding us in real time of the good things we've already been given.

With use, gratitude unfurls in our lives, spreading out through our days like a great net, grabbing hold of ever more moments as we learn how to hold them close, until at last something insignificant as the radiant gradient of a single autumn leaf or the fleeting patchwork of the season's first frost on a car window is enough to bring tears of thanks at the unearned grandeur of this life.

But after learning to feel and practice gratitude, to notice it during my daily, waking hours and then record the various moments at the end of the day, I stumble across a startling quote from William Arthur Ward warning that "feeling gratitude and not expressing it is like wrapping a present and not giving it."[7]

Through the lens of gratitude I discover I have shelves full of thanks tucked away in my mental warehouse, all boxed up and tidied, parcels large and small alike, though most all of them are unsent. And what's more, while many of the things for which I am thankful are intangibles—the way the sunlight bounced its way through the forest, the smell of freshly baking bread on a day of fasting or wood smoke on a snowy wind—a vast portion of the gratitude I feel is because of particular people. People I have known and have been privileged to live my life alongside, people whom I have loved and cherished and who have—whether they knew it or not—had a substantial and shaping impact on me.

So I decide to try delivering one of these "parcels of gratitude" and unfortunately fall flat on my face.

It happens as I am trying to put into words the gratitude I feel for two dear and wonderful people, a husband and wife who are well in their "third act" of life and whose presence, wisdom, and availability have had a hugely shaping effect on nearly all aspects of my life.

Midway through our time together I start voicing the long list of things for which I am thankful to them, when the wife leaps up from the couch and cuts me off mid-sentence.

"Wait!" she yells out with a sharp wave of her hand. "Stop right there. You don't know the *half* of it. We're all too human, you know. All too human indeed."

And then—under the pretense of needing to go check on something in the kitchen—she literally walks right out of the room.

I glance at her husband, whose face is wearing a bemused smile. "She doesn't do well with gratitude," he says by way of explanation.

"Who does?" I reply, feeling a bit foolish for not realizing this earlier.

"You might consider putting it in a letter to her," he suggests. "While she'll wave you off face to face, she'll absolutely read a letter."

"Would an e-mail work?" I ask, realizing instantly how off-base an idea this is.

"Well . . . ," he says slowly.

"Never mind," I add quickly. "Of course an e-mail doesn't work. It isn't the right medium for expressing something as important as gratitude, is it?"

"E-mail would be better than silence," he says, though his tone is halfhearted. "But maybe there's a better form. Something physical and tangible, something that can be held on to, tucked away in a drawer and remembered later on. I'm convinced that physical things are far better at communicating emotion and intent than is the mere arrangement of pixels on a screen. It puts a bit more weight behind the thing, a bit more permanence. With an e-mail, all it takes is a click and that arrangement of pixels vanishes altogether."

"Huh," I say, bemused. "I've never thought about that before. If it's true what they say that 'the medium is the message . . .'" I let my voice trail off.

"Then the format with which one communicates something is very important indeed," he continues, finishing my thought for me. "It saddens me that your generation will never experience the joy of a hand-written correspondence, sealed with a wax stamp and sent through the physical post. There is something utterly delightful about receiving a *real* letter from someone far away. E-mail just can't quite accomplish that."

"You've sown an idea in me," I say with genuine excitement.

"Have I?" The old man's eyes light up. "Good. Come up with a new word for it, something unique and specific, so you'll know exactly what you're doing." The man furrows his brows a moment, then snaps his fingers. "How about *gratigraphs*? From the Latin root for *gratitude* and the Greek root for *writing*?"

"Oh, I like that," I say. "I like that very much. I'll put all that I was trying to say a moment ago into a *gratigraph* and send to you both."

"We'll be on the lookout for it," he says with a smile.

In many of the First Nations (Native Canadian) cultures on the north-western coasts of British Columbia, there are two distinct ways of saying "thank you." The first is similar to the generic English word *thanks* and appears in common, everyday speech.

The second way of expressing gratitude communicates something much deeper, much stronger, much more substantial than a half-mumbled "thanks." As one First Nations woman explained it, "This second way of saying thank you is accompanied by a specific posture." She raised both hands high, palms up and outstretched toward the heavens, demonstrating evident openness, receptivity, praise. "This second expression carries unrivaled force in my culture. It means *I honor you, for you have changed me. I am a different person because I have known you. I will live from now on in this new way you have opened for me, and I am deeply grateful to you for having changed me thus.*"

It is with this in mind that I set about the most formal aspect of the spiritual practice of gratitude: the writing of thirty *gratigraphs* to specific people who've illuminated the decades I've lived. Although each of the people to whom I decide to write has had a unique impact on my life, not all of them were equally substantial. Some of the impacts were quite large, while others were relatively small. But each of the recipients of a *gratigraph* seems to me to be deserving not just of my *felt* gratitude, but of my *expressed* gratitude as well. And for a few recipients, I try my best to express the posture I'd learned from the First Nation's woman: both arms lifted high with palms open in gratitude.

I begin with the woman (and her husband) who had walked out of the room as I'd tried to thank them for the impact they'd had on me. Then I work my way out from there, carefully combing my decades for people to whom I might send a *gratigraph*.

I write a *gratigraph* to my fourth-grade teacher, a couple of old pastors, several dear friends with whom I've had the chance to journey for a while, a neighbor who has been exceptionally kind to people I love. I write a letter to a family we used to live next to, and to the genius of a man who created the graduate school I attended.

I notice something interesting as I write: thanking people becomes addictive.

It's such an easy way to make someone's day or—dare I say it—even someone's year.

Think about it: How long does it take to write a letter to someone? Fifteen minutes on average? Even if you really go for it and spend an hour bringing into articulacy the way someone has really affected you, isn't it worth it?

Why haven't I been mailing out *gratigraphs* all along?

Two people write back almost immediately, handwritten responses revealing that my simple note of gratitude brought each of them to tears. One pastor says that he is in a particularly discouraging season in his church, and that my note encouraged him to keep on. A seventy-year-old bear of a man who mentored me through an especially difficult period in life tells me that my letter is one of the most sacred things he's ever received.

I even send a *gratigraph* to a used washing machine salesman named Willie.

Deriving from the practice of simplicity, Danae and I recently bought a used washing machine. This was not an easy decision. Especially with big-ticket purchases like this, I'm more than a little worried about getting ripped off and ending up with a three-hundred-pound piece of scrap metal sitting in my garage.

When I wandered into Jana's Used Appliances I was comforted by the fact that the multicolored banner above the warehouse door declared "Celebrating 30 Years!" Jana's husband managed the shop, and he came strolling up to me with an outstretched hand as soon as I'd entered the building.

"Name's Willie Jewel," the man said with a wide smile.

The name was a perfect fit. Willie Jewel was a barrel-bodied man of about sixty-five who had on a Tim McGraw T-shirt, a gold necklace, and a faded green tattoo on one forearm. His leather boots and cowboy hat matched his bowlegged stroll perfectly, and the strength of his southern accent endeared me to him instantly.

"Yessir," Willie said a few minutes later as we stood in front of an old Maytag. "Maytag is one of the best names on the market. They build 'em to last and they jes' keep on lasting. You won't be disappointed with this 'ere piece of equipment. I guarantee it."

Despite his bowlegs and arthritic back, Willie Jewel even helped me lift the Maytag into the back of my car and gave me the rope I needed to keep the back hatch from flying open while I drove. I felt I'd gotten not only a washer but an almost-friend out of the deal.

So you can imagine how deep the gut-punch went when I got home and discovered that this particular Maytag wasn't lasting at all. The cold water worked fine, but the hot water didn't flow at all. Not even a trickle. Nadda. Zilch. Zero. Ask it to fill with hot water and the thing just sat there like it was taking a nap.

I came screeching back into Jana's parking lot red in the face, feeling my neck veins pop out a little as my blood pressure spiked.

"Willie Jewel!" I shouted, kicking open my car door. "I want my money back. All of it. You guaranteed me Maytags were built to last, you said you'd inspected this thing *yourself*, and I haven't even had it for an hour yet and the stupid thing doesn't work!"

"Now, now," Willie Jewel said bowlegging his way to the back of my car. "Let me take a look at it and see what's the matter with it."

"I trusted you, Willie Jewel," I almost shouted. "You made me feel *good* about buying this lousy piece of scrap metal off you, but now I know the truth. I want my money back."

"Now look here, young man," Willie Jewel said tilting his cowboy hat down just enough to sharpen his blue eyes into razors beneath it. "Just settle your horses a minute and let me get 'Bessie' into my shop and have a look. I ain't been in business for thirty years by ripping people off. If it's broken I'll fix it. And if I can't fix it you can have your money back, okay? Just trust me."

And do you know what?

Willie Jewel fix that old Maytag, and the thing is *still* washing.

More than that, he *quadruple* the thirty-day parts-and-labor warranty on it as well. In so doing Willie Jewel restore a bit of my faith in humanity. Not everybody is out to make a few hundred bucks off a soapy piece of scrap metal.

So I write Willie Jewel a *gratigraph*, drop it in the mail, and almost forget about it entirely.

"Are you the man who wrote me this thank-you letter?" the southern accent asks when I pick up the phone. There was no "good morning" on Willie Jewel's part this time. No chitchat.

"Is this Willie Jewel?" I inquire after a moment's pause.

"Are you the one who wrote me this thank-you letter?"

Definitely Willie Jewel. He's the only southerner I'd written.

"Yes sir, I am," I answer. "You treated me well and fair, and in today's world that's a rare thing indeed. I owed you a thank-you."

"I took your letter home and showed it to my wife, Jana," Willie Jewel says. "Would you believe it brought tears to her eyes?"

There is a long pause, and I hear Willie Jewel draw in a deep breath before he starts speaking again. "Makes a man feel good to be thanked every now and again. Even an old bowlegged appliance salesman like me."

"Well, Willie Jewel," I say. "I meant every word."

❦

Saint Ignatius of Loyola—the founder of the Jesuits—has a thing or two to say about gratitude. The saint suggests that not only should gratitude be a defining characteristic of our lives, but that in forgetting to be grateful we open ourselves up to a whole host of malicious paths. He writes:

> It seems to me, in light of the divine Goodness, though others may think differently, that ingratitude is one of the things most worthy of detestation before our Creator and Lord. . . . For it is a failure to recognize the good things, the graces, and the gifts received. As such, it is the cause, beginning, and origin of *all evils and sins.* On the contrary, recognition and gratitude for the good things and gifts received is greatly loved and esteemed both in heaven and on earth.[8]

Just in case you missed that, in Ignatius's mind ingratitude is "the cause, beginning, and origin of *all evils and sins.*" It doesn't really get any stronger than that.

Given Ignatius's dire warning, the scholarly evidence presented in the *Journal of Personality and Social Psychology,* and the reciprocal letters I keep receiving in the mail from people to whom I've sent a *gratigraph,* I think I'm going to head to the store and buy myself a head of cabbage, holding both hands up high as I go.

CHAPTER 16

All for It: The Practice of Protest

Even the King may not override the immutable, unwritten laws of heaven.

—SOPHOCLES (ANTIGONE)[1]

Unjust laws exist: shall we be content to obey them,
or shall we endeavor to amend them?

—HENRY DAVID THOREAU[2]

We should never forget that everything Hitler did was legal.

—MARTIN LUTHER KING JR.[3]

Tucked back into a corner of what used to be a major religious epi-center—Saint Paul's Cathedral—in the heart of one of the most important cities in the world—London, England—there is a 150-year-old painting by William Holman Hunt called *The Light of the World.* It stopped me in my tracks early one morning as I entered the empty cathedral to attend an all but abandoned prayer service.

In the painting it is night—the background is thick with darkness. A few stars are visible, but otherwise the sky is just deep and empty space: *nihilo,* nothingness. A larger-than-life Jesus stands outside a slammed-shut door, the seal of which is conclusive and absolute as a tomb's. The door-way is overgrown by vines and thistles, and though there is no handle on the outside of the door, the Light of the World is knock-knock-knocking on the door, waiting—patiently and serenely—for the long-awaited day when the spell of death and darkness will at last be broken and the door flung open.

A passage from the book of Revelation has been etched in stone beneath the painting: "Behold, I stand at the door, and knock: if any man hear my voice, and open the door, I will come in to him, and will sup with him, and he with me."[4]

In Jesus' other hand the Light of the World holds a lamp that—despite the night's darkness—burns brightly, heralding the coming day. And despite all the chaos of the darkness, dawn is itself evident behind the Christ; just there, in fact—a hint on the distant horizon.

Standing in front of the painting one can't help but see that the moment the door opens will of course be the very same moment the sun finally breaks free from the horizon, when the seemingly endless night will at long last give way to day.

"Do you know why there isn't enough affordable housing in this city?" The well-dressed man walking hand-in-hand with his young daughter has stopped at the crosswalk where I've been standing for the past hour, handing out pamphlets. There are four or five of us stationed at every corner of this rainy Vancouver intersection on a Saturday morning. We've done our best to make our protest obvious—flying signs and banners, handing out flyers, inviting others to participate. All of this is aimed at decrying the deplorable lack of affordable housing in one of the most difficult-to-afford cities in the world. Most people just scurry past my outstretched pamphlets without making eye contact, or stare with mock interest at the concrete two feet in front of their feet, pretending they don't know I'm there. Every now and then somebody points an umbrella at me like a shield, warding me off like any old storm.

The pedestrian who just posed this sharp question is an exception to the indifferent norm. He's staring me straight in the eyes, letting his question hang in the air, just like his cologne. Struggling to figure out how to respond, I know that I only have about thirty seconds before the stoplight changes and the man and his daughter are gone.

"There are lots of reasons why there isn't enough affordable housing in Vancouver," I say. The man's daughter peers up at me from a safe distance, tightening her tiny fingers around her father's.

What I've said is true, of course: every city is complex and multifaceted, and we should resist simplistic solutions to complicated problems. But I'm willing to bet this man's question is more rhetorical than literal. And besides—some people (especially the "Type A" personalities) ask questions not because they care what your answer is, but because they think you should care what their answer is.

I have a feeling that is what's happening now, but I decide to play along. "Why do *you* think there isn't enough affordable housing?"

The man smirks. "Because there aren't enough people planting car bombs in front of the banks and developers' offices."

My mouth falls open, and I laugh nervously, wondering if he's really an anarchist or if he's slyly trying to see if I am. The crosswalk shifts from the solid red hand to the forward-moving white man. People swirl around us, but the guy stays rooted in front of me. Maybe it's because I've had only a limited amount of caffeine that morning, but my thoughts are tripping over themselves like toddlers.

"Do you mean that?" I ask at last.

"I'm dead serious," the man says impatiently. "If you want to get someone's attention, you have to *get* their attention."

All I can do is stare in open-mouthed astonishment at this expensive-smelling man.

The crosswalk starts blinking red again.

"You're right that we need to get people's attention," I say at last, my words finally coming to me. "But isn't there a better, less destructive way than car bombs?"

"Maybe." He shrugs, looking up at the buildings around us. "But do you know how much money we're talking about here?" He stares me hard in the face again, ignoring his daughter's impatient tugs.

"Lots," I say.

"Yeah," he says sardonically, unblinkingly. "*Lots and lots.* If I knock down a low-income housing unit and build a high-end condominium complex, I personally will bank hundreds of thousands. Every single time. Why on earth wouldn't I want to do that?"

"You're a developer?" I ask, surprised.

The streetlight turns red; the people now move perpendicularly.

The man gives a half-smile and nods. "Hundreds of thousands on the small ones, maybe a million on the big ones. And over the next few decades this city will make millions, too, in taxes and the additional income that high-end real estate attracts."

"Doesn't that value dollars over people?" I ask, finally straightening out my thoughts enough to form a coherent question. "Shouldn't a city be affordable for all of its inhabitants?"

The man shrugs again. "So what if a few useless bums are forced to move on?"

"But doesn't that seem wrong to you?" I stammer. "Or at least unkind?"

"Who cares about kindness?" the man scoffs. "It's about survival, right? Call it capitalism or economic Darwinism or whatever you want. It's all the same: the strong eat the weak."

I'm speechless now, as two moral frameworks collide like armies in the battleground of my mind.

The man shrugs. "Hey, don't get me wrong. I don't like it any more than you do. I used to *be* you. I'd take to the streets for my ideals, used to believe there was something worth fighting for." The man grimaces, as though what he is about to say is painful. "But sooner or later you'll grow up and realize that Profit is the only god this world worships."

He leans in close for emphasis, engulfing me in the incense of his cologne. "And all gods demand sacrifice."

The traffic light cycles again from red to green, and the bright-eyed, forward-moving white man lights up. A horn honks, and tires screech.

"Daddy, come on!" The man's daughter is hauling on his hand now, trying desperately to get him to cross the street.

"Car bombs," the man says as he steps off the curb. "You have to *force* me to listen if you want me to change."

They disappear into the crowd.

Nearly three centuries ago, philosopher and statesman Edmund Burke allegedly warned that "the only thing necessary for evil to prevail is for good people to do nothing."[5] In a similar strain Henri Nouwen wrote not that long ago that:

> You are Christian only so long as you look forward to a new world, so long as you constantly pose critical questions to the society you live in, so long as you emphasize the need of conversion both for yourself and for the world, so long as you in no way let yourself become established in a situation of seeming calm, so long as you stay unsatisfied with the status quo and keep saying that a new world is yet to come. You are Christian only when you believe that you have a role to play in the realization of this new kingdom, and when you urge everyone you meet with holy unrest to make haste so that the promise might soon be fulfilled. So long as you live as a Christian you keep looking for a new order, a new structure, a new life.[6]

Unfortunately, far too many of those who would agree with sentiments like Burke's and Nouwen's take their conviction and "holy unrest" as a license to multiply violence, to heap bodies upon bodies, to pour out blood upon blood. Thus a well-dressed developer in Vancouver suggests that car bombs might be the most expedient way to effect change, and politicians around the world suggest that ever "smarter," more expensive weaponry will at last perfect our conquest against evil and usher in a world that is "safe."

On the one hand, violence does sometimes seem like an appropriate course, doesn't it? How will things change unless we *make* them change? If the strong eat the weak, mustn't we make ourselves stronger? Lest we be eaten?

But on the other hand, what are we to make of Jesus' warning to Peter in the Garden of Gethsemane that "all who take the sword will perish by the sword"?[7] And not only that, what about Jesus' refusal to call to arms those "legions of angels"[8] that could have been summoned to his defense against the death and torture that lay before him? Utilitarian arguments abound: If ever there was a moment for Jesus to utilize force, wouldn't that have been it? Surely it was "justifiable" to defend himself, or at very least his hapless disciples? Wouldn't it have been better to continue his ministry? To keep healing people, keep spreading the good news?

Don't get me wrong. I'm *not* proposing we adopt the all-too-common caricature of pacifism: the fingers-in-the-ears, head-in-the-sand, pretend-like-everything's-okay impotence. Instead, I'm suggesting that it is precisely here that the voices of luminaries like Martin Luther King Jr. or Dorothy Day or Mahatma Gandhi have so much to teach us about the so-called "third way" between blind indifference and coercive bloodshed.

Each of these individuals sought to learn from and follow Jesus' example: they believed that the world needed to change, but they also believed that change could only be found through a different—albeit hidden and difficult—way, an alternative to mere brute force. This is why Martin Luther King Jr. wrote from the Birmingham jail,

> Returning hate for hate multiples hate, adding deeper darkness to a night already devoid of stars. Darkness cannot drive out darkness; only light can do that. Hate cannot drive out hate; only love can do that. Hate multiplies hate, violence multiplies violence, and toughness multiplies toughness in a descending spiral of destruction.[9]

It's why Gandhi warned that "mankind has to get out of violence only through non-violence. Hatred can be overcome only by love. Counter-hatred only increases the surface as well as the depth of hatred."[10] And why Dorothy Day prayed, "Prince of Peace, Christ our King, Christ our Brother, Christ the Son of Man, have mercy on us and give us the courage to suffer."[11]

The spiritual practice of protest, I've been learning, is a potent way of engaging and practicing this "third way," of living into the seemingly irresolvable tension between the world's brokenness and Jesus' refusal to use force to bring about the Kingdom of God.

Protest is a rare and fascinating word, one of those oddities in the English language whose meaning has literally spun around 180 degrees during its lifetime, so that now it means *exactly opposite* what it originally meant.

Like most people, I once thought *protest* basically meant "to be against." The word brought to mind hippie-looking people with unkempt hair, dancing outside a nuclear arms base or an oil pipeline, clad in hemp sweaters and Birkenstocks.

Frankly, this kind of protest wasn't of much interest to me. But then a friend pointed out how the word *protest* is the offspring of two parent words: *pro* meaning "toward" and *test*, which is the same root that *testify*, *testimony*, and *testament* all come from.

The point: the original meaning of *protest* is "to testify *toward* something"—not against.

Perhaps this is a small distinction, but I have found this shift, this reorientation of the *why* propelling my actions to be of an importance as simple and extraordinary as the dawn: just a little bit of a shift and the difference is substantial as day and night.

Picture Yazid.

Just a boy, fifteen years old and fatherless, scaling rugged mountains in the shadowlands between Iran and Iraq. It is night, and Yazid is alone and cold and hungry. His clothes are torn and ragged, his feet bloody from the strain of the endless miles he has run. He has been running—always running—for more than a month now, fleeing the brutally oppressive Iranian government.

He flees because he has hope. Hope that perhaps tomorrow will be better than today, hope that perhaps there is a land in which he might live freely, hope that there just might be a place out there worthy of the elusive word *home.*

But this night is a crossroads for Yazid, and now everything will begin to be different.

As Yazid rounds a bend in the moonlit road, a man with an automatic weapon steps out from behind a dark boulder. What happens next happens fast. Shouts. Fists. More and more guns, their barrels flashing like cold daggers in the deadly moonlight. Now Yazid is on his knees. Now on his face. Now choking on dust, chewing on gravel.

His hands are bound, and all goes black.

The next weeks are hell.

Captive, Yazid is beaten, tortured, and given only just enough food and water to keep him more or less alive. This is all "part of the program." When his captors are satisfied that he has been sufficiently "initiated" into the brotherhood, he is given a bit more food and allowed to become a slave, doing whatever they command him to do.

Yazid is now considered a member of the People's Mujahedin of Iran, or Mujahedin-e-Khalq, aka the "MEK," a group of resistance fighters living in the mountains of Iraq, committed to fighting to the death against the oppressive Iranian regime Yazid fled in the first place.

There is only one problem with Yazid's association with the MEK: according to the revolving database on a government computer half a world away, Yazid will now forever be identified as a member of a terrorist organization.

Fast-forward through two years of a slave's day-to-day life. Yazid is seventeen years old at the beginning of the first Gulf War, and soon after the United States' invasion of Iraq, Yazid finds a moment to break free of the MEK's stronghold and flees under a white flag to the US troops for help.

Yazid is but a boy. He needs protection, he needs medical attention, he needs refuge, he needs help. When the soldiers hear his story, they immediately refer him to the United Nations High Commissioner for Refugees (UNHCR) officials where he is granted Convention Refugee Status by the highest-ranking intergovernmental authority in the world.

But this does not matter much to the immigration officials in every country Yazid bounces through over the next decade. They see his documented history, his "association" with the MEK, and conclude his backstory is tarnished. He "belonged" to a terrorist organization. Never mind that he was forced at gunpoint to join. Never mind that they tortured him. Never mind that he was their slave. Never mind that he fled them as soon as the opportunity presented itself.

Never mind.

Fast-forward again. December 1, 2012, is a cold and stormy day in Vancouver.

The snow begins falling around 11:00 a.m., the clouds smothering the land even as they tear across it.

And it is cold.

Very, very cold.

A man with dark skin and red scars on his back grits broken teeth as he walks toward the bridge, pulling a faded jacket tight about his shoulders. Despite its height, it does not take long to reach the bridge's deserted apex, for he has been running—always running—for a long time now, searching for refuge, searching for a place worthy of the name *home*. The man's heart is pounding as he heaves himself up onto the railing.

To be or not to be? It is a simple question, with such massive ramifications.

His heart says yes, but his mind—his mind is weary from the long, long struggle, weary of the mountains of impossible paperwork, the muscled border guards with crossed arms and faces of stone.

The man catches sight of a single snowflake amid the storm, watches it bouncing along for a moment.

But then it is gone, vanished amid the one hundred billion other singular gifts.

A car has stopped behind him, honking its horn. Someone is shouting.

But Yazid can't make out the words above the roar the darkness below him makes.

Ever so slowly, Yazid leans forward, forward, out into the darkness.

And is swallowed by the storm.

℘

"Shame!" the black-haired woman bellows through angry tears. "Shame on government!" She is a friend of Yazid's, an Iranian herself, whose grief and rage have today compelled her not to weep in private but instead to take to the streets and cry out for a world that has not yet arrived. A world in which the most vulnerable are not driven to suicide but rather given the refuge they desperately seek. The poster of lament that hangs from her neck was made with care: Yazid's photo, his full name. Both his birthday and death day are there as well.

"No refugee should suicide," she screams in broken, poignant English. "Shame on government!"

We are a gangly group, only fifty or so, walking through the indifferent city this frigid Tuesday afternoon. Someone has a megaphone and together we chant as we walk: "*JUST-ICE FOR REF-U-GEES. JUST-ICE FOR REF-U-GEES.*" We have put our kids in daycare or called in sick or taken an extended lunch break in order to block traffic, in order to lament Yazid and the system that made his life a living hell, in order to protest.

It's surprising how many other Vancouverites are hostile and impatient as we exercise our rights to gather in public, march, and hope for a better world. Surprising but understandable: we are blocking traffic, clogging streets, interrupting their smoothly running days as we hope for a world that welcomes and protects the most vulnerable instead of slamming the door in their faces. Horns blare and people hang out of their car windows, making obscene gestures and shouting colorful phrases.

The goal of our meager march is the government office that coordinated and ultimately denied Yazid's continued refugee claims: the Immigration and Refugee Board at the Canadian Border Security Agency. This is the most obvious place to go, but perhaps not the best. After all, democratically elected government is really just the institutionalization of the majority's will. So perhaps we should instead be knocking on every citizen's front door with our posters and our chants, waving the photographs of Yazid and the tears of the wailing women, trying our best to thaw hearts of stone into hearts of flesh, doing whatever we can to diffuse the culture of hate and xenophobia directed at nearly all "people from away."

"Innocent until proven guilty," would be a good basis to start from.

So, too, would be "welcome until proven otherwise."

This is a long road, a lengthy pilgrimage indeed, given all the best-selling, fear-mongering pundits. Given our hyperphobic culture.

So we distill our protest and our passion and our hope into this symbolic act and arrive at a tall, brick-faced building with mirror-finish windows that bring to mind the interrogation chamber in which Yazid spent many hours being questioned by nameless, indifferent agents. Despite his Convention Refugee Status, Yazid's claim for refugee protection in this country was rejected again and again by the government on the basis of his unwilling association-at-gunpoint with the MEK.

"A tragic turn of events just occurred," a fellow protestor tells me as we walk.

"Oh?" I ask, wondering what could be worse than a refugee-claimant's suicide in his country of refuge.

"Just last month, the MEK was removed from the terrorist watch list. Yazid would probably have been granted permanent refugee status."

I gasp at this news, feel the tears stinging my eyes.

"He was so close," the woman says.

We crowd into the foyer of the government offices, carrying our signs and posters and placards high. The room is small and sparse. Before we're all inside the room is full, so the rest crowd outside the double doors and press their faces up against the windows. We've taken the uniformed security officers completely by surprise. Over our chants for *"JUST-ICE FOR REF-U-GEES"* they are frantically trying to regain control, hurriedly punching buttons on the grey, government-issued telephone, requesting backup from this department and from that one as well. Desk drawers open and close, and one of the guards finds what he is looking for—a yellow roll of CAUTION tape. He stands up and attaches the roll to one of the walls and then tries to herd all of us into a corner so that we don't obstruct the walkway from the elevators, but there are too many of us for the security guards to corral. Someone tears the CAUTION tape in two, and we keep on chanting.

A new person takes hold of the megaphone and suggests that we sing a song as a symbol of unity and peace. He is an old man, wrinkled and greyed, but there is a fire in his eyes as his amplified voice fills the foyer.

"It's an old song," he explains. "Sung by those who were crying out for civil rights back in the '60s in the United States as *they* marched, demanding that their government change. It's an appropriate song for us to adopt today, and a simple one too. Sing along once you know it."

And then his voice—a low baritone—fills the foyer with a deep, solid resonance. As the rest of us join in singing "We Shall Overcome," the windows of the foyer and even the very foundations of the building itself begin to shake with the sound of our voices, the sound of our protest.

Despite the cold and the dark clouds, the streets are packed with people from rainy-grey wall to rainy-grey wall. Most (but not all) are women; most (but not all) are of indigenous origin. People are holding signs and posters, potent memorials bearing witness with photographs and nicknames—"Raven," "Queenie," "Jay-Jay"—to the lost-but-not-forgotten.

I catch sight of a poster for a girl named Mary whose death day is just one day after her sixteenth birthday, the same year I was born. A woman—Mary's daughter? Mary's sister?—is here today, nearly thirty years later, remembering Mary. The ink on Mary's poster is running in black streaks, mirroring the mascara marking her memorialist's face.

The woman finds a friend in the crowd, calls out to her.

They embrace. Hold on tight. Weep.

From somewhere in the center of the crowd a drum begins, deep and powerful as a heartbeat—*boom! ba-boom! ba-boom! ba-boom!*

It is February 14—Valentine's Day.

And instead of worrying about dinner reservations or what they're going to wear tonight, or where to find the last available box of chocolates, a thousands-strong crowd has gathered in one of the most dangerous and difficult parts of Vancouver to march in remembrance of the lost and murdered women of the Downtown Eastside.

Of the hundreds of women who have disappeared from this part of Vancouver, many (most?) have vanished without even an official police inquiry or really much public notice at all. These are the people for whom there are no milk carton campaigns, no Amber Alerts, no missing posters placed in every thinkable location. These are the doubly lost: the ones whom—in the eyes of the "respectable public"—no one will miss.

I am protesting again today, believing that a different world is necessary and indeed possible, a world where the weak and the vulnerable are not disregarded but instead treated with a unique and particular honor. The crowd I've joined is one of the largest I've ever been a part of. We have real energy, real vitality today, despite the cold, despite the storm that threatens overhead. That said, I do feel a little out of place right now, for in so many obvious ways, I stand on the side of the guilty: I am white, I am male, I am young, I am strong.

All I can hope to do is learn more about what it means to be a "white ally," a "male ally," a "young ally," but of course these are not easy questions—my kind's past has so often been bloody and cruel.

Suddenly a beautiful, pungent white smoke reaches me, and instantly I'm caught up in the visceral, subconscious euphoria of the smell, transported to the local Anglican church's confessional where I have been going at regular intervals during this Sacred Year.

"What is that?" I wonder aloud, turning toward the source of the smoke.

A wise old First Nations woman is just a few steps away, holding up a burning clump of herbs. She has braided hair and braided crow's-feet tiptoeing around her old eyes. She looks at me with a kind but piercing gaze.

"It's white sage," she says. "Our people believe it has cleansing, purifying qualities. And there is so much in this city, so much in our world, that is not yet as it should be. I had to bring it with me today on this protest. As a symbol. As prayer. Crying out for Creator to cleanse us from all our faults and failings. Crying out for Creator to make us whole."

I nod, and swallow hard. *Yes*, I think to myself. *Yes, that's it precisely.*

"Cleanse me, *Atsoo*?"[12] says a young man emerging from the crowd, now standing in front of the wise old woman.

"Of course," she replies. She raises the smoking white sage up and—starting at the man's head—anoints his shoulders with the smoke, then his hands, then his hips, then his feet, until he is wreathed in white. She speaks as she anoints him. "The Creator is before you and behind you, on your right and on your left, within and without you.

"Turn around," she continues. She follows the same pattern again, moving from head to toe, bathing him clean in the white smoke.

"Now," she says once she's finished, "walk in peace."

"Thank you," the young man says, turning to look at her. He places both hands together at the bottom of his chin in a posture of prayer, bowing in gratitude for the gift of cleansing that he has received.

"Cast your whole vote," Henry David Thoreau advises, "not a strip of paper merely, but your whole influence."[13]

True, protest is not the most "efficient" way to bring about change. But then again, whoever said efficiency was the main goal? After all, car bombs, smart bombs, and atom bombs are all "efficient" ways of coercing people into conformity.

But it is worth noting, isn't it? Jesus' complete indifference toward the apparent "inefficiency" of the cross?

The rhythm of the drum beat quickens, sounding strangely like a knock-knock-knocking on a mighty, long-shut door: *boom! boom! boom! boom! boom!*

There, in the middle of the thousands-strong crowd, I reach into my pocket, grab hold of the hazelnut, and lift it up toward the sky in an open palm. A snowflake lands next to it, small and insignificant, melting in a moment. Another falls beside me, then another, and another. The fragrance of the white sage is everywhere, embracing us all, as the old woman cleanses another penitent: "The Creator is before you and behind you, on your right and on your left, within and without you. Walk in peace."

Like a rising tide, the crowd around me begins to sway and then—all at once—we begin walking through the cold, indifferent city, protesting toward a world that is yet to come.

As we make our way I can't shake the feeling that the dawn of a new day is coming, just there, in fact: evident behind the Light of the World, a hint on the distant horizon.

CHAPTER 17

Unto Others #1: The Practice of Pursuing Justice

Seek justice. Love mercy. Walk humbly.

—MICAH 6:8 (PARAPHRASE)

If you love peace, then hate injustice, hate tyranny, hate greed—but hate these things in yourself, not in another.

—THOMAS MERTON[1]

Jesus heals our hearts through the gift of the Spirit, and then he calls us in turn to work toward the creation of communities of love; a church of compassion, more committed to living in solidarity with others, particularly with the poor; and a society where people struggle to bring peace and justice.

—JEAN VANIER[2]

Rats and roaches live by competition under the law of supply and demand; it is the privilege of human beings to live under the laws of justice and mercy.

—WENDELL BERRY[3]

Aware of the depth of suffering in the world,
we can vow not to live superficially.

—THÍCH NHÂT HANH[4]

I am in northwestern Uganda, about an hour's drive and then a quarter-day's walk outside of Liratown. Danae and I are here for a month, living in our backpacking tent in two villages called Otongo and Otellenyor. We're on a research trip of sorts, trying to learn more about the ramifications of unsafe water on the lives of families and children in this part of the world.

From the start the hospitality and welcome we've received from the village members has been astonishing. Beyond energetic waves and broad smiles, food is the foremost indication of their welcome toward us. As we make our way around the landscape taking notes, interviewing families and trying to wrap our minds around the fact that more than a *billion* people don't have access to safe water, people are always stuffing eggs or mangos into our pockets as tokens of their welcome. Every evening we are invited to join members of the village under the Bell Tree to enjoy a simple yet abundant meal of cassava dipped in boiled greens that have been "mingled" with tahini. We sit up late under the multiplying stars, faces lit by firelight. Talking, telling stories, laughing.

One especially hot afternoon a village leader named John Ludy invites us to walk with him.

"I want to show you something," John says.

Our repeated questions and attempts to discover what it is that John will show us are only met with his quiet, sober face. "You will see," John answers.

We are reluctant to leave the shade of the Bell Tree in the heat of the afternoon, but something in his tone suggests a gravity we shouldn't ignore.

So we follow John out from beneath the shade of the Bell Tree toward the northwest, tracing our way along well-worn footpaths as we go. We walk and we walk and we walk. It is beyond hot—literally: the last threshold on my keychain thermometer is 110 degrees Fahrenheit, and when I stop to check it the thin red column has surpassed it and reached the end of the line. Have you ever experienced *heat* goose bumps before? I didn't know it was possible, but here I am, walking beneath an unthinkable sun, feeling my skin prickle with gooseflesh even as my shirt darkens with sweat.

"We are very close," John says, pointing ahead of him. "Just beside those boulders there."

A few hundred yards ahead of us there is a small heap of greyish boulders, rising up from the otherwise flat plain, stacked in a pile as though an absentminded giant had passed this way not long ago.

The footpath gives way to a rutted road, the indentations of heavy trucks evident and surprising given the distance from the nearest town. Another five minutes and we reach a desolate clearing in the center of the boulders.

The reality of what John has brought us to see crushes down upon us with more weight than the heat.

"Oh no," is all I can think to say. It's all I can do to keep from weeping, or from screaming.

Five people are at work there amidst the boulders, beneath the brutal sun: a father, a mother, and three children of descending ages. A long and heavy chain binds them all, attached to each person at the calf by a leg iron.

The father and mother take turns with the sledge hammer, swinging it against the largest of the boulders, shattering it slowly into smaller-sized rocks. The parent who isn't currently swinging the sledge picks up the rocks and carries them to a pile stacked in front of the eldest son, who is swinging a carpenter's hammer, cracking the rocks into smaller, baseball-sized stones. The two smaller children work with two rocks each, crushing the smallest stones into quarter-sized pieces of gravel.

In a semicircle around the family there are chest-high heaps of each grade of stone, four-foot records of countless hours of human misery and suffering, here beneath the savage sun. "Oh no," I say again, feeling my words crack and fail utterly before such a scene.

Our presence hasn't disrupted them one bit: the family continues swinging their hammers and stones, the rhythm of their work jackhammering into my consciousness the awful truth of what injustice does: make life intolerable.

"Do you see?" John asks from beside me. "When I said that I want justice for my people, this is just one thing to which I speak. People should not be forced to live like this."

"Why are they here?" I ask. "Who has done this?"

"They owe money," John says. "To the man who owns this gravel pit. They have been here for two years. One day, perhaps, they will be free. But then there will be another debtor to come and work in this place, another family forced into this kind of life."

"Why don't you stop it?" I turn to face John. "Can't you do anything about it?"

But John just sighs and shakes his head, and turns his palms up toward the slavish sun in resignation. "He is a very rich man. Very powerful. In my language we call him a 'wide one.' What can I do?"

"A wide one?"

John nods. "Wide ones are not easily moved. Many people must push them if they are to stand aside and make room for others."

John steps toward the mother and the father and motions for us to join him. "Let me introduce you," he says. "They have names, though the wide one does not care to know them."

Justice is a rare and precious thing—a pearl of great price—hard won wherever it is found. Great gains have been made in certain respects, but whenever I open my eyes and really start looking around, it's clear that justice is *far* from universal in our world.

The popularity of the word *justice* these days doesn't help much either. Countless campaigns advocating for "justice" spring into existence every year, and some—even the strongest supporter of the *idea* of justice must admit—are really a way of pimping the notion of "justice" as an avenue to profit or prestige.

Why do I say that?

Telecommunications companies have a significant stake in whether or not Internet access is considered to be a fundamental human right, whether it's a "justice issue." Pop stars are followed around by hoards of paparazzi as they "fight for justice in the world" by adopting children or making high-budget films that pose as documentaries. Warring politicians claim that *their* policies are "just" while their opponents' are (obviously!) not. And, so the story goes, if *they* get elected, we might have a chance at a more just world, but if their opponent is victorious—well then so, too, shall injustice and oppression be.

Back at the monastery, I'm sitting in Father Solomon's office, trying to find some ground on which to stand amid all the conflict-of-interest ridden "justice washing" that goes on in our world.

"What does *justice* even mean?" I ask. "Justice on *whose* terms? My terms? God's terms? The politician's terms? The law of the land? And if we mean a particular land's laws, which land are we talking about? The United States? The United Nations? Iran? Ancient Rome?"

Father Solomon nods as he listens to my questions, and thinks for several moments before responding. "You're right to point out the differences between these competing versions of justice. One of my favorite philosophers puts the question this way: 'Whose justice, which rationality?'" Father Solomon smiles, and pauses before continuing.

"But mustn't we—if we choose to adopt the title *Christian*—mustn't we seek to make our first allegiance to the justice found in God's Kingdom, rather than the law of the land in which we live? And I know that's a complex idea in our world today, and oftentimes the words *God's Kingdom* have been used as a justification for horrific injustice. But in my life I've found a stronger, more abiding sense of what justice must mean by looking to the theologians than to the politicians."

"That's interesting," I say, mulling on Father Solomon's words. "So many people talk about politics as though their politician is God's politician. That the policies of their candidate are directly in line with God's own. The thinking becomes, if we just get the right candidate in office, or just pass this particular law, or repeal that particular bill, then everything will sort itself out and we will have arrived at a just and perfect society."

Father Solomon shakes his head. "I don't want you to think I'm diminishing the importance of political engagement. Struggling for a more just society—just in the broader sense that its laws align with the laws of heaven—is very important. But the pursuit of justice is a long and complex struggle. Pretending like a particular candidate can be the solution to all our problems is foolish at best and idolatrous at worst, especially when we think about the overwhelming power of lobbyists and the mass-media marketing machines on *both* sides of the political spectrum."

"It's a mess," I say, hearing the confusion in my own voice. "What does it even mean to 'seek justice' in our world today? What does it mean to work toward the kind of justice that the Kingdom of God entails?"

"A good question," Father Solomon admits. "Certainly it will mean advocacy on a broad level. Working with others, calling the politicians who are in power, signing petitions, and making your voice and opinions heard. But from the theological perspective, I think justice means something much more than that as well."

"How so?"

Father Solomon pauses, pulls on his beard, and looks at me under raised eyebrows.

"Are you familiar with the Henry David Thoreau quote: 'If I devote myself to other pursuits and contemplations, I must first see, at least, that I do not pursue them sitting upon another man's shoulders. I must get off him first, that he may pursue his contemplations too'?"[5]

I let Thoreau's words roll around in my mind for a few seconds, feeling their impact.

"So justice means not sitting upon another's shoulders?" I ask.

The old man nods. "To be human is to be interdependent—no one is an island. But to be a *just* human is to be rightly related to all others. So yes: I would say that justice in its fullest sense prevents us from being parasites. Justice precludes us from making our way in the world at the expense of another's well-being, at the cost of another's blood."

"But what about economic Darwinism and survival of the fittest and all that?" I ask. "Doesn't that apply to our world today? Isn't that justification for those who have power to use it for their own benefit?"

"Blaming victims for the violence perpetrated against them is one of the clearest signs of pathological violence," Father Solomon says bluntly. "It has occurred in every period of history, just as it occurs in ours as well. But all that gets relativized if Jesus is *the* Dominus, *the* Lord. For if Jesus is the model of what dominion is meant to look like, the power structures are turned upside down, and the fitter you are, the more you are called to be like the God-Man who is 'servant of all.'[6] Power, dominion is *not* a warrant to parasitize and tyrannize everyone and everything around us for selfish gain. It is *not* permission to survive whatever the cost and thrive on the destruction of whatever stands in our way. It is *not* permission to slash and burn forests, to send countless species into extinction, to rape the land and the poor for our own short-term gain and mindlessly induce the suffering of tens of millions of people for our own profit. And until we realize that the invitation to *dominion* found in our Holy Text is a call to self-sacrificial service, I fear that suffering and death will only continue to multiply in our world."

I've never seen Father Solomon lose his cool before. But now his breath is coming in short gasps and his eyes snap back and forth between me and the monastery's orchard.

"I'm sorry. I didn't mean to upset you," I say, searching for words.

Father Solomon waves his hand, silencing my apology. "There's no need to apologize, Michael," he assures me. "If there is anything worth getting upset about in our world, it is these kinds of misunderstandings that justify horrific acts of violence and oppression. The biblical narrative invites us into something so much better than just survival of the fittest. A role of co-laboring in God's world to bring everything into right relationship, everything into flourishing life. A role of naming and relating and nurture and careful service. A role that sees everyone and everything as part of an interconnected whole—a *cosmos*—not just a bucket of 'raw material' that we can use as fuel for the insatiable engines of our economies. A role that seeks the flourishing of all people and places and cultures alike, rather than their annihilation in the name of whatever ideology happens to be most prevalent at the time. Such a role would be truly *just*, therefore full of faith and hope and love instead of fear and greed and death."

"But then how do we measure justice?" I ask. "Is there a way we can decide what is just and what isn't just?"

"I believe so," Father Solomon says, holding up a hand toward his eye and looking through it at me as though he held a lens there. "The right questions can act like lenses, bringing everything into focus. Does this lead to life for all? Does it help all people and places and species flourish? Not, *is it profitable*? Not, *is it efficient*? Not, *is it what we've always done*? But rather—*does this lead to life for all?* Note that I did not say life for *some* at the expense of *others*, or that some flourish while others perish. These kinds of questions might help us move away from being parasites and toward mutually empowering relationships, toward synergy, toward a way of being in the world where everyone involved is better because they're in it together. Biologists talk about symbiotic relationships, and we should look to this as a model. A just world is a world in which everyone and everything in it flourishes *because* everyone and everything else is flourishing as well."

"A just world is a world in which everyone and everything flourishes because everyone and everything else is flourishing as well," I echo Father Solomon's words, hearing sadness creep into my own voice where there was hope in his. "We're a very long way from that, aren't we, Father Solomon?"

"Of course we are," Father Solomon answers. "And don't let any politician fool you into thinking otherwise. We've got a long way to go and a lot of work to do. Why do you think we monks pray so much? We pray—to quote the Psalms—in the hope that justice and peace might kiss. That the Kingdom of God might at long last come on earth. That God's justice might fill the land like light fills the day."

"But '*Ora et Labora*,' isn't it?" I ask. "Prayer *and* work? We ought to pray, yes. Of course. But how do we *work* toward that kind of world?" I ask. "It seems so overwhelming, so complex. Where do we even start?"

Father Solomon nods and loses himself deep in thought for a few moments.

"Write letters to politicians, advocate for policies you believe will help others—not just yourself—flourish, vote for the candidate you feel will do similarly . . ."

Father Solomon's voice trails off, and I can tell he wants to say more.

"And?" I ask.

Father Solomon tilts his head down and looks at me over the top of his glasses. "Michael, if what we've been talking about is true, and justice is about being *rightly related to everyone and everything else*, perhaps a part of this includes asking ourselves this question: How is my life parasitic? Where might my own well-being currently depend upon another's suffering, another's blood? How might the manner in which I live oppress or suppress or depress another's God-given invitation to life and to flourishing?"

I am surprised by what Father Solomon is saying. "But my life doesn't depend on others' suffering, on another's blood. Not at all."

"Are you sure?" Father Solomon asks, letting the question hang in the air a while.

"I—uh," I stammer, "I don't *think* it does."

"Beware here, Michael," Father Solomon says. "For you are now touching one of the greatest dangers in the pursuit of justice: the temptation to decry *someone else* as guilty rather than seeking to amend your own life. Though I was blind to it for a long time, I am now convinced that my own life—even here in the monastery—is all too dependent on the blood and suffering of others. Given the nature of the world in which we live— and the fact that you and I are well-off citizens in a very complex world where billions of other people are subsisting on less than two dollars a day—I have a hunch that I may be crushing down on another's shoulders without even really seeing clearly how it is happening. This is the nature of the world in which we find ourselves: the rich profit at the expense of the poor, globalized systems of supply and demand enable atrocities to be bought and sold by clueless consumers, trade agreements all too often benefit the richest countries and crush the poorest."

I am silent for a while, wondering if I am crushing others with my life. I certainly don't *think* I am, but how do I know? "I don't think I am living parasitically. I don't *think* I'm crushing others. But how can I be sure?"

Father Solomon looks at me and nods. "Examine your life closely, and ask questions. Lots of questions. For questions will lead you forward. Where does your food come from? Who grows it? How is it grown? How much were they paid to grow it? Were they paid fairly? Justly? Where do you get your energy, your electricity, your gasoline? These are just two areas of your life, and there are many more besides. Examine your life closely enough and you will begin to see how connected and dependent your life is upon others, and only then will you be able to see whether you are living toward a just and rightly related world, or living your life on the backs and blood of others."

"Wow," I say bluntly. "I guess I've never thought of those things as justice issues before."

"And that's why injustice keeps on existing in our world," Father Solomon adds. "Because good people like you have their eyes closed and aren't interested in peeling back the layers of their lives to discover how they actually affect other people."

We sit in silence for a brief moment, and then Father Solomon notices the clock on the wall and stands up abruptly.

"You'll have to excuse me, Michael," he says, shaking my hand in a quick good-bye. "Prayers are about to begin."

I descend from the monastery with questions piling up in my head like a train wreck.

Am I living parasitically?

Is my life dependent on the blood of other people?

Am I a "wide one," like the gravel-pit owner who chained the family together in Uganda and made them work endlessly?

There are so many questions I'd never thought to ask before. But I commit to not let ignorance be my excuse. Instead it will be my invitation, a chance to ask hard questions about how my life impacts other people.

On the drive home I decide to dig deeply into the two areas Father Solomon mentioned, committing to a "justice audit" on my life. This will mean plunging as deeply as possible into food and energy, to find out where two of the most basic things in my life come from.

This idea of a justice audit might seem a bit intense.

But I can't get the Uganda gravel-pit family out of my mind. Nor the sinking feeling that I just might unknowingly be a "wide one."

The logic is simple enough: if I want to live a just and rightly related life, I need to seek to live just and rightly related days.

Food

I've contemplated exactly fourteen apples during the Sacred Year, paying absolute attention to each one—how it looks, how it sounds, how it feels and smells and tastes. But as I'm sitting here this morning eating my breakfast, I wonder if I might step outside the box a little and try contemplating the banana that is lying here next to my bowl of oatmeal.

But today I'm to go beyond noting simply how the banana strikes all of my senses.

Thanks to Father Solomon, a new question has come into my mind, a new manner of contemplation, built upon one fundamental question: How did this banana even get here?

Who grew it?

Where did they grow it?

Under what conditions?

Were they paid justly?

Essayist, poet, and author Wendell Berry has noted that "how we eat determines, to a considerable extent, how the world is used."[7] And, given the nature of the international agricultural and distribution networks that make it possible for me to eat a banana today in the middle of the Northern Hemisphere's winter, I must add to Berry's comment: "how we eat determines to a considerable extent how both the world *and other people* are used."

After breakfast is over I peel the label off the banana and get to work.

Turns out this particular banana was grown in Ecuador. Or so says the label. I don't have any reason to believe this isn't true, but just to make sure, I call up the company's headquarters to ask a few more questions.

"Hi there," I say as cheerfully as I can. "I'm working on a project right now, and I'm trying to learn about where a particular banana was grown and who grew it. Can you help me?"

"Hold please," comes the response.

I'm disconnected twice and then directed to three different people, each of whom says they're unable to help me and directs me somewhere else within the corporate Rolodex. I leave three messages, follow up again the next day and the day after that, and still haven't actually been able to get ahold of anyone who might be able to help me sort out where this individual banana has come from.

That's a shame, because when one door closes, I do what everybody else looking for information does: I start poking around on the Internet.

Asking the questions I'm asking is like opening Pandora's box, with each subsequent question exposing another tangled mess.

The simple fact of the matter is that a great deal of our world's food distribution is funneled through a few multibillion-dollar corporations who work with subsidiaries in each of the countries where their agricultural production actually takes place. Some might call this the most efficient way to go about things, but what it also does is provide neat little firewalls that protect the corporations from any sort of litigation or legal action. All the corporation has to do is claim plausible deniability: "*We* didn't know what was happening. It is our subsidiaries' problem. Our suppliers' problem. Our partners' problem. Not ours."

Many agricultural products originate in countries facing all sorts of issues—from poor governmental regulation to vicious paramilitary organizations to rampant child labor—that make the question of justice fiercely difficult to untangle.

The situation is made even more complex by the fact that many companies are actively championing corporate social responsibility initiatives aimed at making their business practices *seem* more equitable and just. Some activists laud this as a necessary step toward reforming global supply chains, while others decry it as mere corporate "greenwashing": a corporation's clever marketing strategy designed to appease consumers' consciences without actually requiring any fundamental changes.

Given the complexity of the world in which we live, probably both opinions are accurate to a certain degree.

Then I stumble across a documentary about bananas, and the plot thickens to the consistency of overcooked oatmeal.

The documentary focuses on Nicaraguan banana farmers who were exposed to a dangerous pesticide *after* it was banned in the United States. The makers of the documentary highlight the legal proceedings between the farmers and the multibillion-dollar corporation they're seeking damages from.

But before the first documentary can be shown at the Los Angeles Film Festival, the corporation's lawyers take up arms and start threatening libel lawsuits to everyone associated with the film. Then the corporate lawyers went after the Los Angeles Film Festival, where the documentary was going to premiere, pressuring the festival to not allow the film to be shown at all. Thankfully, the festival resisted the threats and allowed the screening to continue, albeit in a different venue and with a significant legal disclaimer read beforehand. After the initial screening at the film festival, debates raged about whether this scenario was a classic example of a big-bully-for-profit-corporation attacking a tiny documentary maker, or if—as the multibillion-dollar company alleged—the lawsuits the documentary maker had followed were based on fraud.

Things get thicker and thicker: although a California jury originally found the company guilty and ordered them to pay millions of dollars in damages to the farmers, a judge soon threw the jury's ruling out on the basis of alleged fraud on the part of the plaintiff.

Three things make this exceedingly strange: (1) the witnesses claiming the fraud were "anonymous"; (2) these "anonymous" witnesses weren't cross-examined in court; (3) counter-accusations exist that the food company *paid* to acquire the testimony of the "anonymous" witnesses.[8]

Mainstream media sided with the judge,[9] while independent sources cried foul at the "coincidence" that soon after the judge threw out the ruling she received a substantial promotion from a state politician who received campaign donations from—you guessed it—the multibillion-dollar corporation.[10]

(If you're wondering why I haven't named the company or the documentary here explicitly, it's because I'm worried about getting sued myself. So is my publisher. Am I the only one who finds it tragically ironic that—despite the First Amendment—I have to tiptoe around getting sued while writing a chapter on the spiritual practice of justice? It seems like the systems of our world trend in a particular direction, and it isn't toward the weakest and most vulnerable but rather the "wide men.")

What can we conclude from this? There's nothing at all straightforward about eating a banana.

Nor eating chocolate either, apparently.

Over a conversation about this justice audit, a friend mentions another recent documentary called *The Dark Side of Chocolate*. Intrigued by the title I watch it online and am shocked to learn about the rampant child labor and human trafficking in Western Africa that fuels much of the chocolate industry. More than three *billion* pounds of chocolate are consumed every year, almost half of it in the United States alone. And those countless tons we Americans glut ourselves on annually—who knows what percentage of it has been harvested by modern-day slaves or trafficked children?

Did you taste the tears and blood when you bit into that last bar of chocolate? I'm sorry to ask such a blunt and indelicate question. I'm just trying to be less of a wide one.

The more I contemplate the banana I ate for breakfast, the more I feel like I'm living inside *The Hunger Games*, where the weak and poor are forced at gunpoint to sacrifice their very lives to provide the entertainment and luxuries for the rich to consume. What I'm shaken to discover, though, is that *I live in the Capitol* (the epicenter of decadence and over-indulgence in Suzanne Collins' dystopian world) and have been gorging myself on bananas and chocolate my whole life without ever even questioning the process that brought them from seed to plant to fruit half a world away and then to the shelves of my local supermarket.

So what to do?

Three things regarding food in particular stem from this justice audit: (1) buying more locally; (2) buying more organically; (3) buying more fairly.

A good way to integrate all three of these presents itself in the form of local farmer's markets and CSA (community-supported agriculture) programs. Danae and I begin visiting our local Saturday farmer's market and buy our groceries there instead of at the large box stores, where finding out who grew them and where and under what conditions means calling more 800 numbers and getting dead-ended at every turn. Through buying at the farmer's market we begin to develop actual relationships with the people who are growing the food we're eating. Quite a difference from the impersonal fluorescent labyrinth of the supermarket and the unknowns of the processes hidden behind billion-dollar organizations, flashy logos, and shady labor practices.

With a few friends we join a local CSA program and begin receiving a large tub of vegetables every week. The vegetables are grown by a local farmer named Paul, a lanky, amicable guy who has a thing for garlic. When I last saw Paul he launched into a ten-minute explanation of the two-year process required to adequately prepare an organic garlic bed. Paul's eyes were alive and his tone adamant—he *likes* the thought of this careful work. Relishes it, in fact.

"It's good work," Paul says. "And because of the CSA model, I'm fairly paid and can actually afford to do the work well. That's a rare thing in our world today, and I'm grateful for it."

The more Danae and I open our eyes, the more there is to see. Someone tells us about a fantastic website—www.LocalHarvest.org— that is a searchable online directory of local farmers, co-ops, and CSA programs. Turns out that beyond the vegetable CSA there is a local wheat CSA we can join as well, and a local pork/beef/dairy/egg co-op we could become a part of. There's even a local fruit and nut co-op to boot. After examining our budget and examining our local food options, we make a few decisions that allow us to move toward sourcing the vast majority of our calories from more local, sustainable, personable, and—I use this word carefully but intentionally—*just* sources.

Buying more locally, buying more organically, buying more fairly.

These are not imperatives but invitations. They aren't be-all, end-all solutions. But I'm convinced that they *are* a step in the right direction toward a more just life, toward a less parasitic life, toward a life that isn't built on the backs and blood of others, toward a more *rightly related* life.

And here's a surprising thing: the process of learning and researching and doing all this work hasn't felt like a dogged, toilsome thing. I *like* knowing Paul on a first-name basis. I *like* being able to go and see his farm, walk through the long rows of vegetables in various stages of their life cycles. I *like* shaking his hand as the sun is setting over the golden rows of wheat and asking how his garlic-bed preparations are going. I *like* that I know I'm paying him fairly for the good work he is doing and that he can feed his family from it and that he isn't using toxic chemicals that will likely harm him and his family and all the surrounding area besides. It makes me feel connected, rooted, established in this place.

But it's about more than just "liking" it. It seems right and good as well. Deeply good, in fact.

ENERGY

"Most of the electricity used in your portion of the grid comes from coal originating in the Powder River Basin," Jake explains to me over the phone. Jake is an employee of the parent corporation that owns the utility company I buy my electricity from. I've called him up on a snowy Monday afternoon to ask a few questions, a continuation of the justice audit I'm trying to work my way through. I started contemplating a light bulb, and this is where it's led me.

"Where's the Powder River Basin?" I ask.

"Wyoming and Montana," Jake responds. "But that's not where all of the coal comes from. The rest is from Appalachia."

The terms *originates* and *comes from* are relatively simple ideas that refer to unbelievably complex processes. And the more I dig the dirtier it gets. I've had a dim notion that mining and mineral extraction techniques can be devastating to both land and people, but I had no idea what all it entailed.

Mountaintop removal (MTR) is a process as destructive as it sounds, and it's a common method to get at the coal seams in the Appalachian Mountains. Once the standing forest has been slashed and burned, high-powered explosives are used in a systematic manner to detonate the top off a mountain. Heavy machinery dumps the rubble into adjacent valleys, burying streams by the mile. When the coal seams have been laid bare, still more heavy machinery descends like a swarm of locusts, extracting the coal ton by blackened ton.

The coal must be washed before it can be used to heat the water that turns the turbines at a power station. This washing typically takes place close to the actual MTR site and results in millions of gallons of toxic sludge. At least one of three things typically happens to this sludge: (1) it sits in a massive open sludge pool; (2) it leaks out and pollutes whatever unburied streams might still be flowing nearby; or (3) it leeches down into the aquifers, poisoning the drinking water for miles around. Even after "reclamation" projects have been completed on destroyed areas, toxic pollutants are still prevalent.[11]

MTR pretty much turns living forests into barren wastelands. To put it in terms of Tolkien's Middle-earth, Rivendell becomes Moria. And we switch on our lights.

And then there's the deplorable human impact of MTR.[12]

If you haven't seen the movie *Erin Brockovich* it might serve as an adequate introduction, though in a different context than Appalachia. According to an aggregate of twenty-one peer-reviewed studies, when compared to the general population, people living near MTR sites have a 50 percent greater risk of fatal cancer and a 42 percent greater risk of birth defects.[13] Whenever the people try and rally together against the distant tyranny of the mineral extraction corporations, armies of lawyers descend waving hundred-page legal documents like batons.

We've heard this story before, haven't we? David versus Goliath?

Only now Goliath is the multibillion-dollar mineral extraction corporation and David is a tiny group of cancer-ridden citizen-miners too sick to stand up and fight. And David doesn't have any stones, much less a slingshot. Not that it would matter, for while Goliath is there, he isn't really within range, given the swarm of lawyers and dirty laws that circle around him in a slippery, insulative layer.

Similar kinds of catastrophic environmental and human effects result at another major source of American coal: the Powder River Basin in northeastern Wyoming and southern Montana. The method here isn't MTR but rather open-pit mining, but it still does a number on the surrounding landscape, wildlife, and people as well.[14]

I phone up a lawyer working at a local resource council, a group of concerned members trying to protect the natural resources that exist in this part of our country, and ask her about the effects of the mine in her area.

"They use an extraordinary amount of explosives at the mine sites," she says. "The dust created by these explosions and the mining activity in general coats everything for miles around. Every now and then one of the explosions doesn't fully detonate or the ground is too wet, and we'll get these massive clouds of orange, highly toxic material that emerge from the pit like a plague."

I hang up the phone with the lawyer and call up Jake again at my utility's parent company.

"Are there any non–fossil-fuel based energy technologies I might make use of?" I ask Jake. "You know, like wind power or solar or something like that?"

"Absolutely. And we're working hard to expand wind-based generation in your area. We have two new projects coming online in the next five years, in fact."

"Brilliant," I say. "So what portion of my electricity will then come from renewable sources, once these projects are complete?"

"Hold on one moment," Jake says. I hear him clicking around in search of the answer. "Five percent," Jake answers.

"Five percent?" I ask. "That's all?"

There's a long pause on the other end of the line. "It isn't much," Jake admits. "But at least it's a start."

It's a start, yes. But a long way from anything like a nonparasitic existence, from a life that might be called *just*.

Decimated forests.

Obliterated mountains.

Open pit mines.

Forgotten streams.

Toxic sludge pools.

Contaminated aquifers.

Orange toxic clouds.

Fifty percent increases in cancer rates.

Higher incidents of birth defects.

There's no way to spin it: my use of coal-derived electricity contributes to the destruction of people and places. I hang up the phone, walk to the wall, and switch off the light.

Suddenly I don't mind sitting in darkness.

What to do?

Small decisions matter. Thanks to an initiative happening in my area I'm able to replace all the incandescent bulbs in our house with more energy-efficient ones, reducing the amount of raw material I burn when I need to see at night.

"Have you heard of *vampire loads?*" a friend asks me.

I shake my head. "Nope." As he explains the term to me, I can't help but wonder how I have never known about these before.

Vampire loads are the imperceptible electric drain that devices in standby mode continue to consume. Computers, stereos, microwave ovens, flat-screen TVs, basically any advanced electronic device that can be powered on with the press of a button is probably drawing "phantom power." And get this: vampire loads account for 5 to 10 percent of the electricity usage in the United States every year, to the tune of around $10 billion annually.[15] That's a lot of cash and a lot of coal—seventeen coal-fired plants' worth.[16]

I install a few power strips and start switching devices off or unplugging them whenever they aren't in use: laptops, wi-fi, printers, stereos, and the like. Even cell phones will draw a bit of power if they're plugged in past their 100 percent charge. It seems a little inconvenient at first to have to remember to turn the power strip on and off all the time, but I just picture the top of a mountain getting blown off next to someone's home, and then it doesn't seem like a big task.

In the climate I live in, keeping the house warm is one of the most substantial demands of electricity. I look around online, find a reasonably priced wood stove with a high EPA efficiency rating, and install it with the help of a few friends and several phone calls to friendly customer service agents.

I find a nice guy named Don on Craigslist who sells the firewood he and his son harvest every year off their property just fifteen minutes away, and ask him if he can deliver two cords before the end of summer.

These steps help reduce our electricity consumption to around two hundred to three hundred kilowatt hours per month, which is between 25 and 30 percent of the average US household.[17] Far from a truly sustainable electricity consumption, but certainly a step in the right direction.

But even as I'm doing these things something said by the lawyer at the resource council in the Powder River Basin keeps coming back to me: "These smaller actions by individual consumers are of course good and necessary steps. But the real question is whether or not we're going to be able to change the larger systems that are in place in our world, systems that protect corporate interests at the expense of local communities, whether or not we're going to be able to align our national energy policies with our stated environmental policies, et cetera. And this only happens when we band together as people and pressure our politicians—both local and national—to begin addressing these issues directly."

I go online, sign several petitions on coal-reduction websites, and call up my local representatives to be sure my concerns as a citizen are heard.

"These are all very good things," a friend named Ryan suggests when he and I are discussing my justice audits. "But why not have some fun with it as well? It doesn't have to be only about reduction and limits, you know. Austerity has a bad name, and I think that's all wrong. There are ways to make this kind of simpler, more *just* living rich and fulfilling as well."

"What, you don't think installing power strips is fun?" I ask.

"Not really, no," Ryan says dryly.

At Ryan's suggestion Danae and I have a candlelit Advent, leaving the lights off in the evenings and instead making our evening meals by candlelight and then eating them in the light of the woodstove. It is strange at first, and we both have to learn anew how to find our way in the soft light of a candlelit kitchen. But our eyes and hands adjust, and I only end up breaking one plate during the month of Advent.

Without music and TV shows and electric lights—convenient and entertaining as those things are—the evenings in fact become like mini Sabbaths. We sit together on our couch and read, play cards, and go to bed earlier.

"Think we can keep doing this into the New Year?" Danae asks me as Advent moves on toward Epiphany.

"I hope so," I say. "On multiple levels."

∽

About this time I am speaking to my dear friend Matthew over Skype about all the realizations these justice audits have been generating.

"It feels good and right to be trying to move in this direction," I say. "We've not arrived at a just life, by any means, but even trying to move toward justice just seems right—interpersonally, emotionally, spiritually."

"I hear you," Matthew says. "And at the same time we've got to hold this together with the fact that we've got such a very, *very* long way to go, in just about every area of our life in the West."

Matthew is en route back from the Democratic Republic of the Congo (DRC), one of the most notorious countries on the planet in terms of human rights abuses. He was sent there as part of a videography team by an international aid organization. Their mission: to document the abuses and chaos that tyrannize the men, women, and children in one of the country's mining regions. The hope was that their team's work might not only highlight the work of the aid organization, but also help raise awareness about the injustices and perhaps someday inspire people to press politicians in Washington to wake up and pay attention.

I ask Matthew to tell me more about his work.

"Where do I start?" he says. "It was astonishing and terrifying and shocking. I've never been that close to live gunfire before, and there were a few points where we weren't really sure what was going to happen."

I'm silent for several long seconds. "I didn't realize it was that intense," I say at last. "You're glad to be alive?"

"My emotions are so frayed right now," Matthew admits. "It's hard to put it into words, you know? I've just interviewed a huge number of women who were victims of rape. Rape as *a weapon of war*. One of the local warlords gives his soldiers permission to rape the women in villages."

"Is it a tribal conflict?" I ask. I have no idea what the cause of the conflict is, and I'm asking out of total ignorance.

"Well, here's the thing," Matthew explains. "Sort of. But it's so complex. The different parties in the conflict sometimes work together, sometimes work against one another. It's a mess. Some five million people have died, and nobody in the West really knows about it."

"What?" I interrupt Matthew. "Five *million* people?"

"At least," Matthew says. "And hardly anybody is talking about it."

"How is it that we don't hear about this every day on the news?" I stammer. "Five million people is one of the largest conflicts in the last fifty years."

"Since World War II," Matthew agrees. "I don't know why we don't hear more about it. Maybe it has something to do with the fact that we love our electronics in the Western world."

This is a total surprise to me. "What do you mean?"

"The computers we use, the cars we drive, the planes we fly on, the cell phones we talk on," Matthew says. "All of them require minerals like those that are mined in the DRC. They're called the *three Ts:* tantalum, tungsten, and tin. And the mines where these things are found are controlled by the local warlords who have a stranglehold on people in the area, forcing them to work as slaves, killing the men, raping the women and girls. It's hell on earth. Then they sell the minerals to middlemen who export them to Western electronics companies. We have our electronics, the companies make their profits, and nobody asks any questions."

The image of the family in the Ugandan gravel pit comes rushing back to me, darkened even further by the horrors Matthew is describing.

He continues. "And every time we fly or get into our car or power on a computer or talk on a phone, chances are that we are doing so—at least in part—as a result of the kind of warfare whose effects I've just spent two weeks documenting. And it makes me want to vomit. It makes me want to throw away everything I have that is soaked in the blood of others. I want to walk everywhere. Not fly. Not drive. I want to write with a pen and paper, not use my laptop."

We fall silent for several long moments.

"You see the tragic irony of this, don't you?" I ask, feeling my stomach sink. "You're returning from Africa, and you aren't walking home. I earn my living as a writer and as a public speaker, daily dependent upon laptops and airplanes. Even this very conversation is made possible by a global IT infrastructure, computers running on those exact minerals. Everywhere we turn, everything we do is in some way dependent upon the blood of others."

My stomach drops as I'm speaking and I see now why Father Solomon said his whole life was parasitic, even there in the monastery. "No matter what we do, we're complicit somehow, aren't we?" I say.

Matthew pauses before responding. "Yeah, we are. I don't see any other logical conclusion. That is the nature of the systems we've built in our world today. They are enormous. They are multinational. They are highly profitable. Our whole society depends upon them, our whole culture, our whole civilization. We've built a world in which it is virtually impossible to live, move, and have our being without stepping in someone else's pain and suffering, without slipping in, soaking our hands in someone else's blood."

∽

Soon after this conversation with Matthew I confess my despair to a friend and theologian named Jonathan Wilson. A group of us have gotten together at another friend's house for dessert, and the conversation has gradually turned to the topic of justice.

"I don't know what to do," I say. "Sometimes it seems so overwhelming that I can't think of doing anything but throwing my arms up in despair."

"It does seem overwhelming at times," Jonathan agrees. "Given the state of our world and the complexity of the systems in which we are all both willing and unwilling participants."

We all nod, and I glance down at the chocolate cake, and wonder about the cacao beans from which it is made.

"But might I offer another way of thinking about it?" Jonathan asks.

We all nod, hopeful.

Jonathan begins, and sheds a new and hopeful light on the conversation. "I like to think about it this way: if the Kingdom of God is actually coming—the Kingdom in which justice shall prevail and everything shall be rightly related to everything else—then when we seek to live more justly, no matter how small the action may be, we are actually proclaiming, and heralding the advent, the arrival, of that Kingdom even before it comes in full. It's like the first hint of dawn on the eastern horizon. We may not be able to see very well yet, and may become overwhelmed by how crushing the darkness continues to be. But the fact that the day has not yet come in the full is by no means a reason to despair that it is only dawn. We must herald the dawn. Proclaim it. Seek to participate in it in every way we can and encourage others to do so as well. Yes, we have a very long way to go. Yes, there is much that is wrong and broken and vicious in our world. But another world is coming. A just world. A rightly related world. And it is in that that we put our hope, and in the One whose Kingdom it is, even as we work toward it in the here and now."

I've tucked Jonathan's words into my pocket alongside my hazelnut, and I've found them more comforting than I'd even hoped.

Yes. The road toward justice is long and winding and difficult.

Yes, despite my best efforts I am still caught up in systems that perpetuate injustice and make me complicit in the blood and suffering of others.

Yes, I am still a wide one.

And I am not okay with this.

Far from it.

These small justice audits have convinced me that I must continue such work, asking hard and uncomfortable questions about many other things besides.

My response will not be despair, nor inaction, but rather resolution: a commitment to continue seeking to live more justly, in a more rightly related way, for as long as I have breath.

Until the Kingdom of God at last comes in all its fullness, and justice finally fills the land.

CHAPTER 18

Life Together: The Practice of Community

*What should young people do with their lives today? Many things,
obviously. But the most daring thing is to create stable communities
in which the terrible disease of loneliness can be cured.*

—KURT VONNEGUT[1]

*We have all known the long loneliness and we have learned that
the only solution is love and that love comes with community.*

—DOROTHY DAY[2]

*It is in community that we come to see God in the other. It is in
community that we see our own emptiness filled up. It is community
that calls me beyond the pinched horizons of my own life, my own
country, my own race, and gives me the gifts I do not have within me.*

—JOAN CHITTISTER[3]

*There is actually no more dangerous solitude than that of the
man who is lost in a crowd, who does not know he is alone and
who does not function as a person in a community either.*

—THOMAS MERTON[4]

I believe that the community—in the fullest sense: a place and all its creatures—is the smallest unit of health and that to speak of the health of an isolated individual is a contradiction in terms.

—WENDELL BERRY[5]

Community is a trendy word these days, but not all versions of community are created equal. In the monastic world, entering into a shared life, into community, is a relatively straightforward if utterly demanding process: you sense God's leading, give away all your stuff, enter the cloister, and then after a set period of discernment along with the community members there, you make your vows and become an official member of that monastery or convent.

Things are a little harder to define outside the cloister.

Some people think community is really just about having your name on a membership list. Once you've signed up, you're basically in. And this is true in some regards, I suppose. It works this way at a country club (though you have to pay the annual dues, of course) or a school (though you have to pay the tuition) or even at a gym (though you have to pay the monthly fee).

But belonging to an organization that I have to *pay* to be a member of doesn't really seem to fit with the idea of a spiritual practice. I'm looking for something that is going to have a lasting and shaping influence on me, that is going to require me to change, to begin thinking differently about things, that is going to invite me toward being a different person.

I'm not ready or able to jump into the cloister, but I'm not interested in joining a country club either.

I'm searching for a *formative, shaping* community.

This is how it happens.

Danae pauses the movie we're watching and turns to face me, a sure sign I'm about to get hit with something significant. "I think we should move to East Vancouver," she says. "And become a part of the neighborhood and community around that church." She stops for a second, but then continues before I even have time to respond. "Maybe we can even live in one of the community houses."

I blink a few times.

Then a few more.

"That's a long way away," I say at last. It was the best I could come up with on such short notice.

We've been living a ten-minute bus ride from our graduate school. The idea she's just blindsided me with would mean living on the opposite side of the city from where we both spend our weeks, effectively quadrupling our daily commute.

"If we are serious about really becoming rooted in a community, proximity plays a role," Danae says.

"Yeah," I respond, trying to get my brain out of the movie and into gear for an argument. "Proximity does play a role, but I'm not sure I'm ready to move across the city just because we're intrigued by a particular church."

"I feel like we're sort of stuck in the middle here," Danae explains, "between two potential communities: between our school where we spend our days, and the life people seem to share together within that church community in East Vancouver. This apartment here just feels like an in-between, like we're splitting the difference but missing the point. With so much distance between the core of each group, we don't even have to *see* other people unless we intentionally plan to do it, don't have to interact with anybody if we don't want to. We aren't really experiencing *life together* with anybody by living here."

"What do you mean?" I say. "We live in a great apartment complex. People here are really nice."

"They're nice," Danae agrees with a nod. "But do you know anybody's name?"

"Sure," I say. "There's Don and Jane, and . . ." But my voice trails off.

"Do you mean Doug and Julia?"

"R—Right," I stammer. "That's what I meant. And then there's what's his name."

"Do you know Doug and Julia's last name?" Danae asks. "Or anybody else's name? Do you know anything about anybody? Because I don't. And I don't feel *known* here either. This apartment complex feels like a transit bus, and we're all passengers who just happen to be on it together. That's not a community."

I look up at the ceiling, racking my brain for the name of the guy who has held the door for me a couple of times.

"It is a bit lonely here, isn't it?" I say at last. "Even though we've lived here for almost a year, I do still feel distant and disconnected from other people."

"We're living *completely* autonomous lives," Danae says. "All we do is work at school and eat and sleep here. I don't feel connected at all. I don't know anything about anybody's life—what they're doing, what they're experiencing, how it's going for them. I want to try living in a more connected way. Less independently, more interdependently."

"Are you sure about that?" I ask. "Although I like the *idea* of trying to live more interdependently, there are parts of it that would be really difficult. There are plusses and minuses on both sides, don't you think? Plusses and minuses to living more interdependently, plusses and minuses to living more autonomously."

"I know," Danae says, nodding. "And we've lived most of our adult lives independently. What if we gave living interdependently a chance? See what it's like?"

"It would be intriguing to explore." I am slowly starting to come around to the idea. "How will we know if we never put ourselves in situations that force us to learn more about it?"

"We won't," Danae says definitively. "We have to dive in and see."

Danae again pushes Play on the movie, but my mind isn't really in it.

All that night and for the rest of the week I'm pondering this idea of intentionally moving toward a *shared life* with a group of people, a way of doing *life together* that would be categorically different from the total anonymity and autonomy with which we currently live. Because despite living in that "great" apartment complex and despite my gym membership and being a graduate student and even my previous "commuter" church experiences, there is still an aching sense of loneliness. A felt need to become more thoroughly rooted and interconnected with a particular community of people.

I want to know and be known in a network of relationships that go beyond mere exchange, beyond mere nicety, beyond mere anonymity. I want to enter into the kind of interwoven relationships that begin to slowly emerge when a particular group of people in a particular place intentionally decide to lower their facades and stop masquerading long enough so that they might actually get to know one another. I want to live into the kind of collective rhythms and habits that grow slowly out of a shared vision and set of values. I want to be formed within the ethos and atmosphere that comes from an explicit and intentional commitment to *do life together.*

"Let's try it," I say a few nights later. "I have no idea what this will mean, what it will require of us, but I want to give this *life together* thing a try."

"Are you sure?" Danae asks.

"No," I admit with a laugh. "Of course I'm not sure. But I don't think you really can be sure ahead of time about something like this. I think we'll have to grow into it, you know? Find out what our capacities are, learn a bit more about where our blind spots are, what ways we need to grow. But like you said . . . we'll never find out if we don't dive in and see."

Thus begins one of the most challenging and illuminating seasons of the Sacred Year, or more accurately, of my entire life.

Within the month we move out of our apartment in West Vancouver and across the city into the neighborhood of Grandview Calvary Baptist Church—"Grandview" for short. Neither of us have ever lived within walking distance of our church before, much less just two doors down, but that's where a room in a community house opens up. After two phone calls and a long meeting over coffee, we decide to move in together with a group of people we don't even know.

Upon making that decision we go from feeling like two anonymous passengers on a transit bus to marveling at how thin walls and floors could actually be.

After spending most of the weekend unpacking our boxes and learning a bit about the people who are now our new housemates, we head next door for the Sunday afternoon church service at Grandview.

As I walk into the church I can't help but smile at what a ragtag bunch of people we're moved to do "community" with. Amid a *very* post-Christian Vancouver, Grandview is a medium-sized church, even though there are only a hundred or so people sitting in the pews this afternoon. For Danae and me this feels small and intimate enough to suggest that we might actually get to know and be known by the others in this place, instead of just swimming weekly through another anonymous crowd.

"Hey you two!" a jovial Iranian man cries as we begin making our way down the main aisle. Though we've only met this man a couple of times, he nonetheless runs up to us with a big smile stretched across his stubbly face and throws his arms around both of us. "I heard you've just moved next door. Welcome to this place. I am so happy, for you are now close to all of us."

Before we even have a chance to respond, he steps past us to embrace another person as they enter the church.

This place cuts through most of the "normal" societal boundaries like a scythe: education levels, age groups, race, language, and socioeconomic class all cease to have their "normal" effect here. On any given Sunday homeless people sit next to millionaires. People who haven't completed high school pass the peace of Christ with people who've earned PhDs. People whose first language is Spanish, French, Korean, Chinese, Japanese, Swahili, Amharic, Arabic (just to name a few), and of course English all worship by singing hymns and songs in a multiplicity of languages and reading the Scriptures aloud in their own language. People of First Nations origin, of European origin, of African origin, of Asian origin all walk down the center aisle together to receive Eucharist. People who are employed and people who aren't are all welcome here, as are people who are clean and sober and people who smell strongly of cheap vodka or keep nervously patting their pockets.

We walk down the main aisle, slide into one of the rows of pews, and take a deep breath.

Here we are.

⁂

Despite all the differences that exist between members of Grandview, several things in particular help knit us all together into a formative community.

I was shocked to discover after moving into the neighborhood that about half the members of Grandview live within a ten- to fifteen-block radius of the church building. Although it isn't a "parish church" in any formal sense, living among such a large number of people who share Sunday pews reveals the lost wisdom of such a model: living so close to many of the people I worship with weaves our lives together in ten thousand strong yet subtle ways. We keep seeing one another everywhere. Every Monday, Wednesday, and Friday I see my pastor sweating on the elliptical machine at the local gym. At the coffee shop I order my double shot from the woman I sat two rows behind just a few days ago. I round a corner in the grocery store and practically knock over the person who baked the Eucharistic bread. As I'm biking home one afternoon a whole crew of fellow members are hanging out on a front porch, so I stop and sit awhile. When I almost get hit by a car on the way home, my anger is cooled by the realization that I "passed the peace of Christ" to the driver not even twenty-four hours ago.

Then there is Grandview's formal rite of membership.

This rite isn't binding in any constrictive sense. What it *is* is an explicit invitation to *be here with us for a while*. It's a way for the community as a whole to say, let's seek to live life here together in this place, with one another, for as long as we're able. Let's worship together, laugh together, feast together, lament together, work together for the good of our community, our neighborhood, and even our city. And it's a chance for the new members to agree and acknowledge publically that they desire to join with the others and do just that.

A few weeks after our arrival in East Van, one of Grandview's biannual church meetings is announced. A Membership Rite is planned for that evening, and we're invited.

"Will all of you who are becoming members please step forward?" the pastor announces when the time has come.

About five or six of us come up to the front of the room and stand there shoulder to shoulder, looking out at the motley crew of people we're committing to doing life with. I've stood up in front of innumerable crowds before, but this is the first time I've stood in front of a church and felt like I might actually know and be known by most of the people looking back at me.

The pastor goes down the line, asking a few questions of us all: where we're from, how we've come to Vancouver, how we spend our days.

After each person's interview the church recites the Membership Litany that is on the overhead projector, the call and response that formally affirms our membership and place in this formative community.

The pastor invites Danae and me forward, and after we've answered the questions, we look out at the group of people and hear them welcome us into their midst:

All: Michael and Danae,
We thank God for who you are!
We welcome you!
Pastor: May God's strength pilot you,
God's might uphold you,
God's wisdom guide you,
God's eye look before you,
God's ear hear you,
God's Word speak for you,
God's hand guard you,
God's way lie before you,
God's shield protect you,
God's host save you
All: Together we will be
Together we will see

the Kingdom of God
In this place.[6]

When I first heard about all that the Membership Rite entailed, I thought such a formal thing seemed a bit overdone: litany for litany's sake.

But having gone through it and experienced the massive effect such intentionality has, I'm firmly convinced that many of these formalities—like the vows the monks and nuns take when they become part of *their* communities—have significant psychological implications both for the people who are being welcomed in and for the people who are doing the welcoming.

These rites are like punctuation marks in life. Without the use of commas and periods and exclamation points, it all just runs together into a jumbled stream of consciousness. We lose our places, lose the line of logic, lose the flow of the narrative.

But with punctuation, with these kinds of rites and other significant markers to help guide us along our way, we're reminded *who* and *what* and *when* and *where* we are living and moving and having our being.

Knowing all that goes a long way, even if the *why* of it all is only visible in outline form.

And then there are Grandview's twin practices of hope and lament.

We all know those people who seem to think being hopeful means walking around with smiles and blinders on, those places not at all willing to acknowledge the real state of things in our world, turning a blind eye toward the pain and the fractures and injustice and death that are evident all around us. I innately sense this to be a kind of "cheap hope." Something just as antithetical to the real thing as the "cheap grace" Dietrich Bonhoeffer warns us about in his book *The Cost of Discipleship*.[7] This is the kind of hope that is naive, simplistic, foolish.

I'm chapped and chafing from all the counterfeit and cheap hope in our world today. I'm weary from the kind of bogus hope that refuses to read the lament psalms and focuses only on the happy-clappy ones. The kind of hope that recoils from the pain and suffering in our world and exists inside a fragile bubble of denial.

The Jesus I read about in the Gospels doesn't at all seem to close his eyes to the reality of things as he's walking around, healing people of diseases, calling the power structures to account, weeping outside the city of Jerusalem.

Jesus doesn't really strike me as a head-in-the-sand kind of guy.

So why are so many of those who claim to follow him?

If hope is to have any ground on which to stand, it must get its head out of the clouds and be firmly rooted on the earth with and alongside the broken and battered and bruised world in which we live. Real hope starts precisely there—in the *real* world—staring reality straight in the face, naming it for what it is and *then* looking toward and working for the coming of a different kind of Kingdom.

When a local neighborhood man dies—a fifty-year-old named Mike—after being attacked outside the homeless shelter he volunteered at regularly, the Grandview community assembles to lament Mike's death at the very place it happened. This senseless violence sends shock-waves through the whole neighborhood, as a beloved man's life is cut off in a moment.

As our ragtag group gathers in the parking lot of the shelter, people stream out from inside. People who knew Mike and people who didn't. People who had worked with him for years and people who got to know his face only because of the memorial established in his honor.

Once we have all gathered together, there is a moment of silence and then the litany begins:

> Leader: Lord Jesus, we cry out to you now because our world and our own community and even we ourselves are still caught up in this same terrible lie of violence. We are still actors and bystanders in a world that does not cherish life, that regularly leads the innocent to their deaths. We remember Mike, who died not very long ago here in this very place, because of the brutal lie of violence. And

we remember also all those who have died from violence in our
city, in our country, and in our world.

**All: O Lord, you who know the violence that is in our world and
in our hearts.**

Have mercy upon us, and show us the way of love.

For we long to be a people of peace.[8]

It is this kind of acknowledgment of the brokenness of our world, of
the pain and the suffering and the lies that we are all willing and not-so-
willing participants in, that legitimizes any community's hope.

On a Friday afternoon—Good Friday, in fact—most of the Grandview
community gathers together for the neighborhood stations of the cross
walk.

We all come from our various tasks and varied weeks and gather
in the church's parking lot, atop the labyrinth a community member
painted there. It's a good reminder—that labyrinth—of what community is all about: that we're all on this pilgrimage together, journeying
with and alongside one another for a while, toward whatever it is we'll
find when we reach the center.

We stand here together in the parking lot, shield our eyes against the
shockingly bright spring sunlight, and strain to hear above the roar of the
nearby traffic what the leader is saying at the front of the group.

Turns out the First Station is actually the plot of recently tilled soil
next to the parking lot.

The soil is glorious, black and rich as brownies, tilled and waiting to
be sown.

"This plot wasn't always so fertile," the leader of this station explains.
"Its life-giving power is itself the fruit of long labor by many members of this community. Heavy amounts of compost and manure have
been mixed in. So, too, have shredded pieces of paper that contained
the written record of our community's regrets, sins, and failures. You
may remember how you were invited one Sunday, last fall, to write them

down and then feed them into a paper shredder as we approached the altar to receive Eucharist. Now those shredded regrets have been composted all winter and have been mixed into this soil. Your regrets and sins and failures have become part of the life-giving soil into which we are about to sow these seeds of hope."

The leader invites us to join in on the call-and-response:

Leader: Standing in this garden, Lord Christ, may we remember how you groaned on our behalf in another garden. As we plant this wheat, remind us of your death on the cross, your entombment, and your words of encouragement:

All: "Unless a kernel of wheat falls to the ground and dies, it remains only a single seed. But if it dies, it produces many seeds." Today we plant our hopes in the darkness of the dirt, waiting for your life and light to shine upon us.

Leader: Lord Christ, bless this land and this wheat. We pray that the harvest would feed your hungry people and nourish us with your filling love. Amen.[9]

And then we all step forward. One after the other, we grab a handful of bone-dry wheat berries from a bucket and embody hope by scattering seeds broadcast onto the fertile soil.

Knowing a bit of the stories and struggles of the people with whom I am doing this infuses great potency into the act. For everyone here, each physical seed is also a symbol of deep yearning and hope. Of hope for reconciliation with loved ones. Of sobriety. Of employment. Of some sense of meaning—however faint—amid all the swarming meaninglessness.

As the winter fades away and spring pushes up in full, the wheat takes root and grows. First tiny shoots, thin and short as green straws, poke their heads through the black earth.

They are almost knee-height as midsummer nears, and in July the heads of grain slowly begin filling out. Once the days have become noticeably shorter, the stalks and heads of grain hue slowly toward a dry, golden brown. And when at last the leaves are falling, the wheat is ready to be harvested, the welcome fruit of a carefully sown hope and a lengthy patience.

Several of us take an afternoon to harvest the wheat, laying it in the autumn sun to dry as much as possible before the winter rains begin to fall.

"Remember where this wheat came from," the pastor says on a snowy Sunday, lifting up the freshly baked loaf of bread high before the congregation. "This wheat is borne of your regrets and your hopes, seeded into the darkness of the soil, raised to new life by the power of God at work in our world through the many mundane mysteries that undergird our very existence. This is the body of Christ, which was given for you. All of you, take and eat, and may God grant you the good hope of everlasting life."

Of course I'd be lying if I made it seem like *life together* is all easy and simple and beautiful. Nothing but lovely litanies and shared meals and no bumps along the road.

Make no mistake, *life together* is messy.

How could it be otherwise, when we are all messy and in-process beings?

None of us have yet become all that we should be, and not everything that is awry within us has been healed. Living in such close proximity to people in the neighborhood and in the context of community houses means others come to see our blind spots and foibles, up close and personally, even as we get to know theirs.

Conflict becomes inevitable.

Some conflict is rather humorous, like when one of our housemates keeps frying up pounds of discount-aisle kidney and making the whole house reek like baked urine for days thereafter.

Other conflicts, however, are deep and wounding on every level, for all involved.

Up until now we've never really had to walk those tumultuous paths of conflict before. Without the million little alchemic moments weaving us into the warp and woof of a formative community, it has been relatively easy to keep people at arm's length. To never get close enough for either intimacy *or* friction to emerge. Or when friction did emerge, to just back away a little so that there was enough space and distance separating us so that we didn't need to actually address the grievances. We could just let space heal the wounds.

But when you are committed to doing *life together*, you see one another *all the time*—in the morning making coffee, and then again in the afternoon while coming or going, and in the evening around the dinner table, and then again in the middle of the night while coming out of the bathroom. Or in the coffee shop and at the grocer, in the gym as well as in the pews. And then it becomes a lot harder to just let grievances lie.

Left unattended in such close proximity, wounds will fester and boil.

That's when Danae and I find ourselves caught up in the long and fragile process of acknowledgment, apology, forgiveness, and reconciliation. Such a long and fragile process is the only balm, the only salve that can heal the wounds we inevitably inflict on one another as we seek to participate in life together.

Some of these conflicts have run their course, and the old wounds have healed.

Others—I must confess—are still ongoing. And though the sharpness of the pain we have inflicted and had inflicted in us may have dissipated some, there is still the dull ache of resolution not yet fully achieved.

Like I said: life together is messy.

An older woman and her daughter—both First Nations women—are setting off on a long and challenging endeavor within our city to work for reconciliation and peace between First Nations communities and the European settlers whose ancestors rapaciously acquired the land on which we now all live. Theirs is a long road, an important road, working against many aspects of human frailty, oppression, and unhealth that are mixed viciously into our society. These women know the challenges that lie ahead of them and are all the more determined to work for peace and reconciliation.

But they need a community behind them in order to do so.

So they ask all of us at Grandview to support them, to walk with them, to encourage them to keep on when they become weary.

Midway through the Sunday service our pastor asks the two women to come into the center aisle of the church.

"Please stand and come toward these two women," our pastor instructs. "Let them feel your presence surrounding them, standing with them, empowering them to do the good work they feel God calling them to do."

And we do. All of us. Rich, poor, uneducated and educated, housed and homeless, North American, First Nations, Middle Eastern, African, Asian, Oceanic. We lay aside our differences in order to come together around these two whom we love and care for, these two we support, these two whom we long to see succeed.

As we surround them the pastor prays and invites us all to speak words of affirmation over them, words of prayer on their behalf.

When we conclude, the older woman in the center of the group looks around at us with tears in her eyes.

"My ancestors had a practice," she says in a strong, emotion-filled voice. "A practice where—if there was a danger drawing near, they would put all the children in the center and then form a tight circle about and around to protect them. This was to enable the children to grow strong and to live the life that was ahead of them, to do the good work Creator had for them to do."

Tears are streaming down her face now.

"You have done this for us here today, standing around and with us. Helping us grow strong and do the good work Creator has for us to do. Thank you for being our people."

A fellow community member named Shadrach and I meet for a beer soon after the service. He opts for an amber ale while I go straight for a stout. It doesn't take long for our conversation to land on the extraordinary thing, the deeply empowering encircling we've both just witnessed and participated in.

"It's astonishing what's happening on multiple levels, isn't it?" I ask.

"Not just that the community is metaphorically standing with them, but that we are actually, *physically* standing beside and around them as well. That we speak words of wisdom and power and goodwill and affirmation over them, that despite all our differences we come together to bless and encourage and support one another for the good work Creator has for us to do."

Shadrach finishes a sip of his beer and nods. "Who doesn't need that? To know that you have a whole community of people around you, supporting you, standing with you and alongside you?"

"To know that whether you succeed or fail," I add, "you are welcomed in by a group that seeks to hold you up, and to do that with goodwill and great hope."

"I know that place isn't perfect," Shadrach says, taking another sip of his beer. "But we all need to feel like we belong to something, to keep the gnawing sense of loneliness at bay. Outside of my family, this is the best place I've belonged in a long time. One of the most hopeful, one of the most formative communities I've ever been a part of."

"Me too," I agree, feeling a potent gratitude grip my gut. "Like you said: Who doesn't need that? Who doesn't *want* that? A formative life together with a particular group of people, in a particular place, for a particular time. No, it isn't perfect. But it is very, very good."

CHAPTER 19

Unto Others #2: The Practice of Caring

To care means first of all to be present to each other.

—HENRI NOUWEN[1]

You can find Calcutta anywhere in the world. You only need two eyes to see. Everywhere in the world there are people that are not loved, people that are not wanted nor desired, people that no one will help, people that are pushed away or forgotten.

—MOTHER TERESA[2]

To love someone does not mean first of all to do things for that person; it means helping her to discover her own beauty, uniqueness, the light hidden in her heart and the meaning of her life. Through love a new hope is communicated to that person, and thus a desire to live and to grow. This communication of love may require words, but love is essentially communicated through non-verbal means: our attitudes, our eyes, our gestures and our smiles.

—JEAN VANIER[3]

To evangelize a person is to say to him or her: you, too, are loved by God in the Lord Jesus. And not only to say it but to really think it and relate it to the man or woman so they can sense it . . . But that becomes possible only by offering the person your friendship; a friendship that is real, unselfish, without condescension, full of confidence, and profound esteem.

—BRENNAN MANNING[4]

Love is never abstract. It does not adhere to the universe or the planet or the nation or the institution or the profession, but to the singular sparrows of the street, the lilies of the field, "the least of these my brethren." Love is not, by its own desire, heroic. It is heroic only when compelled to be. It exists by its willingness to be anonymous, humble, and unrewarded.

—WENDELL BERRY[5]

I'm eavesdropping outside a patient's room at St. Paul's Hospital. The conversation is about me, so I feel somewhat justified in doing this. To make myself look busy I pull a pen from my fire-engine red "Volunteer Vest" and start scratching meaningless notes on the standard-issue notepad.

"I can't believe it," Lyle—the patient I've just spent fifteen minutes chatting with—says from inside his room.

"Believe what?" his nurse asks. I can hear her tidying Lyle's room, picking up his bedpan.

"That guy," Lyle says.

"Who?" asks the nurse. "The volunteer?"

"Yeah," says Lyle. "I mean, you nurses and doctors, you're paid to take care of us. It's your job. You all *have* to be here."

"Well," the nurse muses, "most days it doesn't feel like an obligation. I actually enjoy working here."

"Doing something while getting paid for it is one thing," Lyle says. "Doing it for free is another thing entirely."

"I guess so," the nurse agrees.

After a moment of silence Lyle wonders aloud, "Why do you think he does it?"

"I don't know." The nurse stops her tidying, musing over the question. "People volunteer at St. Paul's for all sorts of reasons. Some are trying to boost their chances of getting into med school, some are doing it as community service after a minor offense, some just because they're bored and looking for something to do, or because they want to give something back to their community. Why don't you ask him next time?"

"Maybe I will," Lyle says. "Regardless, I really enjoy talking to him, you know? It's like he cares about me. He's got no agenda. No expectations. It's just a conversation. It's nice."

"I'm sure it is, Mr. Smith," the nurse responds, finishing her tasks. "Now let me get rid of this, and I'll be back in just a minute with your medication."

By now I've finished crossing the t's and dotting the i's on my notepad three times over. I turn to head down the hall toward the next patient's room when all of a sudden the nurse comes racing out of Lyle's room—bedpan in hand—and we nearly crash right into one another.

Thankfully she's an expert at keeping things afloat, and we both raise our eyes in glad astonishment that everything has stayed where it should.

"I'm *so* sorry about that," I say sheepishly.

"Not nearly as sorry as you might have been," she jokes with a wry smile.

I give her a wide breadth and continue on down the hall, Lyle's question ringing in my ears.

Why *am* I doing this?

It's a question I ask myself every Tuesday as I frantically try and finish up a few last-minute tasks, cut short the phone call that's dragging on longer than it ought to, and hurriedly rifle through the refrigerator looking for something to grab for a late lunch en route to the hospital. Why halt a busy, productive, too-much-to-finish kind of day in order to venture thirty minutes across town to a hospital? After all, most people avoid hospitals like those other infamous institutions that pepper our landscape—*prisons*. "I'll only go when they *make* me go!" most of us say.

Why would anyone *intentionally* spend time wandering the labyrinthine, florescent-lit, antiseptic-smelling hallways, wheeling patients around or running somebody else's errands or just sitting beside the bed and chatting?

The answer to this question has been obvious every afternoon I've spent here: doing this is perhaps the most sobering thing I've ever done in my life. It is very, *very* good. And I'm not talking about the kind of moral, pat-yourself-on-the-back, holier-than-thou kind of sobriety or "goodness," but the heart-quickening, meaning-engendering, enlarge-your-soul moments that take your breath away even as they bring tears to your eyes and make you hope that someday—*someday!*—you'll be a person worthy of the goodness you sense might be there way-down-deep in the heart of the universe.

Don't get me wrong—volunteering at the hospital is by no means a walk in the park.

In fact it's gut wrenching: two of the patients I've known at St. Paul's have left the hospital via the morgue in the basement. Many are still there, watching the clock tick-tock in increments of months, not hours. Even those who seem like they'll recover and soon be going home provide a weekly, head-on encounter with the bare and basic fact that we are all frail, fragile, beautiful people, that we are all weak sometimes, that we are all in need of compassion and love.

A typical volunteer shift at St. Paul's is about two hours long and involves visiting with around ten patients, doing everything from fluffing pillows or wheeling people down to the cafeteria for a coffee, to getting books from the basement library or just sitting together in silence with them. I'm a member of what's called the "Flying Squad," an illustrious catch-all term for the crew of "filler" volunteers: we go wherever we're needed, whenever we're needed.

Practically, that means I spend a lot of time in the stairwell.

Ad-hoc development over more than a century has left St. Paul's Hospital with a smorgasbord layout that is more mash-up than design. Teams of engineers and architects are constantly at work improving the place. Such constant "improvement" is commendable in theory, but in practice, it only adds to the madness.

During the time I've been volunteering here the elevator systems in the main building have all been under rotating renovation, and so the nine intended elevators have been reduced to only four. On really bad days, only two or three actually work. Given the number of high-priority patients that must be shuttled between floors—from, say, Emergency to the OR or from Recovery to Radiology—most of the staff and volunteers have learned to avoid the sometimes ten-minute wait and instead use the stairwell in order to move up and down through the hospital.

One especially busy afternoon I have already ascended and descended about fifty floors in total. I am literally dripping with sweat as I make my way up to the tenth floor to respond to one final patient request before calling it a day. A fellow red-vested volunteer stops on a landing to let fast-moving doctors and nurses pass her by. I stop, too, thankful for the chance to catch my breath before I see the last patient.

"This Stairway to Heaven is a killer, isn't it?" the volunteer says with a smile.

"Stairway to Heaven?" I ask between gasps. "What do you mean?"

Out of the corner of my eye I catch a quick smirk on the face of a passing doctor.

"These stairs," the volunteer says, a little surprised. "You know that's what they're called, right?"

I shake my head.

She laughs. "Yeah, it's pretty morbid, but think about it: Palliative Care is on floor 10, Maternity is on three. The people at the top are almost finished with their time here, so they put them way up high—you know, closer to heaven."

Wiping a drop of sweat out of my eye, I have to laugh.

"The original Saint Paul would be proud," I respond with a grin. "But yeah, the ascent is a killer."

"Well," she says, checking her watch. "I was paged to Maternity five minutes ago. I should get down there."

Finding an opening in the traffic on the stairway, she merges back into the flow, descending toward the great big ENTER HERE sign hung over the third floor, while I continue ascending toward the EXIT.

I check in at the nurse's station in Palliative Care.

"It's just about dinner time," the head nurse says as I arrive in the ward. "We're swamped this evening. Would you be willing to help Beatrice with her dinner?"

"What does that entail?" I say tentatively. Other than my niece Tirzah, I've never helped anybody eat before, and I'm doubting my skill.

But my hesitation doesn't seem to dissuade him.

He pushes Beatrice's rolling dinner table toward me, and I stare down wide-eyed at the variety of things it contains.

"You'll get the hang of it," he assures me with a smile. "It's just applesauce and mashed potatoes and a little fruit juice. She can't handle much in her state. Just keep the bites small, and she'll do fine."

With that he spins on a heel and walks back to the nurse's station to answer a ringing phone.

"You're late," Beatrice says with a half grin after I've knocked on the door to her room. The strain of those few words sends her into a bout of intense coughing. Opening the door a little, I hear a vaguely familiar song playing from her bedside table, though I can't immediately place it.

"That I am, Beatrice," I reply with a nod. "I'm sorry." I accidentally run the hospital table into the door with a loud *bang!*

"Oh, it's you!" she says, recognizing my voice. "I thought you were the nurse. From the sound of things you've brought me my dinner, so I guess I'll have to forgive you." Beatrice's eyelids are half closed as always, but she has a smile on her face. I've been getting to know Beatrice for the past several weeks, stopping by and chatting for as long as I'm able.

"What are you listening to?" I ask as I position the hospital table across her bed.

"*Les Misérables*," Beatrice answers. "Do you know it?"

"Of course," I say. The whole sweep of Victor Hugo's epic storyline comes rushing back to me. "Shall I pause it while you eat your dinner?" I ask, placing the napkin over Beatrice's hospital gown.

She shakes her head. "No. Let it be. It will be like dinner theatre!" She laughs a little, but the laughter turns into coughing.

"What's on the menu tonight?" Beatrice asks when she's at last found her breath.

"Mashed potatoes, applesauce, and fruit juice," I say, picking up a fork. "What shall we start with?"

"Is that even a question?" Beatrice asks with mock surprise. "Mashed potatoes, please."

"Okay," I say, unwrapping the plastic fork. "I've never helped anybody eat before," I confess as I begin mixing the mashed potatoes. "So just let me know if the bites are too big."

"Right," Beatrice says. "You'll do fine. I'll let you know when I'm ready for the next bite, okay? It's like the *Ready, Aim, Fire!* game parents play with their kids to get them to eat. Only now it's an old lady that's being fed."

I have to smile at the simple, forthright joy this dying old woman exudes. "That sounds very good, Beatrice."

"Ready . . . ," Beatrice says in a loud voice. "Aim . . ." Her volume increases. "*Fire!*" she practically shouts, ending with her mouth open.

"Fire!" she says again, before I've even had a chance to gather the second bite.

"Fire!"

"Whoa, slow down!" I say, scrambling to fill the fork again.

As we finish the mashed potatoes, the finale to *Les Misérables* begins, with Jean Valjean's powerful voice filling Beatrice's small room.

"This is my favorite part," Beatrice shares with a sigh. "It's my constant prayer these days, you know. I'm ready to go home, tired of all this waiting around to die, delightful as it has been to get to know you and the other volunteers."

"Beatrice, I—" I stumble, at a total loss for the right words to say in response.

"Shhh!!!" Beatrice hisses at me. "*Listen!*"

I put down the fork and listen as the dying Jean Valjean's song of longing for his true home fills Beatrice's tenth-story hospital room, high atop the Stairway to Heaven.

As the song continues, tears begin flowing down both of our cheeks, especially as Fantine and Cosette join in harmony with Jean Valjean for the culmination of the entire production, expressing in perfect harmony the linkage between loving others and knowing God.

∽

A couple of weeks later I'm back at Beatrice's room on the tenth floor.

Turns out Beatrice would like to go for a "walk" today from her ward to the windows in order to look out at the city and "get some fresh air." She's too sick and too weak—too close to the end of her time here in this world—to be taken down to the fourth floor where the rooftop gardens are located. Nevertheless, gazing out the west-facing windows toward the sea has been refreshing and restorative for her in the past, and I'm happy to help however I can.

The nurse and I help Beatrice sit down in the blue transport wheelchair. She's become too weak today to lift her own feet, so I take one and the nurse the other, and we gently lift each leg up onto the footrests of the wheelchair, Velcroing them in so they'll stay put as we're moving.

"Ready, Beatrice?" I ask, releasing the emergency brakes on the wheelchair.

Because today is an especially low-energy day, my question receives no audible response, just a barely perceptible nod of Beatrice's thinly haired head.

"Okay," I say with evident flair. "Here we go!"

I wheel Beatrice out of Palliative Care and into the main corridor, toward the radiant west-facing windows. Sunlight is pouring in thick as honey. I position Beatrice's chair right in the center of a generous pie-wedge of radiance and pull up a chair beside her.

"What a *gorgeous* day!" I exclaim, blinking in the sunlight. "This sun is a welcome change after all the rain we've had this winter, isn't it?"

"Yes," Beatrice agrees with a labored nod of her head. She turns her face—only slightly—deeper into the warm light. A faint smile comes across her thin lips, but I can't help wonder how many smiles she has left in this life.

We settle into several minutes of comfortable silence, while Beatrice just closes her eyes there in the warm sunlight.

Looking out at the sea I'm struck by how odd and yet simultaneously extraordinary it is for two people who hardly know one another to sit quietly together like this. It makes me thankful for all the time I've spent trying to cultivate silence in my own life during this Sacred Year.

For meaningless chatter—as I learned early on at St. Paul's—doesn't really work in hospital wards.

Sometimes silence is the only appropriate response.

I found this out the hard way on my first volunteer shift, when I bounded into a patient's room and said in way-too-chipper a voice, "Hi, Mr. Lawrence, how's it going today?"

Mr. Lawrence's long stare bristled with evident anger.

"I've been here for three months," Mr. Lawrence said at last. "And I will probably be here for at least another three. Six months of my life has been lived in this place. How do you *think* it's going?"

I had nothing to say, except a feeble, embarrassed apology.

"Hi, Mr. Lawrence, it's a pleasure to see you today" is what I've said every week since that first-day disaster of a learning curve.

This seems to work relatively well, for it solicits a somewhat less prickly retort from Mr. Lawrence. It's the best I've been able to come up with. What *are* you supposed to say to a person who lives in chronic pain, or who has just learned they have cancer, or who has just been told her baby didn't survive the complicated operation? "Have a nice day"? "See you next week"? What if they've made their last ascent up the Stairway to Heaven by next week?

Suddenly Beatrice clears her throat, snapping me back into the brightly lit present moment. She inhales deeply and speaks. "May I ask you something?" Her voice is hard to hear, barely more than a whisper.

I lean forward. "Of course, Beatrice. Anything."

She draws in several more wheezing breaths, and her eyes remain half closed. "Do you enjoy being able to stand?"

I frown, unsure of what she's asking. Would she prefer I not sit here next to her? "Yes, I like standing," I say. "But I like sitting well enough also."

"No!" she responds sharply, smacking the armrest of her wheelchair. "That answer isn't good enough. Do you enjoy *being able to stand*?"

I suddenly feel like a student who has just learned there's going to be a pop quiz. I sit up in my chair, thinking about how to answer Beatrice's question. "Yes," I say slowly. "I enjoy being able to stand. Very much."

"That's better," Beatrice replies. "Now." She turns her face toward me, though her eyes remain half closed. "Do you enjoy being able to feed yourself breakfast, lunch, and dinner? Three full meals per day?"

I'm starting to catch on to the fact Beatrice is trying to teach me something priceless, trying to give me the hard-won wisdom of those who remain contemplative even as they are sick and nearing death.

"Yes, I enjoy being able to feed myself very much."

"Good," she responds again, nodding slowly. Then, with a sinewy, translucent old hand Beatrice grips the armrest of her wheelchair and squeezes until her knuckles turn white. "Do you enjoy being able to walk?" She is barely audible now, but her meaning is loud and clear.

"Yes," I say softly, as the tears begin stinging my eyes. "I enjoy walking very much."

Beatrice nods her head in satisfaction, pleased that her student is beginning to understand what she is offering.

"Good," she says, letting her eyelids close all the way. "Never take your health for granted," she continues, with a long sigh. "It is an easy thing to do, of course. All my life I hankered after money, yearned for a bigger house and a nicer car, sought a better lover. Nobody ever advised me to be overjoyed at the health I just took for granted."

She shakes her head at this, but then another fit of coughing breaks over her. It is nearly a full minute before she regains enough breath to speak.

"I never realized it before, but I see it now so clearly. If you can stand and feed yourself and walk, then whatever else is happening in your life, you have a great deal to be thankful for."

I remain silent, knowing now that this is a perfectly appropriate response.

Beatrice extends a hand toward me. I take it in my own, and the two of us sit there in the sunlight at the top of the Stairway to Heaven for a long while, holding hands and gazing out at the infinite sea.

"Look at all those sailboats," I say after ten minutes or so of silence. These aren't filler words. Beatrice told me earlier about her childhood by the sea in England, and the long afternoons she would spend on a grassy hill with her brothers and sisters, counting the sailboats as they came into harbor. I'm hoping the memory might be pleasant for her. The sea is vibrant now, radiant in fact, sparking like frying diamonds. "It's a perfect day for sailing," I add.

"How many are there?" Beatrice breathes.

"How many sailboats?" I say. "Hmm, let's see." I fall silent for a moment, counting the tiny triangles of white tracing their way across the infinite blue, carried along by the invisible Wind. "Twenty at least. And that's just close in. There are many more farther out, just there," I point out a different spot on the window, "toward the open ocean."

Beatrice nods and sighs, and closes her eyes halfway again, remembering.

"Do you enjoy being able to see?" Beatrice asks at last.

Her words steal my breath, as the meaning behind her question practically slaps me across the face.

I have nothing to say, as I sit here beside a dying old woman.

"I have been . . ." Beatrice opens her eyes wide, and I see for the first time something I should have picked up on long ago. "I have been blind a long time now," she says.

I am silent for several more long seconds. "Beatrice," I say at last, astonishment evident in my voice, "what's the point of sitting by a window if you can't see?"

"There are many ways to experience the light," Beatrice answers with a smile. The sunlight braids its way down through her thinning hair, onto the side of her once elegant face. The light refracts through her radiant brown iris like light through a prism so that—for a brief moment—I'm blinded by the colors that flash out from her unseeing eye.

"Michael," Beatrice says, reaching out in search of my hand, not minding at all the flow of tears coursing down her wrinkled cheeks.

"Yes, Beatrice?"

"Do you remember that line from *Les Misérables*? 'To love another person is to see the face of God'?"

"I remember it," I say.

"Have you learned to see yet?"

Why do I do this? Why am I seeking to make a habit of being with people atop the Stairway to Heaven?

Because of countless tiny-yet-seismic moments like these, sitting at the tenth-story window, holding the bony hand of a blind old woman who is helping me see things I've never noticed before. Because every time I walk out of the hospital I'm overwhelmed by a deep sense that life and health are great though finite gifts. Because I find even the darkest parts of my soul lifted and buoyed by deep gratitude for the fleeting finitude of this life, for the extraordinary gift of a heart that works (for now) and kidneys and lungs that do too (again, for now). And a brain to guide it all, and a spine and a muscular system, and immune system to protect it all, with eyes and ears and nose and tongue and skin—those five little windows—that reveal at least some of the glorious extravagance of the world that is literally overflowing with beauty.

I do this because coming face to face with the reality of death and sickness and being with the people who are nearing the tenth floor of the Stairway to Heaven is a tonic that sweetens and sanctifies the rest of my life, a catalyst that engenders not only deep gratitude but also humility, a lens that brings into focus the beautiful truth that Frederick Buechner points out, that we all

> hunger to be known and understood. We hunger to be loved. We hunger to be at peace inside our own skins. We hunger not just to be fed these things but, often without realizing it, we hunger to feed others these things because they too are starving for them. We hunger not

just to be loved but to love, not just to be forgiven but to forgive, not just to be known and understood for all the good times and bad times that for better for worse have made us who we are, but to know and understand each other to the point of seeing that, in the last analysis, we all have the same good times, the same bad times, and that for that very reason there is no such thing in all the world as anyone who is really a stranger.[6]

An unexpected sound greets me as I walk into the church's banquet hall: Chicago club–quality jazz riffs being hammered out on a piano and the sounds of friendly conversation. Laughter, lighthearted banter, friends shouting out greetings to friends. This is one of the most interesting "meals for the marginalized" I've ever been to, and I've participated in more than a handful, both as a recipient and as a provider. Something unique is emerging here: there is none of the drudgery of institutionalization, none of the bickering in the lineup, none of the dehumanizing switchbacks as you "take a number" and wait. Even the tables are exemplary: not rectangular cafeteria-style, but rounded King Arthur style, and neatly decorated too: table cloths, central vases with fresh-cut flowers, ample silverware, clean plates, and ice water with lemon.

This is an experiment of sorts, an adventure in rehumanization. The people who help organize this weekly meal at Grandview Church here in East Vancouver got together about a year ago and decided they were going to revamp the structure and format of the evening in order to try and make it more of a family-style, sit-down-and-eat-together meal, rather than an industrialized, "move it or lose it" sort of thing.

The effect has been impressive.

"You want some mashed potatoes?" Kyle says, reaching for my plate as I sit down. I can see the grime under his fingernails and am thankful he's wearing plastic gloves. Despite his shabby clothing, his unkempt hair, his broken teeth, Kyle's excitement at being able to serve another is overwhelming.

I nod with evident gratitude. The smell of Yukon-Gold potatoes overwhelmed me when I walked in, and my mouth hasn't stopped watering since.

"These are the best mashed potatoes I've ever had," Kyle exclaims with a smile, heaping my plate full. I wonder how long it might have been since he's done something for someone else.

"That's more than enough," I say, after the second massive spoonful.

"Nah," Kyle says with a smile. "These are too good to pass up. Here, just one more. You can thank me later."

"Thank you!" I say with wide-eyed surprise as he hands the plate back to me. It weighs at least three pounds.

The difference between the take-a-number, assembly-line approach and the family-style approach couldn't be more evident. By empowering people with the opportunity to care about one another—gasp!—we actually care. Serving one another dinner *encourages generosity* instead of inciting greed or jealousy. Not perfectly, of course, for people are never perfect, but it begs an interesting question: Could it be that the *ways* we go about caring for one another have the ability to foster either kindness or conflict, to solicit selflessness or breed selfishness?

"This is incredible," Kyle says once he's taken his own seat.

"What is?" I ask.

"This . . . ," Kyle answers, motioning toward the rest of the room with his fork. "I've never been to a meal like this." He takes another mouthful of mashed potatoes. Judging by his appearance I assume Kyle has been to lots of these sorts of meals, and I'm curious about what he's getting at.

"These mashed potatoes are extraordinary," I say, taking another bite of my own.

"They are," Kyle agrees, while shaking his head. "But that's not what I mean."

"What then?"

"Usually I'm the one receiving from other people. It feels really good to give, though, to be the one to serve you your meal too.

That's when something snaps sharply into focus for me: giving back, caring about others, is astonishingly uplifting, joy-inducing, humanizing work. We were *all* made to love. As Jean Vanier points out, "we come to this earth to open up to others, to serve them and receive the gifts they bring to us."[7] What pain might I have inadvertently caused by always *doing* the serving, instead of allowing myself to be genuinely cared for as well? Despite my best intentions, might I have inadvertently dehumanized the people I've been trying to care for by always enforcing a hierarchy where *I'm* the benevolent one and *they're* merely the recipient of my magnanimity?

"It is no good at all to do everything for those you love, and not give them a share in the doing," writer George MacDonald warned more than a century ago. "It's not kind. It's making too much of yourself."[8]

Why have I been so slow to see that "every human being has a great, yet often unknown, gift to care, to be compassionate, to become present to the other, to listen, to hear and to receive"?[9]

The truest sort of life-giving care—I'm beginning to see—must be bidirectional: it must not only be given but also *received* from others. For care is not just a process, but a fabric. A great tapestry into which we are all invited to be woven and by which we are all invited to be held. Care is multifaceted, adaptive, wonderfully dynamic and fluid, a *Dance* that—if we'll but let it—can carry us up into uncommon realms.

Like I've said before, words are verbal Velcro. If they're kept clean they are wonderfully useful, holding thoughts together, making ideas and stories stick. But also like Velcro, if you use words indiscriminately, sticking them to anything and everything, they become so chock-full of random bits of fuzz and lint that their capacity to adhere diminishes. Soon words are all but useless, merely cosmetic reminders of once functional realities.

Sadly, *love* has become so chock-full of detritus from carelessness and poor usage that it's nearing uselessness. We love anything and everything these days: our cars, our bicycles, our houses. That new T-shirt, or a nation, a favorite TV show or a baseball team, a friend or a spouse or a child.

But like Velcro, it is possible to pull the lint out of words, to restore some of their stickiness.

Though it is longer and clunkier, the phrase *caring deeply* is acting like a stiff brush, helping scrape the lint out of *love*. I'm doing my best to only say that I *love* something or someone if I really care deeply about it. I thoroughly enjoy ice cream. But I do not care deeply about it. Take it away and I will be just fine. So, too, with my bicycle and even my favorite shirt. But my family? My friends? The patients I've been getting to know at St. Paul's?

I care deeply.

To deeply care about someone or something is to find yourself invested in its well-being, rejoicing when it does well, saddened when it does poorly. Maybe this is what is meant by "rejoicing with those who rejoice," as Saint Paul says, and "weeping with those who weep."[10] So much so that you not only abstractly desire but also manifestly work toward the well-being of those whom you care about, and can't but help lament when things go poorly.

Mother Teresa said, "Love, to be true, has to hurt."[11]

Of course it does. Real love asks something of us, requires something of us, demands that we cease our stoic indifference and impenetrability and instead be open, vulnerable, *affectable*.

I weep when I learn Beatrice has died.

The nurse seems surprised. "She wasn't expected to live long," he says. "You knew that."

"I know," I say, wiping away a tear. "Of course I knew. But even so."

"You've spent a lot of time with her these past few months, haven't you?" The nurse's voice is kinder now.

"Yeah," I nod. "And I'm deeply grateful for that time."

Caring deeply is what the Greek word *agape* seems to be getting at, what it's trying to stick to. When John 3:16 says that "God so loved the world," it doesn't just mean that God has an affinity for the world, or that God is mildly pleased by the world, or that God likes the world in the way we enjoy a cup of coffee or that favorite T-shirt, but rather that God *cares deeply* about the world, that God is yearning for and working toward the world's well-being, that God is rejoicing with those who rejoice and weeping with those who weep. So much so, in fact, that God gets involved, gets down and dirty with, gets wrapped up in this cared-oh-so-deeply-about world, and in fact sends his only Son into the world, in the hope that the world might flourish.

Perhaps this is the greatest indication of God's omnipotence, the divine capaciousness and might. We needn't bother asking whether God is able to create a boulder too big to move, for here's a more illuminating enigma: Can God create anything—anything at all—and not care deeply about it? And not be affected by it?

"Even the sparrow,"[12] assured Jesus.

And by extension each of the four hundred billion stars in all those one hundred billion galaxies, sown like seeds amid the *tremendum*.

Beloved hazelnuts, every one.

Even you.

Even me.

Singular gifts, all of us.

Melting snowflakes though we are.

CHAPTER 20

Year-End Review

God wills that our occupation shall be in striving to
know and love him until we are made whole.

—JULIAN OF NORWICH[1]

Either you look at the universe as a very poor creation out of which
no one can make anything or you look at your own life and your own
part in the universe as infinitely rich, full of inexhaustible interest,
opening out into the infinite further possibilities for study and
contemplation and interest and praise. Beyond all and in all is God.

—THOMAS MERTON[2]

Glory be to him whose power, working in us, can do infinitely more
than we can ask or imagine; glory be to him from generation to
generation in the Church and in Christ Jesus for ever and ever. Amen.

—EPHESIANS 3:20–21 TJB

During the last week of my Sacred Year, I trudge in a flurry of inattentiveness down our community house's two flights of creaking stairs into the basement, where the washer and dryer reside. Much to my frustration, a housemate has carelessly (to my mind, anyway) started a load of laundry earlier in the morning and then forgotten it there before going off to work. This means I have the responsibility of first emptying the washing machine before I can get to my own chores. A tiny oversight—true—but stress always doubles an insult.

Mumbling my frustrations I quickly yank the damp and wrinkling clothes from the machine and leave them heaped high atop the dryer. "Not my problem," I say to myself, leaving them to mold.

I then cram my own clothes down into the machine, whirl the nobs, toss in a half scoop of the snow-white detergent, and pull so hard on the Start dial the whole thing comes off into my hand.

Then I fly back upstairs to keep hacking away at my to-do list, forgetting entirely about the hazelnut in the pocket of my jeans that are now in the wash.

If I think about the hazelnut at all during the next few chaotic days, it isn't conscious enough to motivate a search. In fact, this week is so particularly stressful that I don't even notice its absence.

A few days later, long after the sun and wind has dried my jeans on the clothesline, long after they have been folded and put away, I at last wear that pair of jeans again. I slip them on over my feet and hoist them up as usual, ready to get going on my day. But I encounter something strange as I try to smooth down my pockets, something familiar and yet now suddenly strange. Changed.

I close my hand around the hazelnut and gently coax it from my pocket. Holding it there in the hollow of my hand, my mouth falls open in astonishment.

The hazelnut has sprouted.

Soaked by the warm water of the wash, awoken by the sunlight while on the drying line, and given a bit of time in the darkness of my drawer, impossibly, imperceptibly, and without a single eye poised to *Selah!* it, the common yet unexpected miracle of new life began taking shape right there in my pocket.

Now a tiny taproot has emerged through a hairline crack in the shell, seeking life and light and nourishment and anchorage. I turn the hazelnut over and over again in the chalice of my palm, wondering at the chance or luck or providence that has brought this moment to me in the final stretch of my Sacred Year.

The next day a friend named Aaron and I are working together in my garden plot, shelling soup peas. We have a whole tangled mess of uprooted vines heaped up into a pile on the sidewalk beside the garden, and we sit here cracking and snapping the peas free from their pods into shopping bags as people speed by us on busy First Avenue. It is slow, steady work, the kind that absorbs just enough mental chatter so as to make it possible to really listen to what someone is saying.

"I used to work on a tunnel crew," Aaron says, dropping another handful of peas into the bag.

"What does that mean?"

"Construction," Aaron explains. "I worked for eight months on a tunnel crew, building a new tunnel up north."

"That's a long time," I say. "How was the work?"

"It was okay at first," Aaron shares. "I was on the night shift, and I used to arrive just after sunset, work all night long, and then come out into the daylight. Bookending your workday with light on both sides is a good thing."

I nod and crack open another pea.

"But after a month I got transferred to the day shift," Aaron continues, disgust obvious in his voice. "They assumed I *wanted* to work the day shift, but it was awful. The only thing I knew was darkness. Light became a memory—a thing of the distant past. I worked all day long in the darkness beneath the mountain, working a front-end loader to load the dump trucks that took away the rock as the drilling machines ground on and on. I'd get there before daylight, and emerged from the tunnel after sunset. Seven months of nothing but darkness."

"Did you get weekends off?" I ask, disturbed by the thought of never seeing daylight. The shortened hours of winter daylight in Vancouver's northern latitude are notorious for causing depression and seasonal affective disorder in the population. I shuddered to think what the effect of total darkness might be on a person.

Aaron shakes his head. "Nope," he says. "The contractor was on a tight deadline. They paid double for weekend overtime, and I needed the money. I worked seven months with only four days off, and every one of those four days it was raining."

"That would have been really hard."

"It was good in a way," Aaron says. "In the end it was all worth it."

"How so?"

"Well . . . ," Aaron begins to explain. He stops shelling peas and looks directly at me. "The moment we punched through was one of the most astonishing things I've ever seen. We were drilling and drilling, scooping and loading, just as we had been for more than half a year. Rumors started to fly that we were getting close, and yet the work kept on for another three or four hours. And then all of a sudden, everybody started shouting, and it was like someone had flipped a switch on the sun. We were *there*. We'd *made* it! The whole crew started cheering and hugging one another and some of the guys actually shed tears—can you imagine that? Big burly construction guys weeping in the sunlight! All of us covered under a solid half inch of the mountain's dust, blinking in astonishment in all that brightness."

I don't say anything for a bit, just hold the potency of the image in my mind for a while. "That's a good day's work," I say at last.

Aaron nods. "That's kind of how I think about this thing called faith. We've got to keep pushing on and on under a mountainous weight, making our way through what feels like interminable darkness, hoping, waiting, watching for the day when we'll finally break through into daylight, when things will finally be the way they're *supposed* to be."

A few days after Aaron and I finish with the peas, I head out to the monastery for one last weekend retreat (a sort of formal closure Father Solomon thought might be a good idea after everything my Sacred Year has entailed). After I've gotten settled into my room Father Solomon invites me to walk with him through the monastery orchard. "It's a beautiful fall day," he says. "The winter rains will be coming soon. Let's enjoy being outdoors while we can."

Outside the air is crisp and cool, with that sharp, spicy note at the edges that marks the coming of fall—it's a perfect afternoon for a walk with a monk.

As we saunter along, several of the other monks are working in teams with ladders, harvesting the abundant fruit—pears, apples, plums, apricots—filling bushel upon bushel that will be stored for the community to eat throughout the winter months.

As we near a high outlook, I recount Aaron's story of working on the tunnel crew to Father Solomon.

"The life of faith is like digging a tunnel under a mountain in utter darkness?" Father Solomon repeats. "Sounds about right. At least half of the time, anyway. Is that an accurate way to describe your Sacred Year?"

"It is," I say, nodding. "The Sacred Year has been profound in so many ways, some expected, some utterly surprising. There have been moments of clarity, *ah-ha!* moments as well, but a great deal of it has just been showing up, putting in the work, slogging through the darkness. It just feels like hard work at three o'clock in the afternoon on the days I'm fasting, or in the early mornings when—frankly—the last thing I want to do is get out of bed and sit silently with a candle, trying to listen and pray."

"Nobody ever said it would be easy. It's more a marathon than a hundred-yard dash. 'Let us run with endurance the race that is set before us,'[3] as someone once put it."

We fall silent for a few moments, listening to the sound of the Wind rustling in the trees, inhaling the rich autumnal fragrances it offers to us.

Father Solomon breaks the silence. "You arrived here almost a year ago out of a terrible storm, Michael. If I remember correctly, you'd just had quite the realization on a plane flight home from the carnival, and through that experience you'd realized that you'd lost the love of life, that you were numb and apathetic and jaded. You said you didn't care whether you lived or died."

I nod, remembering in a quick montage the Change Our World conference and the Shouter and the realization of my own hypocrisy and dry-as-a-desert-psuedospirituality.

"Looking in from the outside," Father Solomon says, "and judging from the conversations we've been having over these past few months, it seems as though you are now in a different place entirely."

"A very different place," I agree.

Father Solomon and I have come to the place where all the bushel baskets of fruit have been stacked, there on a little paved area that doubles as a prime lookout spot from high atop the monastery's hill.

As Father Solomon and I stand there, the fertile river valley stretches out below us toward the west, the river sparkling and shining in the crisp air as it meanders its way toward the mighty Pacific.

"I remember that image you gave me, Father Solomon, way back during our first meeting together. You said that spiritual practices were a way of unfurling the sail of the soul so that the Wind-Spirit-Breath of God might fill us and propel us wherever it wills."

Father Solomon nods and smiles, his habit billowing in the breeze. "It's a good image, isn't it?"

"That it is," I say with a nod. "And so is this." I kneel down, untie my shoes, and slip them off one by one, doing likewise with my socks.

When I'm finally unshod and free, I stand up again and nod down toward the meandering river valley below us. "Peace to you on the journey, Father Solomon," I say, stretching out my hand.

Father Solomon reaches out and grasps my hand warmly. "Peace to you on yours, Michael."

Having returned to the city, I cradle the sprouted hazelnut over to the green rocking chair, where I've been regularly praying during these months, and sit down to contemplate awhile. The implications of what I'm beholding overwhelm me, even as they underscore so much of what I've been sensing, so much of what I've slowly been coming to see.

All of the Sacred Year—all the months of spiritual practice, of learning, of effort and hope and longing—has been but a beginning. Just a taproot, a digging on and on through the darkness, driven by a hungering for life and light and nourishment and anchorage, an anticipation and preparation and foreshadowing of everything else that is yet to come.

While I'm sitting here in this green chair my faithful companion of a dog—a black lab named Elliott—comes to sit beside me. He sighs contentedly, surveying the world, but then suddenly notices *The Complete Works of William Shakespeare* sitting on the half-table beside me. He stands, walks to the table with tail wagging, and begins smelling the hefty volume with evident vigor. He works the whole thing over from top to bottom, does it again for good measure, and at last licks a certain spot on the edge a few times. Eventually he's satisfied or has lost interest, and before long he returns to sit beside me.

And God says to us through the prophet Isaiah, "My thoughts are nothing like your thoughts . . . and my ways are far beyond anything you could imagine."[4]

Even after a year of spiritual practice I'm feeling as though I'm just scratching the surface of things, just sniffing around the edges, just beginning to get a taste.

Each of these spiritual practices—I'm convinced—requires a *lifetime* to come into its full maturity, a *lifetime* in order to bring forth all of its intended fruit. This doesn't strike me as disheartening, though. It's not like the practices are a set of infinitely receding finish lines, forever slipping out of reach. We aren't meant to *accomplish* the practices, to check them off our lists. Rather our capacity for depth and life *increases* as we delve more fully into the practices. It's as though each of these practices *enlarges* our capacity for the divine, even as they help—by God's grace—to bring us in increasing measure into the likeness of God himself.

I'm convinced that just one spiritual practice isn't enough in a life, any more than just one color is enough on a palate or one instrument sufficient for a symphony. These are not isolated silos of focused spirituality. Rather, when taken together, the spiritual practices form an interwoven, mutually reinforcing whole. They're like a landscape—a soulscape, rather—with different aspects and features: mountains and rivers and forests and plains, and everything in between, but forming *one* interconnected whole all the same. Gratitude flows into simplicity, and simplicity reverberates back out in care. Justice and protest and community stand in healthy, invigorating tension with solitude and silence and

Sabbath. Wilderness reminds us of how small and yet upheld we all are, even as embracing mortality infuses individual moments with a quality of potent poignancy. The Examine shares much of the DNA of listening prayer, and both help infuse confession with authenticity, and on and on.

Taken together though, spiritual practices become a lifelong *way*. A *pilgrim path* that will lead our sauntering unto the end of our days. This path we are beckoned down is an invitation to—if I might borrow Saint Paul's language—*co-labor* with Christ.[5] The Greek word Saint Paul used here—*synergoi*—is where we get our English word *synergy*. The unfathomable invitation presented to us in the *way* of spiritual practice is to work *synergistically* with God by walking on that pilgrim path, to meld our hearts and minds and wills and our very lives with God through the ongoing journey until we are at last standing in the full light of day, fully "conformed to the image of his Son."[6]

Who knows how God might show up to us as we walk this *way*? The dying friend whose hand we're holding through the darkest of nights, the Bell Tree from which the old tire rim summons us to a feast, even that single apple resting on the corner of the table just there—each a kindled bush, an invitation to join in and participate in the Great Dance the creating-sustaining-redeeming God has brought and is still bringing into being.

"Join in!" I cry to you. "Join in with eyes and ears and sails open wide, and you just might catch the Wind billowing in your pulses, you just might learn to glimpse the truth that everything and every moment alike cradles a hazelnut in its pocket, a pearl of greatest price, tucked way down deep, just waiting to be brought to blazing life through your both-arms-lifted-high *Selah!*"

Appendix A

Additional Resources

P oet Gary Snyder proposes a delightful metaphor:

> All this new stuff goes on top
> turn it over, turn it over
> wait and water down
> from the dark bottom
> turn it inside out
> let it spread through
> Sift down even.
> Watch it sprout.
>
> A mind like compost.[1]

With this grounding thought in mind, I offer you in the following pages a loose layering of various works that I personally have found nourishing, generative, and/or provocative during this Sacred Year. Obviously there are many more titles that should be added to this list, but I wanted to at least offer a few titles here. And, while I am too particular in my thinking to unconditionally affirm all that is contained in each of these works, I have found each of the following (and many more besides) worthy of inclusion in the compost heap of my mind and heartily suggest that you consider adding them to your shelves and life.

Should you choose to layer in one or more of these works to your own compost, don't be deterred if you encounter something startling in their depths—I certainly did. Instead, let me encourage you to savor it all, to "test the spirits"[2] as we are admonished to do, to be discerning in mind and learn from truth wherever it may be hiding.

Who knows? You may discover that a particularly acidic aspect of your own personality is in fact being balanced by a more basic—albeit unexpected—reality.

Like compost, building a mind—building a life—is work, requiring both effort and patience.

But it is good work. Nourishing work. Necessary work.

And who knows what vital reality just might spring up from the goodness that ensues?

Spiritual Practice/Spiritual Theology

Crossing the Postmodern Divide by Albert Borgmann

Technology and the Character of Contemporary Life by Albert Borgmann

Spiritual Theology by Simon Chan

Celebration of Discipline by Richard Foster

Care of the Soul by Thomas Moore

The Cloister Walk by Kathleen Norris

The Quotidian Mysteries by Kathleen Norris

Monk Habits for Everyday People by Dennis L. Okholm

The Holy Longing by Ronald Rolheiser

Desiring the Kingdom by James K. A. Smith

The Spirit of the Disciplines by Dallas Willard

Mudhouse Sabbath by Lauren F. Winner

After You Believe by N. T. Wright

Living Faithfully in a Fragmented World by Jonathan R. Wilson

Liturgical/Prayer Guides

Celtic Daily Prayer: Prayers and Readings from the Northumbria Community

Common Prayer by Shane Claiborne, Jonathan Wilson-Hartgrove and Enuma Okoro

The Divine Hours series by Phyllis Tickle

God With Us, eds. Gregory Wolfe and Greg Pennoyer

Watch for the Light: Readings for Advent and Christmas

Sabbath

The Rest of God by Mark Buchanan

Keeping the Sabbath Wholly by Marva J. Dawn

The Sabbath by Abraham Joshua Heschel

Sabbath by Wayne Muller

Living the Sabbath by Norman Wirzba

Sustenance

The Supper of the Lamb by Robert Farrar Capon

The Hungry Soul by Leon R. Kass

Dirt by William Bryant Logan

The Good Life by Scott and Helen Nearing

Pilgrimage

The Way Is Made by Walking by Arthur Paul Boers

On Pilgrimage by Dorothy Day

Off the Road by Jack Hitt

The Pilgrim God by Brother John of Taizé

Planted by Leah Kostamo

Creativity

The Writing Life by Annie Dillard

On Writing by Stephen King

Mystery and Manners by Flannery O'Conner

Art and Fear by David Bayles and Ted Orland

Free Play by Stephen Nachmanovitch
The War of Art by Steven Pressfield
Stein on Writing by Sol Stein
On Writing Well by William Zinsser

Simplicity

Sex, Economy, Freedom & Community by Wendell Berry
What Are People For? by Wendell Berry
Better Off by Eric Brende
Being Consumed by William Cavanaugh
The Consuming Passion, ed. Rodney Clapp
Living on Less and Liking It More by Maxine Hancock
An Ontology of Trash by Greg Kennedy
Living More with Less by Doris Janzen Longacre
Diet for a Small Planet by Frances Moore Lappé
Technopoly by Neil Postman
Amusing Ourselves to Death by Neil Postman

Protest

Strength to Love and *Letter from a Birmingham Jail* by Martin Luther
    King Jr.
The Binding of the Strong Man by Ched Meyers
Gandhi on Nonviolence, ed. Thomas Merton
"By What Authority: The Bible and Civil Disobedience," by Ched
    Meyers (essay, *Sojourners,* May 1984)
"Resistance to Civil Government" by Henry David Thoreau (essay)

Caring

The Essential Writings and *Becoming Human* by Jean Vanier
The Long Loneliness by Dorothy Day
Under the Overpass by Mike Yankoski
The Ragamuffin Gospel by Brennan Manning

Justice

The Moral Vision of the New Testament by Richard Hayes

The Better World Shopping Guide by Ellis Jones

The 100-Mile Diet by Alisa Smith and J. B. MacKinnon

Resurrection and Moral Order by Oliver O'Donovan

Justice by Nicholas Wolterstorff

Justice in Love by Nicholas Wolterstorff

Until Justice and Peace Embrace by Nicholas Wolterstorff

Old Testament Ethics for the People of God by Christopher Wright

Pursuing Justice by Ken Wytsma

Documentaries: *Bananas!*, Big Boys Gone Bananas!*, Food Inc., The Dark Side of Chocolate*

Lectio Divina/Spiritual Reading

Too Deep for Words by Thelma Hall

"Meditation in a Toolshed" by C. S. Lewis (essay)

Lectio Divina by M. Basil Pennington

Eat This Book by Eugene Peterson

No Moment Too Small by Norvene Vest

Wilderness / Creation

Desert Solitaire by Edward Abbey

A Timbered Choir by Wendell Berry

Silent Spring by Rachel Carson

Pilgrim at Tinker Creek by Annie Dillard

The Solace of Fierce Landscapes by Belden C. Lane

A Sand County Almanac by Aldo Leopold

God in Creation by Jürgen Moltmann

Walden by Henry David Thoreau

God's Good World by Jonathan R. Wilson

Surprised by Hope by N. T. Wright

Community

Life Together by Dietrich Bonhoeffer
I and Thou by Martin Buber
Irresistible Revolution by Shane Claiborne
The Long Loneliness by Dorothy Day
Plunging into the Kingdom Way by Tim Dickau
The One, the Three and the Many by Colin Gunton
Out of Solitude by Henri Nouwen
Exclusion & Embrace by Miroslav Volf
The Intentional Christian Community Handbook by David Janzen

Prayer

The Cloud of Unknowing (anon)
Prayer by Philip Yancey
Contemplative Prayer by Thomas Merton
Everything Belongs by Richard Rohr
"The Conferences" of John Cassian
The Wisdom of the Desert, ed. Thomas Merton

Appendix B

Almost Answered: A Q&A with the Author

Q: Some people might be uncomfortable with the idea of spiritual practice, insisting that to do so is trying to "earn our salvation" or is a "works-based faith." How do you respond to this?

A: Rightly understood, spiritual practices aren't at all about trying to "earn our salvation." They are not evidence of a "works-based faith." They *are* however, about "working out your salvation with fear and trembling," a process the apostle Paul commends in Philippians 2:12. They *are* about "co-laboring with Christ" (1 Corinthians 3:9). And, by the way, the Greek word Paul uses here is *synergoi*, where we get our English word "synergy" from.

I remember a friend explaining it this way: "All of the Christian life is a *response* to God's initiating action." We didn't create ourselves. We can't coerce God into loving us by how we live. But we can seek to live in particular ways *because* God loves us. Again, to quote Saint Paul in his letter to the Ephesians, "we are [God's] workmanship, created in Christ Jesus *for* good works . . . that we should walk in them" (Ephesians 2:10 ESV, emphasis added). It's essential to get our prepositions right, the direction of causality—what causes what? We are not saved *by* good works but *for* good works.

And spiritual practices fit here naturally: we live in particular ways *because* God loves us and gave himself for us.

A related confusion comes from how we separate God's action in our life from our own. We overemphasize our autonomy and free will in some ways. What I mean is this: many people today think that if I *choose* to do something—a spiritual practice of fasting, let's say—then that is *my* decision, *my* action, and God wasn't involved in my decision in any way. But this is a very new idea of the "will," a very atheistic idea of decision making, actually. It basically assumes that God's hands are tied when it comes to the realm of my own decision making.

I believe this is a false understanding of the human will. Older theologians—Thomas Aquinas, for example—maintained that the human and divine will could actually *work together* in human action to empower and guide us toward the purposes for which we were created. Growth in holiness, conformity with the image of God, becoming like Christ—all of these are processes that I firmly believe (and certainly hope!) that God is involved in in my life. So when I choose to engage in a spiritual practice, I don't at all think it is me just *choosing* to do it, but rather me *responding* to God's prompting in my life.

John Wesley's phrase "the means of grace" captures this beautifully. It's an incredibly helpful way to think about spiritual practices. Spiritual practices are not the "motivation" of grace, nor are they the "end" of grace. Rather, they can each be a "means" of grace, a way through which the life-giving power of God can work in us and through us to help us become more the men and women we have been created and redeemed to be.

Q: You wrote *The Sacred Year* with a three-part structure. The first is "Depth with Self," the second "Depth with God," and the third "Depth with Others." Why this particular structure?

A: One of the awful effects of the Fall we read about in the book of Genesis is the fundamental relational fractures that took place: human beings become separated from one another, from themselves, and from the God who created them, not to mention all the rest of creation as well.

Where there was relationship and a deep harmony in the garden of Eden, after the human beings are cast out there is separation, strife, and an aching loneliness. I believe that one of the most hopeful and surprising "lenses" through which to interpret the good news of Jesus Christ is that God is at work in our lives to relationally *reintegrate* us. To restore us. To take what is broken and make it whole again. This is what I believe salvation is all about: the redemption of all the fractures and broken relationships that are the inevitable result of sin.

We constantly see this kind of holistic relational healing taking place in the gospel accounts of Jesus' life and ministry. Take the leper in Matthew 8, for example. Jesus heals the man, curing him of the horrifically destructive, disintegrating disease. But this isn't just a physical healing. It is that, and so much more. This healing reintegrates the man into his community, restoring relationships that were otherwise nonexistent. To be a leper in Jesus' day and culture was to be forced—by law—into the dim margins of society. The once-leper-now-restored man may be reunited with his family, with his friends, with his community, with his God. That's precisely why Jesus tells him to go and offer sacrifice required for the healing of leprosy. Jesus' healing of the man restored him to wholeness with himself, with others, and with God.

So I wrote *The Sacred Year* with this kind of tripartite structure because I believe the good news is that God is at work even today, even now, in our very lives, restoring that which is broken into wholeness. And this wholeness—I believe the biblical narrative portrays—works along (at least) these three trajectories: wholeness with self, wholeness with others, wholeness with God.

And yet so often we reject this invitation to restoration and wholeness by staying on the surface of things. We glide through, skim through our lives, content to scrape the surface rather than plunging into the depths. I don't believe God is very interested in staying on the surface of things. The incarnation itself is proof of that. God insists on going to the heart of things, of getting into the depths. This isn't about plastic surgery, image management, or makeupping the facade. This is about *true life*: deep and flourishing life with self, with God, with others.

Q: You employ a great deal of metaphor in *The Sacred Year*—there are more stories than propositions. Why is that?

A: Why do I use metaphor, why do I rely on story? Because story and metaphor are the most enduring avenues we humans have yet found for meaning. Because story and metaphor are so much more robust and appealing than mere facts. Because Jesus didn't sit the disciples down in a classroom and give them a systematic argument about what the Kingdom of God was like, but rather said to them, "Follow me," (Mark 2:14 ESV). And when they did that they began to see with their own eyes and hear with their own ears something surprising and wonderful and invigorating about the character of God, about the way God loves and redeems this world he has made. I prefer metaphor and story to mere factuality because the Kingdom of God isn't something we can neatly encapsulate in a theory so much as it is something we must plunge into and discover and experience from the inside.

Q: So are you saying that facts and truth don't matter?

A: No, not at all. Facts matter a great deal, and I hope to come to "see clearly" one day. But as Leslie Newbigin points out in his extraordinary book *Proper Confidence*,[1] "truth" is not some fact or a piece of information, nor even an expansive network of accurate pieces of information, but a Person—Jesus Christ, who claimed, "I am the way, and the *truth*, and the life" (John 14:6 ESV, emphasis added). Coming to know this Truth is therefore much more like getting to know a person than it is like memorizing the multiplication table.

I believe "facts" and "information" are like any tool: within the intended context, they are very useful. But outside of their proper realm, they can become disadvantageous and maybe even outright dangerous. I'm thinking of when we cut other people off at the knees if they don't measure up to our particular doctrinal standards. In this way facts and information are kind of like a bottle of glue. A bottle of glue is a great tool when you want to stick a few things together, to help them congeal. But if you use a bottle of glue improperly—to wash a dish, or help you get dressed, or feed your dog—you're going to end up with a great big mess. Why? Good tool, wrong context.

I believe a great deal of the tragedy of fragmentation we see in our world today, and particularly the disintegration within Christianity, might be helped some if we could grasp the great and overarching story we're invited into with God, as opposed to bickering endlessly trying to get our doctrinal ducks in a row.

Q: Should other people endeavor on their own Sacred Years? Do you want people to follow in your footsteps?

A: Sure. Why not? Now, I realize that I've been extremely lucky in having the opportunity to spend a substantial amount of time delving into these various spiritual practices. And to have the chance to write and reflect upon them has been a great gift and honor. Not everybody will find themselves in a similarly expansive season of life. But I undoubtedly believe that each of these spiritual practices (and there are many more, of course—*The Sacred Year* is only a sampling) has an astonishing, God-given capacity to shape and form us.

Such a Sacred Year will look different for everyone, of course, but I think it would be an extraordinary thing if readers undertook something similar in their own lives—I hope it happens, and happens for many. But of course, it won't be me they're following at all, for I'm just one person amid a very large group of people, stretching back thousands of years, who have all been on this pilgrim journey, following after God, catching astonishing glimpses of Jesus along the way.

My suggestion would be to perhaps select one or two of the spiritual practices in *The Sacred Year* and then dive in for a month to each practice, and explore how they begin to shape and form you. Some of them will probably fit more into your life during this season than others will—and that's okay. We each need different things in different seasons of our journey, so delve deeply into what you sense the Spirit leading you toward.

Q: Any plans to become a monk?

A: Ha! No, not at all! I've discerned a different calling in my life than first-order monasticism, and thus am already happily married! That said, I do believe that the sixteen-hundred-year-old Christian tradition of monasticism has a great deal to offer us amid the problems and questions we are struggling with today in our hypermodern, hyperindividualistic, hyperfrenetic world. That's why I draw so heavily on the history and tradition of Christianity, including the monastics, in *The Sacred Year*. In our tradition I found kernels of strong advice, wisdom, and counsel, all of which seemed to me to be of unparalleled benefit during the Sacred Year.

It makes sense, doesn't it: if it's true that there's "nothing new under the sun" (Ecclesiastes 1:9 ESV)? Even though questions and concerns often come cloaked in facade of newness, wisdom invites us to learn what we can from those who have come before us rather than just trying to come up with new solutions in the present crisis. In the various forms of monasticism there exists a *living tradition* from which we can glean, even if we aren't able or don't feel called into full monastic vows.

That's not to say that all of the tradition is applicable in every situation today. By no means. And of course there have been egregious abuses within monasticism, as within every manifestation of Christianity. And yet so very much of it is true, honorable, and worthy of praise (Philippians 4:8). We should seek to keep the kernels of life and let the chaff go where it must.

So no, I don't want to become a monk.

But I do certainly desire to learn from our brothers and sisters who have committed themselves to seeking God by living the monastic way.

Acknowledgments

Like all good farmers, any writer worth his salt must gladly acknowledge that he is charged with the overwhelming task of stewarding a mystery, with midwifing a miracle. I don't know how to just *write* a book in any exacting, scientific sense. The process is much more organic than that: I do my best to give the project the conditions necessary for its growth, and then try my hardest to not kill it.

Such a role in the world is nine parts vulnerability, one part hope. Tenuous at best.

Despite this tension—or perhaps *within* the space created between vulnerability and hope—new life and fruit and words come into our world daily.

One of the things that has made this tension bearable is the wisdom, advice, and encouragement of many others along the way. Below I seek to acknowledge the vibrant ecosystem of people who have collectively infused *The Sacred Year* with their passion, their time, and their wisdom, and who have done so with great generosity, great endurance, great fortitude.

To each one below I lift both my hands in a posture of deepest gratitude. I am fundamentally changed for having known you, and will seek to live in the way you have helped open before me.

Danae:

Thank you for your love, for your belief in me and in this project, for your longsuffering endurance of all the ideas, all the trials, all the mishaps it has entailed. Thank you for reading and rereading the manuscript. And most of all, thank you for your tireless encouragement and empowerment toward the pursuit not just of a Sacred Year but of a Sacred Life.

The Community of Faith at Grandview Calvary Baptist Church in East Vancouver:

Thank you all for the many countless ways you embody the hope of the Kingdom of God, and for all the ways you've invited me to continue hungering toward and searching after the life of faith. It was a joy and a deep honor to work, worship, pray, welcome, protest, lament, cultivate, and hope in your midst.

The Community of Faith at Regent College, Vancouver, Canada:

Thank you for the rigor and integrity with which you seek to shape and form people more fully into the image of God. Living, working, and studying in your midst for nearly five years was—without doubt—one of the most formative seasons of my life. In many ways *The Sacred Year* is an attempt to spread the seeds of Regent wide in the world. May whatever fruit comes from it be honoring to you.

The Monastic Communities East of Vancouver:

Thank you to all within the monastic communities east of Vancouver, for the life of faith you uphold together. Thank you for your tireless rhythms of prayer, for your regular hospitality and welcome of the weary, for the guidance and direction you offer to others free of charge. Thank you for launching and guiding me on this Sacred Year.

Rivendell Retreat Centre:

Thanks to the Watchkeeper Community for the extraordinary place of hospitality, rest, and retreat that you so selflessly provide to so many people from both near and far. Rivendell is a place worthy of its name, and I am grateful for every hour I have been granted within its sacred space.

DC Jacobson and Associates:

Thank you for all the ways you helped this project become a reality. For your willingness to represent it, for your helpful questions and insightful critiques, for your ideas and enthusiasm, and for all the prompt answers to questions both warranted and unfounded. It is always an honor to work with you, and I look forward to our next project.

The Team at Thomas Nelson:

Thank you for believing in *The Sacred Year* from such an early date, and for your passion and effort which have brought it into the world. It was an honor to work with you all on this project, and I look forward to hopefully working together again soon.

A Brief Note on Anonymity and Privacy

The Sacred Year includes interactions, conversations, and experiences with an incredible variety of wonderful people. Given the nature of some of these interactions and friendships, and motivated by a desire to adequately guard people's identities and privacy, I have done my best to anonymize aspects of many of the stories included in this book. This has been a challenging process, for amid a desire to creatively capture the heart of the matter, I have of necessity sought to hold in tension what actually happened with the measure of creative freedom required to protect people's privacy.

While I hope I have largely succeeded in maintaining this delicate balance, I am undoubtedly working with all the blind spots that are inherent to being human.

If I have in any way failed in what I hoped to accomplish through these anonymizing and privatizing efforts, my only hope is that those who feel I have not done as well as I ought will be gracious and forgiving toward me in this regard.

And that you—dear reader—might find it within you to hold fast whatever vital kernels you've discovered in reading, while letting all chaff blow away in the Wind.

Notes

Opening Quotes

1. Elizabeth Barrett Browning, "Aurora Leigh, Book 7," in *Aurora Leigh*, ed. Margaret Reynolds (Athens: Ohio University Press, 1992), 487.
2. William James, *The Energies of Men: A New Edition* (New York: Moffat, Yard and Company, 1911), 14.
3. Ralph Waldo Emerson, *The Collected Works of Ralph Waldo Emerson, Vol VI: The Conduct of Life*, eds. Barbara L. Packer, Joseph Slater, Douglas Emory Wilson (Cambridge: Belknap Press of Harvard University Press, 2003), 151.
4. Karl Rahner, Attributed. Quoted in Ronald Rolheiser, *The Holy Longing: The Search for a Christian Spirituality* (New York: Doubleday, 1999), 216.
5. Frederick Buechner, *Listening to Your Life: Daily Meditations with Frederick Buechner*, ed. George Connor (New York: HarperCollins, 1992), 2.

Chapter 1: What Color Is Jaded?

1. Dante, *Inferno*, trans. Anthony Esolen (New York: The Modern Library, 2003), 3.
2. Gerard Manley Hopkins, "Justus quidem tu es, Domine," in *Gerard Manley Hopkins, The Oxford Authors*, ed. Catherine Phillips (New York: Oxford University Press, 1986), 183.

Chapter 2: Single Tasking

1. Heraclitus, fragment B30. See Charles Kahn, *The Art and Thought of Heraclitus* (Cambridge: Cambridge University Press, 1979), 44–45. Verbatim translation from the front material of Annie Dillard's *Pilgrim at Tinker Creek* (New York: Harper Collins, 1998).
2. Thomas Moore, *Care of the Soul: A Guide for Cultivating Depth and Sacredness in Everyday Life* (New York: HarperCollins, 1992), 219.
3. J.R.R. Tolkien, *The Fellowship of the Ring* (Boston: Houghton Mifflin Company, 1994), 32.
4. Nicholas Carr, *The Shallows: What the Internet Is Doing to Our Brains* (New York: W.W. Norton & Company, 2011), 114.

5. Henry David Thoreau, *Walden: An Annotated Edition*, ed. Walter Harding (Boston: Houghton Mifflin Company, 1995), 6.
6. John Muir, *The Mountains of California* (New York: Penguin Books, 1985), 174.
7. Ibid., 176–177.
8. Psalm 34:8 NIV. Italics added.
9. Mary D. Leakey, "Footprints in the Ashes of Time," *National Geographic*, April 1979, 453.
10. Joseph Stalin. Contested attribution. See David McCullough, *Truman* (New York: Simon and Schuster, 2003), 510.
11. Matthew 11:15 NIV.
12. Thomas Merton, *Mystics and Zen Masters* (New York: Farrar, Straus & Giroux, 1967), 140.
13. Julian of Norwich, *Revelation of Love*, trans. John Skinner (New York: Image Books, 1996), 9.
14. C. S. Lewis, *The Last Battle in The Chronicles of Narnia* (New York: Harper Collins, 2001), 760.

Chapter 3: Life and Death

1. Saint Augustine, *The Confessions*, trans. Maria Boulding, OSB (New York: Vintage Books, 1997), 197.
2. John Calvin, *Institutes of the Christian Religion*, trans. Henry Beveridge (Grand Rapids: Eerdmans, 1989), 37.
3. Catherine of Siena, *The Dialogue*, trans. Suzanne Noffke, O.P. (New York: Paulist Press, 1980), 63. Original quote: "It is charity that binds you to true humility—the humility that is found in knowing yourself and me."
4. e. e. cummings, "A Poet's Advice to Students," *Journal of Humanistic Psychology*, vol. 12, no. 2 (1972), 75.
5. Owen Barfield, *Poetic Diction: A Study in Meaning* (Middleton, CT: Wesleyan University Press, 1973), 63–64.
6. Richard Rohr, *Immortal Diamond: Searching for our True Self* (San Francisco: Jossey-Bass, 2013).
7. Aleksandr I. Solzhenitsyn, *The Gulag Archipelago: An Experiment in Literary Investigation*, trans. Thomas P. Whitney (New York: Harper & Row, 1973), 168.
8. Augustine, *Confessions*, 25.
9. Rohr, *Immortal Diamond*.
10. Galatians 5:22 ESV.

Chapter 4: Daily Bread

1. Traditional Jewish blessing of bread, called the baracha. Quoted in H. E. Jacob, *Six Thousand Years of Bread: Its Holy and Unholy History*, trans. Richard and Clara Winston (New York: The Lyons Press, 1944), 40.
2. Ruth Reichl. Quoted in the Introduction to Robert Farrar Capon's *The Supper of the Lamb: A Culinary Reflection* (New York: Modern Library, 2002), ix.
3. Capon, *Supper*, 40.
4. Luci Shaw, *Water My Soul: Cultivating the Interior Life* (Vancouver, BC, Canada: Regent College Publishing, 2003), 68.

5. Thomas Moore, *The Re-Enchantment of Everyday Life* (New York: Harper Perennial, 1996), 97.
6. *Dictionary.com Unabridged*, s.v. "cultivate," http://dictionary.reference.com/browse/cultivate.
7. Zoë François and Mark Luinenburg, *Healthy Bread in Five Minutes a Day: 100 New Recipes Featuring Whole Grains, Fruits, Vegetables, and Gluten-Free Ingredients* (New York: Thomas Dunne Books, 2009).
8. See Mark 8:18.
9. Mahatma Gandhi. Quoted in Richard Frazer, "Live as Though You Might Die Tomorrow and Farm as Though You Might Live Forever," *Christian Faith and the Welfare of the City*, ed. Johnston R. McKay (Edinburgh: CTPI, 2008), 48.
10. William Bryant Logan, *Dirt: The Ecstatic Skin of the Earth* (New York: W. W. Norton & Company, 2007), 139.
11. Ibid., 147.
12. Ibid., 152.
13. Romans 8:26 ESV.
14. Wendell Berry, "The Unsettling of America" in *The Art of the Commonplace: The Agrarian Essays of Wendell Berry* (Berkeley: Counterpoint, 2002), 39.
15. PBS-Frontline Online Quiz, http://www.pbs.org/wgbh/pages/frontline/shows/porn/etc/quiz.html. Accessed on 2/24/14.
16. "Key Facts About the Issue: A Serious Problem – Around the Globe and in the USA" Coalition to Abolish Slavery & Trafficking website, http://www.castla.org/key-stats. Accessed on 11/20/13.
17. Patrick Radden Keefe, "Cocaine Incorporated," *New York Times*, June 15, 2012, http://www.nytimes.com/2012/06/17/magazine/how-a-mexican-drug-cartel-makes-its-billions.html?_r=0.
18. "Gangs," Los Angeles Police Department, http://www.lapdonline.org/get_informed/content_basic_view/1396. See also Nate Berg, "The 5 U.S. Cities with the Worst Gang Violence," The Atlantic Cities, January 31, 2012, http://www.theatlanticcities.com/neighborhoods/2012/01/5-us-cities-worst-gang-violence/1095/.
19. Ron Findley (February 2013), "Ron Finley: A guerilla gardener in South Central LA" [Video File]. Retrieved from: http://www.ted.com/talks/ron_finley_a_guerilla_gardener_in_south_central_la.html. Accessed on 5/29/13.
20. Wendell Berry, "Manifesto: The Mad Farmer Liberation Front," *The Selected Poems of Wendell Berry* (New York: Counterpoint Press, 1998), 88.
21. See Romans 12:2.
22. See Mark 4:3–9.
23. Mother Teresa. Quoted in Shane Claiborne and Jonathan Wilson Hartgrove, *Becoming the Answer to Our Prayers: Prayer for Ordinary Radicals* (Downer's Grove: InterVarsity Press, 2008), 50.

Chapter 5: Freedom in Downward Mobility

1. C. G. Jung, *The Collected Works of C.G. Jung, Vol 13: Alchemical Studies*, trans. Gerhard Adler and R.F.C. Hull (Princeton: Princeton University Press, 1983), 16.
2. William Bryant Logan, *Dirt: The Ecstatic Skin of the Earth* (New York: W. W. Norton & Company, 2007), 165.

3. Robert Farrar Capon, *The Supper of the Lamb: A Culinary Reflection* (New York: Modern Library, 2002), 25.

4. R. S. Thomas, "Lore" in *Collected Poems: 1945–1990* (London: Orion Books, 2000), 114. Used by permission.

5. Thomas Merton, *New Seeds of Contemplation* (New York: New Directions Publishing Corporation, 1961), 85.

6. Matthew 6:11 esv.

7. Annie Dillard, *For the Time Being* (New York: Kopf, 1999), 55.

8. Quoted in Erik Larson, *The Naked Consumer: How Our Private Lives Become Public Commodities* (New York: Henry Holt and Company, 1992), 20. Quoted in *Being Consumed: Economics and Christian Desire* by William Cavanaugh (Grand Rapids: Eerdmans, 2008), 17.

9. Jonathan Spicer, "U.S. consumer debt drops in second quarter, continuing post-crisis trend," Reuters, August 14, 2013, http://www.reuters.com/article/2013/08/14/us-usa-fed-consumerdebt-idUSBRE97D0T820130814.

10. Henry David Thoreau. Quoted in Wayne Muller, *The Sabbath: Restoring the Sacred Rhythm of Rest* (New York: Bantam Books, 1999), 200.

11. Abraham Joshua Heschel, *The Sabbath* (New York: Farrar, Straus and Giroux, 1951), 28.

12. "Luxury yachts back on the super-rich shopping list," BBC, October 12, 2013, http://www.bbc.co.uk/programmes/p01jrkc8. Accessed on 10/16/13.

13. 1 Timothy 6:7–8 esv.

14. Luke 9:58 niv.

15. See Matthew 6:31–33.

16. Mike Yankoski, *Under the Overpass: A Journey of Faith on the Streets of America* (Colorado Springs: Multnomah Books, 2010).

17. Doris Janzen Longacre, *Living More With Less* (Scottdale, PA: Herald Press, 1986), 18. Doris Janzen Longacre, *More-with-Less Cookbook* (New York: Bantam Books, 1981), 12.

18. Capon, *Supper*, 69.

19. G. K. Chesterton, *Orthodoxy* (New York: Image Books, 1959), 63.

Chapter 6: Let There BE!

1. Flannery O'Connor, "The Nature and Aim of Fiction" in *Mystery and Manners* (New York: Farrar, Straus and Giroux, 1969), 65.

2. Robert Farrar Capon, *The Supper of the Lamb: A Culinary Reflection* (New York: Modern Library, 2002), 121.

3. Dorothy Day. Quoted in Daniela Gioseffi, *Women on War: Essential Voices for the Nuclear Age* (New York: Simon & Schuster Books, 1988), 103.

4. Attributed to Gene Fowler. Quoted in David Bayles and Ted Orland, *Art and Fear* (Santa Cruz, CA: The Image Continuum, 2004), opening material.

5. Thomas Merton, *New Seeds of Contemplation* (New York: New Directions Publishing Corporation, 1961), 98.

6. O'Connor, "Nature and Aim," 83.

7. Johannes Brahms. Quoted in *Free Play: Improvisation in Life and Art* by Stephen Nachmanovitch (New York: Tarcher/Putnam, 1991), 69.

8. Anne Lamott, *Bird by Bird: Some Instructions on Writing and Life* (New York: Anchor Books, 1994), 21.

9. O'Connor, "Nature and Aim" in *Mystery and Manners*, 80.

10. Stephen Nachmanovitch, *Free Play: Improvisation in Life and Art* (New York: Tarcher/Putnam, 1991), 108.

11. Annie Dillard, "To Fashion a Text," in *Inventing the Truth: The Art and Craft of Memoir*, ed. William Zinsser (Boston: Houghton Mifflin Company, 1987), 53ff.

12. Philippians 2:12 NIV.

Chapter 7: Endless Finite Days

1. Attributed to Schopenhauer. See Lewis R. Aiken *Dying, Death and Bereavement*, 4th ed. (Florence, KY: Psychology Press, 2000), 188.

2. Wendell Berry, "A Poem of Difficult Hope" in *What Are People For?* (New York: North Point Press, 1990), 62.

3. Thomas Merton, trans., *The Wisdom of the Desert: Sayings from the Desert Fathers of the Fourth Century* (New York: New Directions, 1960), 76.

4. Saint Augustine. Quoted in Irvin D. Yalom, *Staring at the Sun: Overcoming the Terror of Death* (San Francisco: Jossey-Bass, 2008), 32.

5. Psalm 8:3–4.

6. Irvin D. Yalom, *Staring at the Sun: Overcoming the Terror of Death* (San Francisco: Jossey-Bass, 2008), 132.

7. Kenneth E. Vail III, Jacob Juhl, Jamie Arndt, Matthew Vess, Clay Routledge and Bastiaan T. Rutjens, "When Death Is Good for Life: Considering the Positive Trajectories of Terror Management" in *Personality and Social Psychology Review*, April 5, 2012.

8. James Boswell, *The Life of Samuel Johnson, LL.D.* (New York: The Heritage Press, 1963), 2:393. (September, 1777, *Aetat.* 68).

9. Psalm 90:12 NIV.

10. Athanasius, *The Life of Antony and The Letter to Marcellinus*, trans. Robert C. Gregg (Mahwah, New Jersey: Paulist Press, 1980), 45.

11. Ernest Becker, *The Denial of Death* (New York: Free Press, 1973), 4.

12. Ibid., 284.

13. Bertrand Russell. Quoted in Yalom, *Staring*, 165.

14. Becker, *Denial*, 70.

15. Ecclesiastes 1:2 NIV.

16. William Bryant Logan, *Dirt: The Ecstatic Skin of the Earth* (New York: W. W. Norton & Company, 2007), 57.

17. Ibid., 17ff.

18. John 20:25 ESV.

19. "Telegram from Anna Spafford to Horatio Gates Spafford re being 'Saved alone' among her traveling party in the shipwreck of the Ville du Havre," Original Western Union telegram, US Library of Congress, http://www.loc.gov/resource/mamcol.011. Accessed on 2/24/14.

20. Annie Dillard, *For the Time Being* (New York: Kopf, 1999).

21. See Isaiah 40:8 and Matthew 6:28.

22. John 20:29.

23. See Mark 9:24 KJV.

24. "Funeral Liturgy for Use in Church" in *The Book of Alternative Services of the Anglican Church of Canada* (Toronto: Anglican Book Centre, 1985), 587.

25. Genesis 2:7 ESV.

Chapter 8: Guilty as Diagnosed

1. Frederick Buechner, *Wishful Thinking: A Theological ABC* (New York: HarperCollins, 1973), 15.
2. Thomas Merton, *New Seeds of Contemplation* (New York: New Directions Publishing Corporation, 1961), 93.
3. Thomas Merton, "Gandhi and the One Eyed Giant," in Thomas Merton, ed., *Gandhi On Non-Violence: Selected Texts from Mohandas K. Gandhi's Non-Violence in Peace and War* (New York: New Directions Publishing, 2007), 19.
4. Merton, *New Seeds*, 73.
5. Saint Augustine, *The Confessions*, trans. Maria Boulding, OSB (New York: Vintage Books, 1997), 16. Full quote: "Matters are so arranged at your command that every disordered soul is its own punishment."
6. Psalm 103:3 ESV.
7. See Luke 4:18–19.
8. Thomas Aquinas, *Summa Theologiae*, 1.104.
9. See Luke 5:31, Mark 2:1–12, Mark 8:22–25, Mark 7:31–37, John 8:1–11, Luke 4:19, Luke 23:34.
10. See Matthew 25:41.
11. Romans 6:23 ESV.
12. Henri Nouwen, *Return of the Prodigal Son: A Story of Homecoming* (New York: Image Books, 1994), 15.
13. George Herbert, "Love (III)," in *The Norton Anthology of English Literature,* ed. M. H. Abrams (New York: W.W. Norton, 1979), 1340–41.
14. "The Reconciliation of a Penitent," *The Book of Alternative Services of the Anglican Church of Canada* (Toronto: Anglican Book Centre, 1985), 167ff. Used by permission.

Chapter 9: Is Anybody Listening?

1. Saint Theresa of Avila, *The Interior Castle*, trans. Mirabai Starr (New York: Riverhead Books, 2003), 57.
2. Philip Yancey, *Prayer* (Grand Rapids: Zondervan, 2006), 153.
3. Henri Nouwen, *With Open Hands* (Notre Dame: Ave Maria Press, 1972), 154.
4. Jean Vanier, *Essential Writings* (Maryknoll: Orbis Books, 2008), 153.
5. Philippians 4:6 ESV.
6. 1 Kings 19:12 KJV.
7. Romans 8:26 ESV.
8. See John 3:19 ESV and John 1:5 ESV.
9. "The Order for the Administration of the Lord's Supper," available from http://justus.anglican.org/resources/bcp/1662/Orig_manuscript/hc.htm. Accessed on 2/12/14.

Chapter 10: Taste and Become

1. Bonaventure, *Hexaemeron 23:21*. Quoted in *Hans Urs Von Balthasar and the Dramatic Structure of Truth: A Philosophical Investigation* by David C. Schindler, Jr. (New York: Fordham University Press, 2004), 281.
2. Eugene Peterson, *Eat This Book: A Conversation in the Art of Spiritual Reading* (Grand Rapids: Eerdmans, 2006), 24.

3. M. Basil Pennington, *Lectio Divina: Renewing the Ancient Practice of Praying the Scriptures* (New York: Crossroad Publishing Company, 1998), xi.

4. Angel F. Méndez Montoya, *Theology of Food: Eating and the Eucharist* (Oxford: Wiley-Blackwell, 2009), 46.

5. See Joseph Pieper, *The Silence of St. Thomas: Three Essays,* trans. John Murray, S.J. and Daniel O'Connor (New York:Pentheon Books, 1957), 39–40.

6. Peterson, *Eat This Book.*

7. Ibid., 4.

8. John 11:39 ESV.

9. Ibid.

10. See Ezekiel 36:26 NIV.

11. John 11:43 ESV. Emphasis added.

12. John 6:68 NIV.

Chapter 11: Resonant Loneliness

1. Blaise Pascal, *Pensées,* no. 136, trans. A. J. Krailsheimer (London: Penguin, 1996), 37.

2. Henri Nouwen, *With Open Hands* (Notre Dame: Ave Maria Press, 1972), 36.

3. See 1 Kings 18–19.

4. Stephen Nachmanovitch, *Free Play: Improvisation in Life and Art* (New York: Tarcher/Putnam, 1991), 130–31.

5. Belden Lane, *The Solace of Fierce Landscapes: Exploring Desert and Mountain Spirituality* (New York: Oxford University Press, 1998), 19.

6. Thomas Merton, *New Seeds of Contemplation* (New York: New Directions Publishing Corporation, 1961), 83.

7. Athanasius, *The Life of Antony and The Letter to Marcellinus,* trans. Robert C. Gregg (Mahwah, New Jersey: Paulist Press, 1980), 42.

8. Ibid., 81.

9. Ephesians 3:17 NIV.

10. Saint Augustine, *The Confessions,* trans. Maria Boulding, OSB (New York: Vintage Books, 1997), 8.

11. Dietrich Bonhoeffer, *Life Together: Prayerbook of the Bible,* trans. Daniel W. Bloesch and James H. Burtness (Minneapolis: Fortress Press, 2005), 83.

12. Mark 1:33 ESV.

13. Mark 1:35, "*eremon topon*" is a transliteration of the Greek.

14. Mark 1:37 ESV.

15. Mark 1:38 ESV.

16. John 5:19 ESV.

17. Thomas Merton, trans., *The Wisdom of the Desert: Sayings from the Desert Fathers of the Fourth Century* (New York: New Directions, 1960), 30.

Chapter 12: A Deep, Deep Breath

1. Robert Farrar Capon, *The Supper of the Lamb: A Culinary Reflection* (New York: Modern Library, 2002), 68.

2. Saint Augustine, *The Confessions,* trans. Maria Boulding, OSB (New York: Vintage Books, 1997), 3.

3. Stephen Nachmanovitch, *Free Play: Improvisation in Life and Art* (New York: Tarcher/Putnam, 1991), 155.

4. Norman Wirzba, *Living the Sabbath: Discovering the Rhythms of Rest and Delight* (Grand Rapids: Brazos Press, 2006), 13.

5. Marva J. Dawn, *Keeping the Sabbath Wholly: Ceasing, Resting, Embracing, Feasting* (Grand Rapids: Eerdmans, 1989).

6. Abraham Joshua Heschel, *The Sabbath* (New York: Farrar, Straus and Giroux, 1951), 9.

7. See Isaiah 55:1–2 NIV.

8. Heschel, *Sabbath*, 30.

Chapter 13: Into the Wild

1. Annie Dillard, *Pilgrim at Tinker Creek* (New York: HarperCollins, 1974), 10.

2. Edward Abbey, *Desert Solitaire: A Season in the Wilderness* (New York: Ballantine Books, 1968), 192.

3. Eugene Peterson, *Christ Plays in 10,000 Place: A Conversation in Spiritual Theology* (Grand Rapids: Eerdmans, 2005), 52.

4. Fyodor Dostoyevsky, *The Brothers Karamazov*, ed. Ralph E. Matlaw, trans. Constance Garnett (New York: W.W. Norton & Co., 1976), 298.

5. Ernest W. Hawkes, *The Labrador Eskimo* (Ottawa: Government Printing Bureau, 1916), 153.

6. Dillard, *Pilgrim*, 17.

7. Richard Louv, *Last Child in the Woods: Saving Our Children From Nature-Deficit Disorder* (Chapel Hill: Algonquin Books, 2008).

8. Henry David Thoreau, *Walden: An Annotated Edition* ed. Walter Harding (Boston: Houghton Mifflin Company, 1995), 308.

9. Letter of John Muir, dated July 26, 1868. Quoted in Richard Louv, *Last Child in the Woods: Saving Our Children from Nature Deficit Disorder* (Chapel Hill, NC: Algonquin Books, 2008), 161.

10. Anne Frank, *The Diary of a Young Girl*, trans. B.M. Mooyaart-Doubleday (New York: Modern Library, 1952), 172. (Date of entry: February 23, 1944)

11. David Abram, *The Spell of the Sensuous* (New York: Vintage Books, 1996), 62–63.

12. Thomas Merton, *A Search for Solitude: Pursuing the Monk's True Life* ed. Lawrence S. Cunningham (New York: HarperCollins, 1996), 190.

13. Saint Francis of Assisi, "The Canticle of Brother Sun" in Eric Doyle, *St. Francis and the Song of Brotherhood and Sisterhood* (St. Bonaventure, New York: Franciscan Institute, 1996), 42.

14. Annie Dillard, *Teaching a Stone to Talk: Expeditions and Encounters* (New York: Harper & Row, 1982), 70.

15. Thoreau, *Walden*, 311.

16. Gerard Manley Hopkins, "God's Grandeur" in *Gerard Manley Hopkins, The Oxford Authors*, ed. Catherine Phillips (New York: Oxford University Press, 1986), 128.

Chapter 14: Saunter On

1. J. R. R. Tolkien, *The Fellowship of the Ring* (Boston: Houghton Mifflin Company, 1987), 72.